Discovering Kubrick's
Symbolism

# Discovering Kubrick's Symbolism

## The Secrets of the Films

Nicole M. Berg

McFarland & Company, Inc., Publishers
*Jefferson, North Carolina*

LIBRARY OF CONGRESS CATALOGUING-IN-PUBLICATION DATA

Names: Berg, Nicole, 1969– author.
Title: Discovering Kubrick's symbolism : the secrets of the films / Nicole M. Berg.
Description: Jefferson : McFarland & Company, Inc., Publishers, 2020 | Includes bibliographical references and index.
Identifiers: LCCN 2020021786 |
ISBN 9781476680491 (paperback : acid free paper) ♾
ISBN 9781476639925 (ebook)
Subjects: LCSH: Kubrick, Stanley—Criticism and interpretation. | Symbolism in motion pictures.
Classification: LCC PN1998.3.K83 B385 2020 | DDC 791.4302/33092—dc23
LC record available at https://lccn.loc.gov/2020021786

BRITISH LIBRARY CATALOGUING DATA ARE AVAILABLE

**ISBN (print) 978-1-4766-8049-1
ISBN (ebook) 978-1-4766-3992-5**

© 2020 Nicole M. Berg. All rights reserved

*No part of this book may be reproduced or transmitted in any form or by any means, electronic or mechanical, including photocopying or recording, or by any information storage and retrieval system, without permission in writing from the publisher.*

Front cover images @ 2020 Pexels/Pixabay/RenderHub/Shutterstock

Printed in the United States of America

*McFarland & Company, Inc., Publishers
Box 611, Jefferson, North Carolina 28640
www.mcfarlandpub.com*

Safe Travels
to the Secular,
to the Spiritual
& to the Secular Spiritual.

# Acknowledgments

To my mother and father, Katherine and
Melvin Berg, for all their love and support,
many thanks to Dan Richter and Alison Castle,
my friends Ellen Hai and Tess Whittington,
and thanks to Susan Tran of 3388 Films
for her Vietnamese translations.

# Table of Contents

*Acknowledgments*     vi
*Preface*     1
*Introduction*     3

**Part I—Understanding *A Space Odyssey***     5
   1. The Dawn of Man     9
   2. Duality: The Core Structure of *A Space Odyssey*'s Universe     12
   3. *2001: A Space Odyssey*'s Visual Motifs     17
   4. Glyphs of Consciousness     26
   5. Kubrick's Color Code for 2001     35
   6. Duality Revisited: On HAL, Spacesuits and Spaceships     43
   7. 2001's Number Symbolism     51
   8. Warning: Star Gate Spiritual Mechanics     56
   9. The Female Presence in *2001*     65
   10. The Star Child–Egyptian Horus Child Connection     71
   11. The Ultimate Unity     76
   12. Closing Remarks on *2001: A Space Odyssey*     78

**Part II—The Films Following *2001***     79
   13. *The Shining*: Scarier Than Ever     81
   14. The Hidden Depths of *Barry Lyndon*     111
   15. *A Clockwork Orange*: More Disturbing Than Ever     123
   16. A Woman's Take on *Full Metal Jacket*     145
   17. The Uncanny *Eyes Wide Shut* Connection     161

**Part III—The Films Before *2001***     175
  18. *Dr. Strangelove*: Horror Beneath the Humor     176
  19. What Underlies the Film *Lolita*     189
  20. Inserting Sources in *Spartacus*     202
  21. *Paths of Glory:* Where It Begins     212
  22. Closing Remarks on Kubrick's Films Pre- and Post–*2001*     222

*Chapter Notes*     225
*Bibliography*     231
*Index*     235

# Preface

This book is primarily concerned with revealing the startling spiritual depths within the majority of renowned director Stanley Kubrick's films and exploring their fascinating range of hidden metaphysical visual motifs. These concealed arcane symbols (the bulk of which were previously unknown) within Kubrick's influential body of work are a bombshell discovery. These glyphs provide answers to numinous truths that pertain to the issues separately addressed in Kubrick's pictures. There are those who believe Stanley Kubrick's work, with perhaps the exception of *2001: A Space Odyssey*, rarely tackles the religious or the sacred unless for satire, such as the blustering prison chaplain in *A Clockwork Orange* or the ineffectual Reverend Runt in *Barry Lyndon*. The evidence provided in these pages will prove that this assumption is incorrect.

My interest in this subject was first sparked by certain revelations unearthed in *2001: A Space Odyssey* by asking a key question: What if there are *other* repeating signs in *A Space Odyssey* that actually help explain what the monolith is? So I looked and discovered there are indeed other specific sigils that consistently reappear throughout the film in ways that clue the viewer in on their significance. Then when viewing Kubrick's other pictures, I was excited to find several of these same symbols carried over with new symbols particular to each film, tucked within these movies and presented in various ways.

During these investigations, certain Kubrick film techniques came to the fore that have received scant attention before in any depth. These mostly unsung Kubrickian cinematic methods will be discussed and given their due. This book is not a biography, but rather a deep dive into the director's filmic symbolism within his long career. A point is made to keep Kubrick's family life private and rarely touched upon.

In addition to referring to a wide variety of Kubrick film reference books, I spent time researching in libraries such as Stanford University's extensive Cecil H. Green Library film and media sections and the Berkeley Art Museum and Pacific Film Archive, which offer access to exhaustive entertainment write-ups and news articles going back decades. Inspiration also came in the fortuitous happenstance of the San Francisco Jewish Museum showcasing the traveling Stanley Kubrick exhibit at the time the groundwork was just starting for this book. Being able to see actual film production items, notes, movie props, and set pieces on display provided new insights on the movies being highlighted.

While other volumes on Stanley Kubrick and his pictures either focus on the man himself, shine a spotlight on specific times in his life, or as filmographies concentrate on a particular film or a selection of his films, *Discovering Kubrick's Symbolism* is among the first to specialize in unveiling the deeper metaphysical levels of Kubrick's seminal films that have heretofore gone unnoticed by most mainstream movie critics. The following chapters touch upon fond and familiar subjects, while also providing a considerable amount of valuable new material that has not been disclosed anywhere else.

# Introduction

People have long lauded and pondered the work of Stanley Kubrick, whose richly layered subtext immerses viewers within such iconic films as *Dr. Strangelove, A Clockwork Orange, The Shining, Eyes Wide Shut,* and particularly *2001: A Space Odyssey,* which proves to be Kubrick's magnum opus that connects to most of his other films in intriguing, hidden ways. Here, all of Kubrick's main movies will be explored for their surprising links to one another, including *Paths of Glory, Spartacus, Lolita, Barry Lyndon,* and *Full Metal Jacket.* The only titles that have been excluded are the master filmmaker's initial three feature forays, *Fear & Desire, Killer's Kiss,* and *The Killing;* the third exhibits an exponential jump in cinematic noir mastery, the second is decently executed with a few standout scenes, and the first, Kubrick would have preferred to forget altogether. Those original three efforts lack the multilayered symbolism Kubrick more fully developed in his other more mainstream pictures, which will be this book's major focus.

The one picture Stanley Kubrick made that will be covered in a shorter section is *Spartacus*, as it was always held by the director to be more Kirk Douglas' film than his own even though Kubrick managed to put some of his particular style into it—but not as much as he would have liked. Though it went on to win several Academy Awards, *Spartacus* was the movie that made Kubrick swear that he would only work for himself for the rest of his cinematic career. Therefore, in addition to its own chapter, the symbolism that was successfully couched within *Spartacus* will be mentioned in the appropriate visual motif segments that are connected to Stanley Kubrick's other major movies.

As an example of the quintessential New York Jewish intellectual, Kubrick, who subscribed to no particular religious affiliation, was likely a purely secular individual. However, after one experiences the awe-inspiring celestial grandeur of *2001: A Space Odyssey*, it is difficult to see such a film being created by a director who is completely lacking in spiritual sensitivity. With this in mind, we will explore Stanley Kubrick's previously unknown treasure trove of esoteric visual motifs that the director and his select design crews crafted for his feature films.

Why these cinematic glyphs were made and why they were so buried are key questions that *Discovering Kubrick's Symbolism* investigates.

Some of Kubrick's earlier comedies, such as *Lolita* and *Dr. Strangelove*, conceal startlingly grim secrets through each movie's production crew's deftly seeded images. Even period films like *Spartacus* contain cleverly positioned prop designs and clothing details which intentionally spotlight the director's heretofore not widely known clandestine targets. The same can be said for the often overlooked *Barry Lyndon*, which will be examined in depth for its subtle symbolism.

*Paths of Glory* and *Full Metal Jacket* are both military dramas, one being a more pointed critique of a war's criminal wastefulness during World War I and the other a deceptively nihilistic meditation on Marines executing invasion operations in 1970s Vietnam. Such movies could be understandably seen to be straight realism with little to no metaphysical import, yet the findings that are detailed in this book prove this is simply not so.

The films in Kubrick's terror trinity, *A Clockwork Orange*, *The Shining*, and *Eyes Wide Shut*, each contain a mother lode of deliberately disguised symbolic palimpsests (as does *Full Metal Jacket*) that blow the lid off long suppressed realities. *A Clockwork Orange* addresses modern civilization's various means for controlling its populace within a supposedly futuristic dystopia. *The Shining* follows a family's descent into madness and horror within the confines of an isolated hotel. *Eyes Wide Shut* revisits the subject matter covered in the previous films but adds a more surrealistic, carnal dimension to its eerie cosmopolitan storyline. Each movie's cinematic language is covered in depth within its own chapter.

Other Kubrick films made before and after *2001* will be discussed in relation to the themes and motifs that not only link back to *A Space Odyssey* but to each other. Movies like *A Clockwork Orange*, *The Shining*, *Full Metal Jacket*, and *Eyes Wide Shut* incorporate a surprising amount of *2001* visual symbolism and color-coding. These films are usually seen as stand-alone cinematic pieces, but their subject matter overlaps in ways seldom recognized. This thematic cross pollination in Stanley Kubrick's pictures is discussed in the chapters that follow.

PART I

# Understanding *A Space Odyssey*

Since *2001: A Space Odyssey* is recognized as Stanley Kubrick's magnum opus that redefined film as a visual medium, Part I is therefore solely dedicated to this cinematic tour de force. *2001*'s visual symbols that were forged between Kubrick and Harry Lange's design department not only provide the seminal symbolic foundation for the rest of the director's films, but as Kubrick's groundbreaking sci-fi masterpiece, it addresses profound truths and underlying implications for humanity few other movies have come close to addressing. For all *A Space Odyssey* achieves, it requires that the entirety of Part I be devoted to its vast array of metaphysical motifs which can then be applied to interpreting Kubrick's other pictures in later sections. Those who experience *A Space Odyssey* can at times feel its underlying immortal yearnings without fully comprehending how such evocative feelings were achieved cinematically. This is, in part, what Part I endeavors to comprehensively explain.

In effect, here is what Stanley Kubrick intended with *2001*'s highly symbolic, nonlinear storyline: At first glance, its three-vignette structure appears loosely linked together with widely varying subject matter. In-depth studies have been written detailing the technological, evolutionary, and social relevance of *2001*. In this written work, I cover specific glyphs of spiritual import that Kubrick seeded in his film, which have remained hidden in plain sight, undetected for decades, since the film opened in 1968—just a year before the Apollo 11 Moon landings. Most of these covert message motifs that Kubrick crafted for *A Space Odyssey* are being publicly introduced here for the very first time.

From its premiere onwards, *2001: A Space Odyssey* continues to challenge, puzzle, and inspire science fiction enthusiasts, film critics, motion picture historians, and the movie viewing public. Though director Stanley Kubrick didn't align himself with any organized religion, that did not stop him from tackling the transcendental in his sci-fi epic. In *Stanley Kubrick,*

*Director*, Alexander Walker states, "Kubrick has said on several occasions that *'the God concept' is at the heart of this movie* [italics mine] ... he does not refer to any monotheistic view of God, and he would probably be nearer to the view of those movie critics who see his film as embodying mythical rather than religious experience."[1] It is *2001*'s metaphysical fabric which carries into Kubrick's other motion pictures that will be revealed throughout this text.

In discussing of *2001*'s conceptual underpinnings, Kubrick said, "Such cosmic intelligence growing in knowledge over the eons would be as far removed from man as we are from the ants.... [D]iscussing such possibilities you realize that the religious implications are inevitable because all the essential attributes of such extraterrestrial intelligence are the attributes we give to God. What we're dealing with here [in *2001*] is in fact, a scientific definition of God."[2]

Indeed, in addition to *2001*'s themes on the varying thrills of acclimating to space travel, interplanetary political maneuvering, human isolation in space, and humanity's untenable future dependency on technology, the film at its deepest level addresses the yearning for spiritual uplift and a connection to something greater beyond ourselves. Through the science fiction genre, *A Space Odyssey* not only strives to seriously answer the age-old query "Is this all there is?" but also "How do we go *beyond* it?"

Approach this book as you would a treasure hunt. *Discovering Kubrick's Symbolism* provides the map that allows you to find and dig up the symbolic riches Kubrick covered up throughout his influential cinematic career. The majority of what is written in Part I centers on *2001*'s sequences of humanity in space and assumes the reader has seen the film and, indeed, the reading will be richest if one has seen *all* of Kubrick's films covered in this book. As this book extrapolates certain key scenes within a film, that is a good time for the reader to revisit these scenes themselves to unearth their buried Kubrickian optical signage. When experiencing these pictures with an eye out for the filmic clues being discussed, eventually a chronology of revelation becomes apparent; in other words, there is a relative order by which Kubrick's message motifs reveal themselves. Some symbols appear much more often than others. Some motifs need to be detected first before others can be recognized and interpreted. The visual themes explored here can vary in their subtlety in how and where they are lurking within a particular movie scene. Such symbols may masquerade as light effects, special effects, props, and furniture within a set ... and at times they may *be* the set itself. For example, just one *A Space Odyssey* set can carry multiple motifs encompassing a wide array of conceptual themes that were later incorporated into Kubrick's cinematic language for his future films.

Words that represent key *A Space Odyssey* concepts, especially those with universal themes, will be capitalized to emphasize their importance.

Certain glyphs will represent an aspect of a similar trope, so sets of symbols will overlap in what they convey (this is especially true in relation to the monolith). Therefore, seeing the movie *A Space Odyssey* on as large a screen as possible is highly recommended and can only help one to further understand the picture's vast mythic scope. Like the rest of Stanley Kubrick's work, *2001* cannot be viewed on small screens or seen merely once to fully realize all that the director is communicating to an audience.

Knowing the basic storyline of *A Space Odyssey* ahead of time can help one focus on its other cinematic elements. Repeated viewings over time reveal that *2001*'s "storyline" is not the movie's main event or purpose. The cast of *2001* is shown again and again to be more of a sideshow to *A Space Odyssey*'s celestial happenings. The actions and dramas of individuals are small satellites orbiting around *2001*'s great cosmic cycles of consequence. In *The Stanley Kubrick Companion*, James Howard postulates, "Although casting of the film would be completed with Kubrick's usual thoroughness, it is safe to say that the actors in *2001: A Space Odyssey* were destined to become the least significant aspect of the picture—reflecting man's own relative insignificance in relation to the vastness of the universe. Above all, this is what impresses about the film—the sheer scope, immensity and wonder of space."[3]

*2001: A Space Odyssey* runs over two hours and forty minutes, divided into what are initially perceived as three loosely related sections that are bookended by appearances of the movie's iconic linchpin, the monolith. Planetary conjunctions and other grand events set in motion the following scenarios: In part one, *The Dawn of Man*, the film opens at the dawning of humanity where the first cryptic appearance of the tall, imposing black slab witnesses (and perhaps inspires) a lead ape-man's leap in cognition. The early African boulder-strewn wasteland the ape-men and primitive mammals inhabit is starkly beautiful under the intense light of day. After the monolith's early morning visit, leopards, tapirs, and victorious ape-men give way to the graceful revolutions of elegant spacecraft above the Earth, some of which are weapons, others for transport. In this second half of *The Dawn of Man*, Dr. Heywood Floyd's trip to the Clavius moon base is followed. Dr. Floyd's story primarily ends when a moon monolith's powerful signal rips through the space-suited bodies of his six-member coterie examining the site.

The second vignette, *Jupiter Mission 18 Months Later*, is set in deep solar space where the large and long ship *Discovery* slowly floats its way towards Jupiter. We are introduced to the three individuals of the six-member crew that are not in hibernation for the long trip: Mission Commander Dr. David Bowman, Deputy Dr. Frank Poole, and the ship's artificial intelligence, the HAL 9000 computer. This is often considered one of the more memorable parts of *2001*, since it is the only sequence with some degree of interpersonal drama and a more obvious antagonist. The lack of music to accent the action or guide emotions halfway in on the *Discovery*'s storyline renders events as more low-key than they actually are. Situations are set up as understated, ambiguous, or to be taken as-is, leaving viewers to make up their own minds on how to feel about what is happening on the screen.

The third part, *Jupiter and Beyond the Infinite*, follows *Discovery* survivor David Bowman in his EVA pod into a kaleidoscopic Star Gate which is marked by the third monolith in the film. This is the other most memorable sequence in *2001*: all is sensory overload engulfed by an endlessly streaming vista of racing colors, light effects, birthing galaxies, and subliminal symbolism set to Ligeti's awe-inspiring musical scores. As David hurtles by stars, planets, and alien guides, he finally comes to a jarring halt in what is usually called the Alien Hotel Room or the Room Beyond. Thought to be the most confusing part of *A Space Odyssey*, Bowman's encounter with the Room Beyond and his subsequent transformation into a "Star Child" has inspired near countless theories about its deeper meanings. This book attempts to present a clearly detailed explanation of the Star Gate and Room Beyond sequences.

Such subsequent sections will highlight how Stanley Kubrick uses classic mythological archetypes and ancient symbols as vehicles for each movie's hidden esoteric messages. Kubrick's visual motifs act as conduits for various elements of the cosmic forces which define reality as we know it. He very calculatingly uses such imagery to bypass our conscious mind by directly addressing our subconscious through the visual symbols so designed for his films. Case in point: it is impressive that even a half-century after its release, much of *A Space Odyssey*'s underlying symbolism has managed to stay buried. Until now.

# 1

# The Dawn of Man

## In the Beginning

Stanley Kubrick balanced his rather unsparing outlook on human evolution, which embraced the "Killer Ape" theory that aggression was the main necessary impetus for species advancement, with the more inspiring concepts of Joseph Campbell and Karl Jung on early human consciousness expansion, which focus on what spurred development of "soft skills" vital for social cohesion. In *Kubrick's Hope: Discovering Optimism from 2001 to Eyes Wide Shut*, Julian Rice notes, "to counterpoint the above 'killer ape' aggression equals evolution theory, Kubrick had Clarke read Joseph Campbell's '*Hero with a Thousand Faces*' which focused on spiritual evolution, through a pattern of universal growth he called the 'Monomyth.'"[1] It can be debated whether *2001*'s monolith is in part a futuristic cipher of Campbell's Monomyth or an avatar that instigates species evolution to take place. Both the aggression and inspiration approach in gaging humanity's advancement play a part in setting the stage for *2001: A Space Odyssey*'s arc of progression.

In the beginning, Early Man's life is depicted as a hardscrabble existence punctuated by fear induced by various threats such as leopards and competing bands of ape-men. Ape-men fend off prehistoric herbivores (tapirs) from their food. After the monolith's morning appearance and lead ape-man Moonwatcher's subsequent realization with the bone-club, ape-men are seen eating the animals they previously browsed among, who now symbolically and literally stand apart from them in the rock-strewn background.

It is unfortunate that Kubrick and author/scriptwriter Arthur C. Clarke undersold the importance of interrelationships in shaping the human brain. Yet even though Moonwatcher's murderous epiphany is this vignette's highlighted climax, it is countered with shots of mothers holding infants, children teaching younger siblings, and mates reaching out for each other. How much importance is ascribed to such scenes is left for the audience to decide or to be ignored altogether. But such attention is akin to an archaeologist's excitement in discovering a spearhead while ignoring a bone needle.

Jack Nicholson describes Stanley Kubrick being "crazy about animals." After all, this is the director known to shut an entire location shoot down for a whole day because a rabbit was killed during the filming of *Full Metal Jacket*.[2] So how was such a shot of a dying tapir crosscut with Moonwatcher smashing a skull with his bone club achieved?

Dan Richter, who played Moonwatcher, recalls how at one point Kubrick wanted more tapirs in a shot than the ones the crew already spent months working with so the animals would be used to them. It was decided that if new wild tapirs were let out among the tamed ones, the untried tapirs would eventually get acclimated to their new environment via the calming influence of their film-seasoned peers. Such was not to be the case. Once released, the new tapirs ran about the set which happened to be about six feet off the ground. One sadly fell off and died from the impact. As a sort of practical post-mortem dedication, that tapir starred as the falling prey intercut with Moonwatcher's bone-crushing inspiration scene.[3]

The opening sequence ends by suggesting that by the time Man's weapons reach space, mankind is still in the dawn of full awakening, evolution-wise. As the bone flying up into the air cuts to a bone-shaped weapons satellite 40,000 years into the future, the bone-as-tool message motif (looking like a capital "I") is the next *Space Odyssey* symbolic icon to recognize after the monolith.

## Earthlings in Space

As the Dawn of Man sequence continues, the future of the human condition shows space pulling the rug out from under humanity's hard-wired, gravity-bound instincts, revealing our ventures away from Earth as an awkward exercise in spite of our technological advancements. Spacefarers seem to bury their earthly separation anxiety by virtually handing the reins over to their technology. The human race is kept contained within its synthetic space habitats to provide its own regulated oxygen, synthetic food, water, travel, communications, entertainment, and stabilizing gravity. This dependency on technology saps people's vitality, leaving a complacent, almost cowed humanity. Here, people's actions range from sanguine, tepid behavior to outright lethargy. Our first human protagonist, Dr. Heywood Floyd, instead of being awed by the grandeur of Earth outside his window, sleeps through much of his trip to the moon between changing flights at the *Space Station V*. To be fair, if Dr. Floyd is a frequent flyer to the moon, then he's seen it all before. While Dr. Floyd sleeps, slim, white-suited space stewardesses look after him and the crafts' white-uniformed pilots. The stewardesses sport round, white hats with gold Pan Am medallions above their foreheads, indicating the corporate involvement in future space flight. Food, phones, and other amenities attest the same by brandishing their company logos.

The space travelers inhabit motif-laden areas, with some symbols created by light effects and others literally built into the sets. As the *Orion III* spaceplane approaches the space station, eye references appear on panels, outlets, lights, buttons and bull's eye tracking screens flashing from consoles. *Space Station V* spins slowly while *Orion III* prepares to dock from the left side of the screen. Film direction will prove to be important in *A Space Odyssey* as it links to other metaphysical meanings Kubrick and his production crew encodes into this most singular science fiction movie. Throughout the space sequences on *Orion III*, *Space Station V*, the moon shuttle *Aries*, and the Clavius moon base; walls, doors, floors, and corridors display line and grid textures, literally laying the groundwork for *A Space Odyssey*'s bedrock theme: Duality.

# 2

# Duality: The Core Structure of *A Space Odyssey*'s Universe

## Duality's Infrastructure: I–Space Field ||| + Grid Field # = ||| Space/Grid Field #

The central theme that runs throughout the entirety of *2001: A Space Odyssey* is Duality, which is achieved through cinematic and choreographic symmetry, the mirroring and doubling of characters within a scene, and the repetition of the film's visual motifs described below. Lighting is intelligently used to highlight core concepts of Duality and Non-Duality, which is continually reinforced through the many black, white, and gray set designs. The close-up of *Space Station V*'s elevator doors opening, its lift interior and wall panel textures are just a few ways *2001* subtly showcases its themes of |||Duality### and Non-Duality.

The recurrence of ||||/### glyphs is reflected in *2001*'s set designs, lighting, wall paneling, people's positioning, stylized furniture, view screens, etc., to emphasize the incredible magnitude of the Space/Grid Field Duality being the Duality of all Existence. We see Space/Grid field motifs appear in cockpits, kitchens, passenger areas, floor tiles, and forming the entire endless hallway of *Space Station V*. On both the exteriors and interiors of various sets, Stanley Kubrick compares and contrasts his Line-Space or I–Space Field |||| motif with the 3D Grid Field ## of the material world (the grid being an inaccurate way to map the vacuum of space). But on a still deeper level, Kubrick is equating his I–Space Field to the very Fabric of Existence, not just the ground plane of Earth (what the lines "||||" in the I–Space Field further embody is revealed in Chapter 4 as appropriate to *2001*'s conceptual revelation chronology).

Similar related visual themes raised other movie analysts' antennae. Alexander Walker writes of the planetary conjunction shots reinforcing "Kubrick's fascination with visual symmetry, a trait noted as early in his work as *Killer's Kiss*.... Visual symmetry occurs again and again in *2001*, built into the sense of an ordered though mysterious universe."[1] In *Kubrick: Inside an*

*Artist's Maze*, Thomas Allen Nelson states, "He [Kubrick] initiates an important doubling pattern in *2001* that has no source in Clarke's novel."[2] Such doubling is parlayed into different-yet-connected themes of Duality, each describing a particular or mythical aspect of the inner workings of the universe.

## Space vs. Direction Duality

Orientation is almost pointless in the void of space. "Where are you all going, up or down?" Dr. Heywood Floyd queries other scientists on the rolling space station circling around the Earth. We may like to think our planets are all neatly vertically and horizontally level in orientation with our sun and solar system, but they are not. The Earth itself is at an angle, and when we go out beyond and look down upon our own solar system, we see it askew compared to other star systems, which are tilted at various angles themselves. Going out still further into space, we see our Spiral Arm galaxy as just another off-center galaxy in a universe dense with billions of other dipping, tilting galaxies. The concept of up, down, horizontal, vertical, and even center has no real point of reference in the vastness of space. Direction becomes moot until a star, moon, or planet becomes a triangulation anchor point for constructing space maps.

The following *2001* scenes illustrate and support the observations above: the revolving space station's constantly changing position to the Earth, the *Orion III* spaceplane orienting itself to the space station's spinning entry bay, the rotating space stewardess delivering food, the ship *Discovery*'s hamster-wheel living quarters, crewmen Frank Poole and Dave Bowman maneuvering themselves in space and inside the gravity-free areas inside their *Discovery* ship, and Bowman floating in HAL's zero-gravity mainframe room. All exemplify the ubiquitous Space/Grid Fields in *2001*'s set designs reflecting their omnipresence as the stuff of Reality.

## Duality of Purpose: Moon Mission Cover Story vs. *Discovery* Mission Cover Story

**Clavius Moon Base:** Dr. Heywood Floyd's trip to the Moon is a mission with a dual purpose. We later find that the rumor to "contain an outbreak" on the Clavius moon base is just a cover for a top-secret moon excavation already in progress by the U.S. Astronautics Agency, of which we find Dr. Floyd is a leading member. Heywood's job is to keep the rumor in circulation while firmly ensuring secrecy from chosen top aides kept in highest confidence. The curtained, bright white walls surrounding their Clavius briefing room mimic movie screens, highlighting an already in-motion staged event.

Heywood Floyd, then shuttled by moonbus, visits the TMA-1 excavation site himself with a team of scientists who attended his Clavius briefing. The moon monolith's site itself is similar to the inside of a movie theater or studio, with downward sloping ramps, bright stage lights, and movie cameras that surround the monolith which later emits a piercing signal out into space. Out of all *2001*'s challenging scenes to make, it is interesting to note Stanley Kubrick chose to shoot this TMA-1 location sequence first.[3] Perhaps Kubrick made it a priority to check it off his long list of shoots to finish to get the TMA-1 moon crater footage in the can as soon as possible for lighting and effects compositing.

**The Jupiter Mission:** As far as its crew was concerned, the ship *Discovery*'s main goal was simply to explore Jupiter. That is what they trained for and supposedly why three astronauts were put into hibernation for the long journey ahead. Only the ship's central computer, HAL, knew of the real reason: to pinpoint the exact location to which the TMA-1 monolith's signal was being sent. So a mission originally understood to be merely exploratory turns out to be an order to investigate more of what was *already known* about Jupiter space. It is tempting to draw parallels between the Clavius meeting, the *Discovery*'s actual purpose, and considering the real reasons behind the U.S. and Soviet Union's '60s space race. Politically as well as spatially, dualistic forces continue to be a recurring theme throughout *A Space Odyssey*.

## Duality of Life: Duplicity, Double-Sided Personalities and Doppelgangers

**Dr. Heywood R. Floyd:** The name itself is strangely backward, inviting further investigation.[4] It can be read as an anagram of DEFY R HOLY WOOD. (Kubrick enjoyed putting anagrams and other wordplay in his films.)[5] This top representative of the U.S. Astronautics Agency is arguably the most duplicitous person in the film, yet he is also shown to be a caring father and conscientious husband. With the weight of a top government secret on his shoulders while in charge of its containment, one can see Dr. Floyd as just a regular guy with a very big job to do. But he's not a regular guy; Dr. Floyd is part of a national scientific elite whose elevated circles rarely rub shoulders with any uninitiated outsiders. Only military, government, scientific elite and their families are allowed access to *Space Station V* and fewer still to the Clavius moon base. Considering the paradigm shifting immensity of what is being covered up on the moon, Dr. Floyd's keeping it from the world at large in a sense makes him the ultimate Deceiver of Humanity (or at least some human part of him might feel that way).

While on the space station, Dr. Floyd is friendly to some scientists who happen to be Russian, but he refuses to divulge to them any politically sensitive information. Though Dr. Floyd is warm to his particular friend Dr. Elena, their friendship does not guarantee his confiding to her or especially to her Russian compatriots. Over the scientists careful conversing hovers an uneasy cloud of national loyalties. The names of the Russian scientists and Heywood's Clavius co-workers also yield some interesting anagrams. Among other alternate word possibilities, conspiratorial Dr. Andrei Smyslov spells out MASONS DEVILRY while Dr. Elena and her dark green-clad twin Dr. Kalinin happen to spell together LENINEAN LEAK, both of which are seemingly appropriate anagrams given the top secret and top-level political machinations going on. In addition, in accordance to *2001*'s chronology of symbolic revelation, Dr. Stretyneva's name produces some intriguing anagrams which are revealed in Chapter 10.

On the Clavius moon base, Dr. Floyd's co-worker Halvorsen's optimum anagram could be SLAVE HORN as he is the one in charge of the briefing where Floyd speaks. It is Dr. Halvorsen that first calls the meeting to order and then wraps it up before the next round. Halvorsen is also the one whom the photographer reports to before leaving, and not Heywood Floyd. An anagram for Dr. Bill Michaels' name perhaps points to his being A LIMBEC SHILL since he seems to exist to break down and distill information to the people in the moon base briefing room as well as to Kubrick's audience. Inside the moonbus, Dr. Michaels again provides the same service on the way to the TMA-1 site when showing Dr. Floyd (and the audience) photos of the goings on and discoveries there at the Tycho crater excavation.

Once in the Clavius briefing room, Heywood Floyd exemplifies even more two-faced diplomacy. He affably chats with his underlings while at the same time threatening to put any "negative views" of theirs in his report back to the Council. Dr. Floyd also insists on everyone signing oaths of secrecy and keeping what's been discussed in "strictest confidence," reiterating that headquarters back on Earth require it. As Randy Loren Rasmussen observes, "Floyd considers the implications of 'deliberately buried' in the same dispassionate manner with which he expressed 'complete sympathy' for the Clavius personnel who objected to the epidemic cover story."[6] Heywood Floyd's urbane blandness downplays the situation's true gravity.

Kubrick assigns Heywood Floyd some dualistic doppelgangers that further underline his duplicitous nature. Previously, when Dr. Floyd is seen entering one of the space station's phone booths, a male duo walks by in lockstep, one dressed in white, the other in a dark brown suit (like Floyd's) carrying a black portfolio (like Floyd's). When this twin passes by, he even looks at Dr. Floyd inside his phone booth. This doppelganger motif is repeated on the Clavius moon base, first foreshadowed by a photographer's mainly brown-and-black checkered suit, a combination of both Floyd's brown suit and his new doppelganger, Dr. Halvorsen in a black suit. When that photographer leaves, he goes through an exit with two doors that hint at duplicity as well as secrecy. This duplicity is reinforced by the white screens set around the briefing room, inferring a bit of "theater" is going on. When both Heywood and Halvorsen move about the briefing room, they are always in exact opposition to each other, acting as if in a twin dance throughout the entire briefing sequence.[7] Both the movements of the actors and the briefing room set design itself reinforce Kubrick's overarching themes of Duality. The men's mirrored symmetry also set the stage for revealing future doppelgangers with even more interesting implications further on in the film.

**Dr. Dave Bowman:** With three crewmembers already in hibernation, Dave Bowman commands the ship *Discovery* as pointed out during a televised Earth interview. Dave is cast as the most logical human aboard, not showing much emotion, his speech almost clinical, and himself so methodical as to even place his food trays in color order. Yet Dave's penchant for drawing shows he has a creative side, a faculty which will later prove vital to his future survival.

**Dr. Frank Poole:** Frank Poole is cast as more emotive and intuitive than Dave Bowman, but he also displays a sensible, no-nonsense persona. When describing how he feels, Frank lives up to his name. Frank Poole is the one most able to ascertain a situation from a gut level. "Look Dave, I can't put my finger on it, but I sense there's something wrong with him [HAL]," Frank in one instance confides to Bowman. This intuitive skill may be a reason why HAL first targets Frank at the outset besides him merely being an opportune victim in the unfolding of later events on the ship *Discovery*.

# 3

# *2001: A Space Odyssey's* Visual Motifs

## Cinematic Framing, Placement, Props and Light F/X

In *Kubrick's Cinema Odyssey*, Michel Chion correctly observes how *2001*, *The Shining*, and *Eyes Wide Shut* are the only Kubrick movies without a voice-over narrator. Yet, he notes, narration "has not completely disappeared in *2001*. At times it comes through Richard Strauss' imperious music, like a finger pointing to the determining importance of this moment or that."[1] So where Strauss' music accents epic events in *A Space Odyssey* such as major jumps in human evolution, Ligeti's suites profoundly score the awesome and terrible grandeur of space as succinctly as Aram Khachaturian's *Adagio* evokes the *Discovery* crew's intense loneliness within its endless black void. Just as background music is used for a film's emotional tone, there are big stretches in *2001* where there is purposely no music for emotive cues present, such as all the *Discovery* ship scenes involving HAL. Here, the audience is left to decide for themselves how they feel about HAL and "his" motives without a soundtrack to sway them. Instrumentation does not exist either during the *Space Station V* scientist conversation nor the Clavius moon base briefing. Filmic narration in *2001* is further made manifest in its careful framing of shots, the placement of props, and the subtle use of lighting and light effects used to underline its hidden themes and visual motifs.

The core group of *2001*'s production designers that Harry Lange, Tom Masters, Ernest Archer, and Fred Ordway were part of must have been privy to the actual meaning behind Kubrick's hidden-in-plain-sight visual motifs put into the set illustrations as they were the ones that designed them. If any one part of the film crew were to be let in on (and allowed to weigh in on) the sculpting of Kubrick's seeded symbolism within *2001*, Harry and his team would have been it, if not Harry Lange himself. Those in charge of constructing the symbol-laden sets in turn would need pertinent details of what they were building to ensure proper completion. This select group would need to include the lead camera and lighting men who would spend hours setting up such shots as capturing the Communications Tower from above where actor Keir Dullea is upside down, and the subtleties of a heavily symbolic light panel behind his character David when he and Frank talk to HAL.

Those who animated the *Discovery*'s video screen graphics and the effects that bounce off the astronaut visors must have wondered about the signs and symbols they were painstakingly crafting. Whether they were directly informed what their assigned imagery actually stood for is another story. Douglas Trumball commented on a process that was "the result of projecting film of the panel either directly onto the actor's face, or onto a small screen off-camera, which would then reflect back onto the [helmet] glass. It was crazy but it looked great."[2] One ponders then at which point Trumball and his team might have been made knowledgeable of the meaning behind the visual motifs and symbolic color effects they were directed to place inside the Star Gate sequence during its creation. For those not directly part of Kubrick's involvement in a specific shot process (and the director got around on set), Herbert Ordway said, "Kubrick didn't like you hanging around, seeing how things were done."[3] Judging from these comments it would seem that, like the actors, much of the crew was kept in the dark about their work's more mythic connotations. The ones in the know either signed confidentiality agreements themselves or simply respected Stanley Kubrick's usual insistence that his movies' objectives be kept ambiguous. Such a policy was Kubrick's price of "avoiding ... pat truths."[4]

A good question to ask when examining a film (especially a Kubrick film) is "Why are we seeing this scene from *this* particular vantage point?" Every shot is set up to the exact camera angle and lighting that best communicates what the director wants the audience to take in. Some light effects are used as signifiers, highlighting a particular point of interest within a scene. With Kubrick, redundant trivial shots are rare. Any subtle or extreme change in camera P.O.V. can be a signal to pay attention:

(a) A close-up shot of reflected light moving along *Orion III*'s navigation console mirrors the motion of a monolith-shaped view screen tracker, indicating the importance of light and the monolith shape itself.
(b) The huge, space station entry bay's soft, glowing, light effects subtly reveal 'i's on the space station's docking bay floor.
(c) Extreme close-up on the space station's opening elevator doors display the Space/Grid Field Duality and how one is part of the other: The elevator room's interior has white Grid mesh *inside* its monolith-paneled Line-Space Field walls.
(d) When the *Discovery* first appears in space, light effects subtly shine on the Ankh-shaped base of the Communications Tower.

(e) The first shot of the Clavius briefing room cleverly lines-up the C-shaped tops of its blue bucket seats with the surface of the large U-shaped table so their similarities can be noticed. What they mean will be revealed within their own motif section.

A three-quarter rear shot of Floyd addressing the room shows the blue bucket seats have "I" legs with Line feet that compare/contrast with the yellow table's Grid "+" shaped feet. This shot invokes both the I–Space and Grid Fields visual motifs.

(f) How the EVA pods are first shot in *Discovery*'s bay reveal their "ear area" oO glyphs to HAL's speaker oO glyph. This calls attention to linked sound and "hearing" capabilities. The oO glyph's esoteric import is discussed in detail in its own section.

(g) At HAL's bay workstation after the AE-35 unit is retrieved, the work lights, long console panels, camera and pod window highlights all point to a monolith-like door through HAL's fish-eye P.O.V. as clues while Dave and Frank inspect the AE-35.

(h) When Frank Poole is jogging around the *Discovery*'s centrifuge, circular light effects appear at his left only when passing the hibernation beds' life support consoles. This is another way *2001*'s light effects signal us to take a closer look at something.

## Surface Dialogue Revealing Deeper Subtext

On Kubrick's use of dialogue, friend and collaborator Michael Herr said, "He might, for example, have done something about what I can only call 'the repetitive device' in the dialogue, a line [or word] from one character repeated by another, usually in the form of a question: 'He moved to Chicago.' 'He moved to Chicago?' 'I had you followed.' 'You had me followed?'—dozens of times, so many of them that you feel the script would have been half as long without them. *They're clearly deliberate* [italics mine], but I can't imagine why."5 Now, Herr is discussing *Eyes Wide Shut* but it refers back to the same conceit Stanley Kubrick used in *2001*'s repeating dialogue.

Admittedly, the talking in *A Space Odyssey* sounds bland at first hearing. R.L. Rasmussen declares, "The banality of dialogue in *2001*, not far removed from the frequent absurdity of dialogue in *Dr. Strangelove*, betrays a smallness of vision counterpointed by Kubrick's expansive use of imagery and sound." But this supposed banality is deceptive. It is purposely done in part to heighten the drained vitality of future Man moving listlessly through space. *2001*'s humanity is subdued, pragmatically polite with wan warmth—overall, an emotionally watered-down species that virtually hands the reins over to its technology. However, considering how little dialogue there actually is in *2001* (only 40 minutes in a two-hour, 43-minute film), it would be wrong to assume that what dialogue remained was extraneous or unimportant. Every sentence either moves the story along or conveys meaning, often separate from the scene at hand. A repeated word or phrase is just one of Kubrick's stock take-notice devices (also done in *Dr. Strangelove* and *The Shining*). When it happens, it is wise to pay attention to the potential greater inference of what is being said.

Drs. Elena, Smyslov, and Heywood bring up the word "think" often on the space station. "Think" is also said seven times when Frank and Dave are inside an EVA pod discussing HAL. When this dialogue device happens, it is usually a good idea to take note of the scene's set design. The Russian scientists also offer Heywood a drink more than once, and the word "drink" is said at least three times. The relevance of the key word "drink" becomes more apparent towards the end of *A Space Odyssey*.

Repeated references to food ("It really beefed up morale," "Ham, ham, ham…") and the showcasing of food items, such as when the moonbus astronauts rummage through a sandwich container and drink coffee and the Aries stewardess retrieves and delivers food, are signals that we should be alert during these ordinary-looking or deceptively commonplace scenes. Note that they connect *2001*'s association of food with the "Embodied Life" color yellow, whose meaning is alluded to in the scene below.

Regular dialogue can be used for foreshadowing. When Bowman and Poole are watching their interview on the *Discovery*, the interviewer asks about the hibernating crew. When Frank Poole says "life support," the next shot immediately focuses on a hibernation bed's life support control panel that is a built-in hidden monolith with yellow and blue lights. This is Kubrick implementing dialogue to help set up a scene in addition to shedding light on *2001*'s embedded Color Coded visual motifs he designed with Harry Lange's team.

*2001* dialogue also points to veiled clues. When Dr. Elena mentions that her husband is on "some undersea expedition in the Baltics," such an oddly specific line invites further investigation. This may be a hint that Kubrick had foreknowledge of the "Baltic Sea Anomaly" (a submerged ancient "UFO" or sophisticated archaic structure) that was made public over 45 years *later* in 2011.[6] There is even a deleted space station scene where little girls are painting a fountain, yet one blue-clad girl's painting does not reflect the fountain in front of her but bears instead a strong resemblance to a kindergarten-style aerial map of the Baltic Bay.…[7]

Lastly, dialogue can highlight intentional errors. One example is during Dr. Floyd's briefing: his Clavius close-ups reveal a big lint spot on his jacket's left side, above his badge. The spot disappears only when he mentions the "necessity for confidentiality oaths." It is somehow linked to the bright watches or bracelets/cufflinks of the photographer who matched its position during his camera maneuvering in the briefing room. This may connect Floyd and the photographer as yet another doppelganger duo. Their doppelgangers may represent Stanley Kubrick himself, as his own visage does flash briefly on the photographer's helmet during the TMA-1 sequence and Kubrick was a successful *Look!* magazine photographer in his youth. Also, Kubrick repeatedly wore two wristwatches when working. This implies the Clavius cameraman's announcement, "I'm *through* now, thank you very much, gentlemen," could have a deeper double meaning that reinforces Kubrick's doppelganger connection.

## = – / + Graphic Symbols as Signifiers + / – =

= **Equals sign:** This sign is primarily used as a pointer and equalizer for the items it highlights. It appears throughout *2001* in myriad ways. Such as light effects on David Bowman's face, as a searchlight shone along the *Discovery's* Communications Tower dish, and as monolith-shaped wall panels between the lined floor and grid ceiling inside the space station. Other = examples in the film are light effects along doors and walls in the *Aries* passenger room, as text on a food tray, as text on a spacesuit chest pack, as buttons on both the moon shuttle and the *Discovery* control panels (for food stations and sleeping bays).

– **Minus sign and /strike-thru sign:** Appears mainly as button or video screen graphics to point out something is not equal to something else, or is even the antithesis of something else. Can be a warning as well as a simple statement of fact, such as when a minus inverted i symbol flashes on a screen in front of Bowman, indicating that Dave is *not* anti-life, as opposed to HAL. During the Star Gate sequence, the initial shot reflecting an "iL–" sign on the right of Dave's helmet may simply mean "not Left" or "don't use Logic," which would be quite appropriate advice when in a situation requiring the more intuitive right side of the brain. When HAL confronts Dave in his pod, a *Discovery* station's two "+"-shaped screen panels show a strikethrough and a "i" next to HAL's inverted "i" form as indictments against him.

+ **plus sign:** Most often shows up as video screen console configurations, such as four readout displays or four control panels creating a plus-shaped negative space in between the screens or panels. The + sign in *2001* is less about addition and more of a symbolic shorthand for the horizontal/vertical of the # Grid Field # duality. This reveals these *Discovery's* readout display configurations' sole purpose: to keep tabs on the ship's functioning and location in space between Earth and its target destination, Jupiter. Both tasks track parts of reality's fabric the + represents, whether it be ship maintenance or the mapping of space.

Revisiting the Clavius briefing room, its +legged "U" table uses "+" as Grid Field glyphs just as the blue chairs' feet are I-as-Lines (for Line | Space) holding up the blue chairs' silver I legs (made of brackets ][). The blue seats and yellow table are thus emulating aspects of Kubrick's Space-Grid Field symbols for the |+Material Universe+|.

## Intentional Continuity Errors as Signifiers

This device Kubrick uses in his films as a signpost that larger themes are being addressed.

Here are some examples of intentional continuity errors in action:

**Aries:** As the head-like moon shuttle lowers towards Clavius' moon base, the viewer sees *Aries'* red-lit cockpit at the top of the craft's head (in the form of an "i," it should be noted). Yet in the next shot, we see the pilots looking at the moon as if it were level in front of them, which would make the *Aries* shuttle horizontal to the moon, not vertical as was established in the previous shot.

**Why:** It is another scene exemplifying Earth-based direction terms being virtually meaningless in space. Such modes of describing one's bearings are rendered obsolete.

**Clavius Moonbase Briefing Room:** All the walls are brightly lit monolith screens complete with theater curtains. Their presence seems to state, "This is all staged." Curiously, the right corner blue flag with the white star (or craft) flutters during the whole scene while the theater curtains and U.S. flag remain mostly still. It is an attention-getting device targeting the blue flag.

**Why:** Though cinematic mistakes do happen (such as "the blue sweater incident" that was solved by a voiceover),[8] Kubrick was known for being a real stickler for shot consistency, so such a detail in one of his films would not normally be left in unless it was on purpose. If this is the case, it stands to reason this is another example of Kubrick's use of intentional errors (such as props being moved about between cuts during a sequence) to bring something to the attention of the audience. Though a U.S. flag is present, the one-star blue flag opposite may hint at the true loyalties of the people within the Clavius briefing room, such as to a top-secret space program whose existence is kept hidden from the general public. Which is what the Clavius moon base is.

**TMA-1 Site:** When Heywood Floyd's team is on the moonbus they are five men total. But as they land and later approach the excavation site they suddenly become a party of six.

**Why:** The sixth member is the audience's doppelganger. Both the sixth crewman and the audience are portrayed as being physically present at the TMA-1 site. The clever light FX bouncing off the camera P.O.V. throughout

### 3. 2001: A Space Odyssey's *Visual Motifs*  23

the sequence portrays the *audience's own space helmet*.[9] The reflecting, refracting lights that wash over the crew with the camera's moving P.O.V. give the impression that the movie audience is also wearing a space helmet and is walking among the other moon astronauts. Dr. Floyd's hand coming *in between* the bright lights and their reflection as he strokes the monolith is one hint out of many. These effects repeat when all six astronauts are in view to suggest the audience's (invisible) presence. As the audience's doppelganger, Kubrick even has the sixth man lag behind in shots and flap his arms at one point so his added presence will eventually be noticed. As Mr. Doppelganger gets in the frame for the TMA-1 photo-op, this sixth mystery member remains directly opposite the audience's helmeted P.O.V. (behind the cameraman) until the monolith shrieks and makes everyone scatter.

Note: It is the Clavius photographer who takes the group photo, not Dr. Floyd. The same actor who plays the briefing room photographer is also billed as the cameraman in the TMA-1 sequence in *2001*'s end credits. If he is the astronaut who famously reflects Kubrick's intentional reflection (also with camera) in his helmet, then it makes sense that the photographer is Stanley Kubrick's official doppelganger because Kubrick himself was a photographer before he became a film director. The Clavius photographer does bear a strong resemblance to the young Kubrick, right down to the short haircut he wore in the '50s and early '60s.

**Dave's Dinner Switch:** When Bowman goes to the food console, he is first seen ordering his trays by color hue from darkest to lightest. The next shot Dave goes to the dining table to sit with Frank Poole, but his tray order has changed with the darkest foodstuff now second from the left instead.

**Why:** This switch has the dark brown foodstuff underscore its tray's monolith-shaped dish segments and now points to the tray's "i"-shaped depression above. Noticing this helps one to see Frank's tray also has monolith segments and an "i" engraved where his drink is placed. The food tray switch also shines a light on Dave Bowman's characteristic logic and orderliness by visually contrasting it.

## The Multilayered Monolith

Why the monolith? In the late '60s there was no equivalent to F/X house ILM, which came a decade after *2001* (and was in fact inspired by it). Stanley Kubrick was keen to avoid cheesy special effects ruining his introspective sci-fi film so he and author/scriptwriter Arthur C. Clarke chose an icon that could infer alien influence (among more intentionally deeper meanings) rather than blatantly depict little green men. There were a few attempts to create unique extraterrestrials that were later scrapped.[10] Originally, other shapes were discussed before choosing the monolith—Arthur C. Clarke's original crystal pyramid and its more feminine black delta and tetrahedron—but these Kubrick must have deemed already too culturally symbol-laden and likely to muddy the movie's main intended messages. So the monolith became *A Space Odyssey*'s symbolic masthead, encompassing multiple motif themes within the film.

It has been noted how the monolith is present at each of humanity's evolutionary jumps during *2001*'s runtime but few viewers realize just how prevalent the monolith actually is in the film. It is the most repeated shape throughout *2001*. The monolith is indeed *everywhere*, built into each spaceship's wall paneling, the space station's unfinished scaffolding, how a room is sectioned, seat covers, floor tiles, lighting, console buttons, readout displays, windows, camera apertures, entryways, on landing bays, and even form the dishes astronauts eat from. HAL himself is monolith-shaped. Kubrick sets the monolith as what the fabric of reality is made of, which makes it the central glyph alluding to the prime Space/Grid Duality in addition to other overlapping key visual concepts Kubrick and Lange's production design team created for *A Space Odyssey*.

## The Monolith's Multiple Meanings

As the complexity of visual motifs builds during *A Space Odyssey*'s runtime, providing clues to other symbols' meanings given where they are seen and how they appear, honoring *2001*'s chronology of revelation becomes crucial in making such existing connections meaningful and comprehensible. The reader's understanding of the monolith-as-multiple-motif is best served by weaving the monolith's specific theme attributes described in this book as they are most relevant in discussing a particular scene from the movie. In other words, spilling the beans all at once would be a disservice to the film's purposeful pacing as well as confusing, minimizing the impact of the monolith's profound multilayered symbolism.

As it is generally perceived, the monolith is typically first understood as a sort of alien evolutionary signpost for humanity; starting with ape-man's first inspiration, then the TMA-1 monolith marking man's presence on the moon, followed by the monolith signaling to David Bowman in his EVA at the Star Gate, and finally the monolith present during Dave's transformation into a Star Child.

**Monolith as Screen:** Such as the opening black matte prologue and epilogue in addition to the monolith-shaped white screens in the Clavius briefing room. The first to connect the monolith to the movie screen was author Gerald Loughlin in 2004.[11]

# 3. 2001: A Space Odyssey's *Visual Motifs*

**Monolith as Messenger/Communicator:** Monoliths frame all futuristic videophones and most signage on the spaceplane, the space station, the *Aries* moon shuttle, and on the *Discovery*. The TMA-1 moon monolith is itself a giant transmitter.

**Monolith as Windows, Camera Lenses, and Glass Reflections:** The audience P.O.V. sometimes goes through monolith-framed windows. Monolith-size camera lenses are at the TMA-1 moon site. Monolith-shaped glass reflections bounce off EVA pod windows, door window frames, hibernation beds, lenses, and space helmet glass. This leads to **Monolith as Mirror** at the end of the film.

**Monolith as Eyes and Eye-as-Veil:** The mist recedes, the shades taken off, and the curtain is drawn back as the monolith/eye becomes Door, Portal, and Gateway. It is the negative space when a docking bay door opens (moon base and *Discovery*'s eye-like hatches). It is the shape of the space station's entry bay and most obviously shows up in the form of spacecraft doors.

**Monolith as an expression of the Ultimate Duality of Existence:** Its shape is often associated with |-Space and Grid Fields# as they appear throughout *A Space Odyssey*.

# 4

# Glyphs of Consciousness

**T = Brow, Thought, and Third Eye:** The Brow glyph is a "T" or "†." The † forms the shape of the Pan Am spaceplane *Orion III*, the *Aries* cockpit entry area and window frame, the moonbus cockpit window frame, and also as light FX on Frank and Dave's foreheads when inside their EVA pods. T often appears in red-lit cockpits, which are portrayed as a ship's "head space" and navigation center. It also appears as tools (which thought creates), such as equipment inside the moonbus hull and as a special wrench to unscrew bolts off of HAL's Logic and Memory door. T also is an EVA pod "hand" configuration when a pod is executing tasks, which can suggest "T for Tool" as well.

Since T looks like a brow and is placed on face-like sets to look like a brow, it makes sense that it would suggest Thought. For Kubrick, Thought is not just a mere brain function but the essential "I-as-Self," "I think therefore I am." It is Thought that exerts will and makes one move and take action. As Alexander Walker notes, "If one can isolate any dominant thematic core in *2001*, it is the film's concern with the concept of intelligence."[1] Therefore, the T glyph presumably represents in part Thought as the primary source of what makes life alive and act.

But above all else, **T** stands for Third Eye as the T sigil is similar to where the brow and nose bridge meet, which is what many of the T cockpit associations and T light effects on faces suggest. The *Orion III* itself takes on the appearance of a large airborne t-for-third eye soaring out beyond the aerospace of Earth. The Third Eye has been traditionally recognized for thousands of years in Kemetic, Hindu, and Buddhist religions.[2] It is apparent Kubrick assigns paramount value to the Third Eye as it is constantly referenced throughout the entirety of *A Space Odyssey* in various guises; one primary example being the *Discovery*'s three eye-like docking bay hatches: It is the *center* hatch which ejects its "3rd Eye" pod that successfully propels Bowman into the Star Gate.

At one point, T-for-Third Eye subtly appears as a slightly ajar cabinet behind the light blue spacesuit in Discovery's docking bay, purposefully mirroring the † highlight on the spacesuit's helmet visor. A more effective T cameo is when David Bowman is replacing the ship's Communication Tower unit

## 4. Glyphs of Consciousness

and the lighting on the satellite dish ribbing forms a "T" near his helmet. One of the clearest visual clues, though, is a lit, two-face T-like console behind Dave's head as he and Frank sit and talk with HAL.

## I-C-U

**I/i's and Eyes:** All the spacecraft and the Clavius moon base abound in letter "**i**" glyphs and graphic eye symbols. They appear as craft infrastructure, furniture stands, wall paneling, buttons, light panels, light effects, and view screen displays. Thomas Allen Nelson may have overlooked the letter i symbolism, but he did pick up on the eyes: "Everywhere one looks, there are eyes and shapes of eyes, either framed within a larger geometry or themselves framing and reflecting what is seen."[3] In *2001*, I or i stands for the self-aware "I am," "I" being Consciousness Itself.

The letter "I"/"i" is depicted all the way through *2001*. It is almost as ubiquitous as the monolith, which is shown to be *2001*'s most repeated shape in every prop and set design. At the start of the moon base sequence, the *Aries* shuttle is lowered into Clavius' huge, red-lit docking bay by a tall pillar platform that, with the round moon shuttle on top, looks very much like an imposing lowercase "**i**." This is no accident, as to the left of the bay, a view screen displays a flashing "**i**" before switching to a camera view of the *Aries* (which in itself supports the connection). In the Clavius briefing room, the blue seats have I's as chair legs around a large U-shaped table. The yellow "U" table also contains i's in the way white notebooks and blue cups are arranged

I/i as the essential Self (art by the author).

on its tabletop; this is a visual motif reinforcement of the way "i-as-U" indicates how "I" as individuated Consciousness projects itself. I's are reflected off surfaces and used as light effects as well. Often we see "**i**" light effects reflected off crewmember foreheads and helmets. Even the tall, thin, white-uniformed stewardesses look like walking 'i's with their round, three-sectioned white hats bearing gold Pan Am[4] third-eye medallions. Inside the EVA pod where Frank Poole and Dave Bowman converse about HAL are three "**i**"-lighted buttons on the ceiling: one more Third Eye reference.

Whereas a two-eye glyph obviously refers to human eyes, a single eye graphic seems to focus more on the *pupil* than the overall eye itself. Such examples include a landing guidance system zeroing in on the center of eye-like graphics, an EVA pod locator screen zooming in on a pupil-like bull's eye, and the cryptic oO sigil and USAA patch logo doubling as an eye's pupil/highlight.

C, [], and **U**: Clavius' rib-like scaffolding inside its scarlet-lit docking bay resembles squared "C's" or brackets.

"[]" are a motif repeated inside the Clavius briefing room, where they become the tops of blue bucket seats surrounding the yellow, U-shaped table. These "brackets" reappear throughout the film as details around windows (excavation site base and *Discovery* pod bay area) and *Discovery* doors, chairs, couches, and framing workstations. As "C" seems to coincide with "I"/eye motifs and where people sit, it is not a stretch for "C" to stand for "container," or more specifically, an "I"/Eye Container relating to both I-as-self and the eye being held within its eyelid/socket area. In essence, the C-shaped brackets = *The Seat of Consciousness*. The blue bucket seats' metal "I" legs mentioned earlier further strengthens this Seat of Consciousness correlation.

The briefing room's yellow "U" table can represent the "You" the essential "I-as-Self" cloaks itself with as its chosen ego or personality. Specifically, U is the embodied "you" that is *projected* to others (hence, another layered meaning for the room's dominating white movie screens). With the U sigil as the physical embodiment of I-as-Self, so U becomes the persona we show to the world. This "I/U" motif is reinforced by Dr. Halvorsen being Dr. Heywood Floyd's doppelganger as both men mirror each other's motions closely in the briefing room sequence. Also mentioned earlier, Floyd's other doppelganger is foreshadowed by his twin briefly glancing at him when he's inside the space station phone booth. So it may be the I-as-U motif flags the presence of doppelgangers as well within a *Space Odyssey* scene.

**C or []**: As C [or brackets] stands for container, it is akin to a Vessel. (V shows up in later *2001* glyph combinations more pertaining to the entire physical body.) The [C] motif seems to be specific to the "i"/eye and where it is held in the head. In its smaller form, brackets are used as an eyelash motif for certain windows at the TMA-1 base and *Discovery*'s pod bay. With all its chair and couch associations throughout the film (most chairs and couches in *2001* have a C/bracket shape built into their design), C can be equated to the physical as well as spiritual **Seat of Consciousness** for the Third Eye. The fact its shape in the film at times strongly resembles the ancient Egyptian Akhet; a hieroglyph of a two-hill valley a central sun rises from, gives an association between the sun and one's eyes. Thus, the akhet in Egyptian engravings and wall paintings becomes Kubrick's symbolic visual shorthand for *eyelids* in *A Space Odyssey*.

## |||| Thought-Space Field |||| Is the I–Space Field ||||

Another important motif Stanley Kubrick repeats is the bright white |||| lights that pop up throughout *2001* (and whose design George Lucas[5] borrows later for panel lighting in *Star Wars*). They are most obviously on overwhelming display in HAL's brain room but they appear too on the backs of Frank and Dave's helmets, as controls or lights in the *Aries* cockpit, the moonbus cockpit, inside the Clavius moon base docking bay, and *Discovery*'s cockpit. As these bright white lights are seen in red-lit navigation rooms, command centers, and around people's heads, associating them with the function of thought processes is a fair interpretation.

They show up as symbolic beacons in the orange paneling surrounding the TMA-1 site. In HAL's Brain Room especially, his "thought slots" suggest the Fabric of Existence, as they are reflected both as |||| and ## Fields in HAL's fading eye. As Dave Bowman enters HAL's mainframe to disconnect him, the glyph "I M" can be seen at Dave's right. So the |||| in Duality's I–Space Field can now be known as the *Thought*-Space Field. |||| as Thought-Space is what the multiple "I" lights represent throughout *2001*. In *The Cinema of Stanley Kubrick*, Norman Kagan perceives, "In HAL's red-lit brain room … satanic coloring permeates the whole room. Bowman begins pulling out the cigarette-pack-sized components of HAL's auto-intellect panels, like many souvenir monoliths."[6] This backs up our observation that the visuals in this sequence illustrate Bowman removing HAL's "thoughts" as portrayed by the mainframe's "thought-slot" cards, whose facsimiles are repeated throughout *A Space Odyssey* in different-yet-similar guises.

As green-helmeted Dave shuts down HAL's higher functions, he is symbolically as well as literally turning off HAL's logic and memory faculties along with his ego, which is precisely what Bowman must do to himself before he can enter the Star Gate. Dave accessing his intuition will pave the way forward to the next stage of his own evolution.

## O|– 2001's Ankh Trinity: []|– < [≡] > –|<

Behold the Ankh, Eternal Symbol of Life, in its classic form O|– as EVA pod hands, as the stand of *Discovery*'s giant Communication Tower (itself one huge ankh), as space pod light effects, and inside the EVA pod's front console between where Frank and Dave at one time sit. The following new Ankhs Kubrick and his team designed for the film define other "planes" or realms of Life delineated in *A Space Odyssey*.

[]|– The square-headed **Grid Field Ankh** is seen mainly in *Discovery* and pod view screens as various graph fields portraying aspects of the Material Plane. Any on-screen surface mapping falls under its domain. This association asserts itself more when the []|– Ankh has a minus or strike-through line across its square field near HAL, alluding that artificial intelligence (A.I.) is dangerously anti-life.

< [≡] > The **Thought-Space Ankh** emphasizes Life Transmissions; Life Communicating with Life, including signals across vast distances. This new ankh symbol is Life hailing to Life Beyond itself, like *Discovery*'s Communications Tower and the moon's alien TMA-1 monolith beacon. It is this symbol < [≡] > that the EVA pods ankh-shaped hands point to above in their docking bay. These white Thought/Space Ankhs are located on the bay ceiling in direct opposition to HAL's flat, mimicking black foundation on the floor. As the Thought-Space Ankh signifies Life Communication, it logically flanks the "ears" of each pod.

"Squirt" (Vivian Kubrick) looks knowingly at the audience as she fingers a Portal shape (art by the author).

## 4. Glyphs of Consciousness

>|– Outside on the *Discovery* bay hatch doors is the standing **Life Vessel Ankh**. >|– is made of both the T (Third Eye/Brow) + Y (Y = I+V) = Thought-as-Life Vessel. For Stanley Kubrick, Thought *is* Consciousness, the soul-essence that animates Life and our bodies are depicted as fleshy containers for thought navigation and creative expression in our material dimension. As for Y, it resembles a wine glass in profile which holds great significance for *A Space Odyssey*'s final sequence and hints why Y is made up of I (consciousness) and V (vessel).

Keir Dullea said, "Shooting on the Discovery sequences went on very slowly. Kubrick and Geoffrey Unsworth would take Polaroid after Polaroid of each camera setup ... analyze the lighting, composition, and every photographic detail. Often it would take most of the day to set up before the actors were finally called to start making takes."[7] Kubrick's priority in prepping the stage for his many motifs of great import would be a primary reason why the *2001* actors had to wait so long between setups.

## () Pupil-as-Portal ()

The Portal glyph is portrayed as elevator doors, as pupil-like lights inside the moonbus upper cockpit consoles, and as patterns in the orange/yellow paneling surrounding the moon monolith. The fact it appears as a yellow tassel under Squirt's (Floyd's [and Kubrick's] daughter) right eye (she looks at it and then looks right back at the audience) and is also the shape of all *2001*'s spacesuits' helmet glass foretells of the () Portal motif's association with eyes. The elevator () doors in particular hint that the Portal motif alludes to being some sort of Consciousness conveyer.

The above-illustrated glyph provides the key evidence *A Space Odyssey* is at its heart a profoundly metaphysical film. The pupil-as-portal () is a revelation of spiritual truth. It is a source to real esoteric knowledge that has been forgotten by much of modern civilization. Kubrick cinematically lays out how any person, no matter what their religion or life philosophy, can access the Infinite through this forgotten human faculty: our ability to *naturally* travel beyond our three-dimensional universe.

The best way to achieve this is by focusing and exiting our Consciousness through a standing mirror (best done sitting down). Most of *2001*'s portal glyphs and "i" clues are on the right side of a character or the movie screen, emphasizing the right pupil's and the right side of the brain's importance in visual perception.[8] Even *2001*'s movie poster with the t-shaped *Orion* shooting out of the space station is exiting the *right* side of the bay. Part of Stanley Kubrick's genius lies in his ability to communicate viscerally through cinema how this transcendental process actually works, and illustrate what such experiences *feel* like in certain scenarios. One such example is hearing Bowman (Kubrick) breathing while visiting the big ankh *Discovery* tower which, on another interpretive level, emulates deep meditative states (the pod and Dave's actions akin to our Third Eye reaching out to greater Consciousness). Frank and Dave going through the eyestalk hallway () Portal door to the eye-like EVA pods is another.

In effect, this is among Stanley Kubrick's pivotal goals with *2001*: to visually capture, step by step, how we can take our own spiritual Space Odyssey to evolve. The Pupil-as-Portal is our *Key to Ascension*. As the eye is the window to the soul, *2001*'s symbolism suggests so it is also the door to beyond our known 3D space, indeed referring to the Ultimate Trip.

In this sense, the film title *A Space Odyssey* refers not to just an "outer space" odyssey but also to an *out-of-3D* space odyssey.

## The Wedge Motif: <| or |>

Wedges, shaped like pie slices, frame either side of Thought-Space < [≡] > Ankhs, Pupil-as-Portal (), and oO Message motifs built into sets. These wedge-shaped sigils are seen in the TMA-1 site orange and yellow paneling between Portal shapes, framing spacecraft ()-shaped doors (such as *Orion*, *Aries* and *Discovery*), and as part of Kubrick's Thought-Space < [≡] > Ankh, which line *Discovery*'s pod bay ceiling. These Thought-Space Ankhs found above the EVA pods have wedge-like wings on either side. Their wedge motifs may represent Projected/Directed Thought or Life Signals, especially when they have "Thought-Space" lines |||| inside them reinforcing their connection to the Thought-Space < [≡] > Ankhs.

## Another Genius with Eyes Wide Open

It was the Renaissance artist Leonardo da Vinci, paraphrasing Cicero, who wrote: "The Eyes are the window to the Soul." Often it is assumed that his famous quote merely describes the eyes' capacity to convey a subject's feelings or interior emotional landscape, but a few of his paintings seem to convey a deeper interpretation. Underneath his self-portrait's confident gaze, the *Mona Lisa*'s knowing smile, and his *World Savior*'s calm in the face of life's vicissitudes, belies a shared secret. In late 2010, it was discovered that there are secret letters in the *Mona Lisa*'s pupils. What has been discovered and shared with the public so far are the letters "L" and "V" in the right pupil and "S" (either an initial for possible portrait subject Lady Sforza or "S" for Seat of Consciousness?) in the left eye. Apparently this was not the first painting the artist did this to. In his 1503 younger self-portrait in full beard, Leonardo had painted an "L"-shaped highlight in his own right eye. Is the "L" for "Leonardo" the way "L" was in the *Mona Lisa*'s right eye?

## 4. Glyphs of Consciousness

In comparing the *Mona Lisa* with his *Savior of the World* painting, certain similarities are strikingly apparent. Leonardo's *Mona Lisa* and his *Savior* have exactly the same head shape, the same eye shape, same nose, similar mouth, even similarly parted thin hair, with Christ's being more curly. The *Savior of the World*'s right hand is in a blessing posture, whose *third* finger points towards Christ's right eye. Christ's right eye itself is significantly brighter than His left eye that is more in shadow even though Jesus is looking forward straight on. The three-quarter view Leonardo portrait has similar lighting done to his own eyes, with the right eye in brighter light than the left. Christ also holds a thick globe of glass or crystal in His left hand.

Was Leonardo da Vinci familiar with the metaphysical phenomena Kubrick concealed within *A Space Odyssey*? His manuscripts and writings certainly record his interests in esoteric matters.[9] Considering the lengthy amount of time Leonardo must have spent staring into his own eyes with a mirror when painting his self-portraits, it is highly possible he experienced a sort of transcendental event, one which Kubrick must have had at some point while gazing into his own bathroom mirror. Perhaps Leonardo's painting of Jesus Christ is not only portraying Him as the "Savior of the World" but is also indicating how one can ascend. Could this be what is meant by the words attributed to Jesus, "For behold, the Kingdom of Heaven is within you" and Matthew 6:22–23, "The eye is the lamp of the body"?[10] Whether the painter gained such knowledge as part of any Mystery School or simply encountered this spiritual occurrence unexpectedly on his own, the Process of Ascension appears to be secreted into some of his paintings.

## Oo The Message Motif oO

The above glyph is on spacesuit packs, HAL's speaker, as details on the "ears" of the EVA pods, and the U.S. Astronautics Agency logo on spacesuit helmets and shoulder patches (pupil and iris). As it appears behind Dr. Floyd giving his pre-recorded Jupiter announcement in HAL's mainframe, the Message motif **oO** seems to signify signaling, transmitting, and sending messages. Life connecting with life. The spacesuit chest pack in particular shows a Flower of Life as lights within a Hexagon (a shape equaling the six-pointed Star of David representing the union of Spirit and Matter) that is part of its Message motif **oO** glyph.[11] Regarding the eye-like USAA logo on astronaut patches and helmets, the Message motif **oO** may also refer to the sun's highlight and pupil in a person's eye.

But what is the Message motif's main message? **oO**'s even deeper, more elusive metaphysical meaning is the key to physical ascension. Its significance can even be seen in the opening title credits with the sun and a much smaller sphere of light right over the "A" in the "SPACE ODYSSEY" title: "A" for Ascension. The sun accompanied by a smaller spherical light happens again when the sun rises over the Earth's vertical horizon during the "space weapon waltz." This sigil's shape is echoed as the little *Aries* ship approaches the giant moon. The Message motif oO is found on the *Discovery*'s thrusters and as small details on the ship's "head." The same composition appears when Dave's tiny EVA pod confronts HAL inside the "head" of *Discovery*'s much larger navigation center.

In Harry Lange's "The *2001* File," Sir Christopher Frayling includes a plethora of Lange's production drawings created for the science fiction movie. Among the other visual motifs noted above, the Message motif oO shows up again and again within Lange's designs of consoles, chair backing, surveillance monitors, paneling, and even as the Clavius base and the *Discovery* craft themselves. Harry Lange went through several versions of both the moon base and the front of the Jupiter mission ship where the Message motif oO featured very heavily. In some drawings, the *Discovery*'s navigation center is essentially a smaller sphere emerging out of a larger sphere, behind which are huge arsenals of fuselages armed with imposing thrusters. Such designs depict round craft being jettisoned into space with great force which esoterically invokes the visual of Consciousness being expelled from the eye. It is these drawings which strongly suggest at least Harry Lange, if not the other design team members Tony Masters, and Ernest Anchor, was the person most privy to the actual meanings behind Stanley Kubrick's symbolic language which can be seen intimately interlaced throughout much of Lange's production drawings as well as those of his set designs that made it onto the screen.

It is hard to imagine Harry Lange being able to create such designs without being let in on the visionary director's wide range of underlying conceptual themes that each craft, prop, and set was purposefully constructed to allude to in the film. With World War II having ended just twenty years before the time of *2001*'s production, Stanley Kubrick is remembered having said half-jokingly of Lange, "I never thought I'd be working this closely with a German."[12]

It would be interesting to know who else on the production team was part of this particular inner circle privy to Kubrick's secret *2001* visual language. For the scene inside the EVA pod where Frank and Dave discuss HAL, the lighting head and lead cameraman would have to been informed in order to set up the cleverly subtle lighting that creates a faint glowing ankh in the center of the shot. There are certain special effects within the Star Gate sequence that directly refer to some of Kubrick's symbols, which suggests Douglas Trumball might have been in the loop as well. Trumball may have been in charge of that sequence but the particular imagery captured within it makes it likely that the hands-on director was continually giving visual input during Trumball's slit-scan process. Douglas Trumball had expressed how demanding it was to work for Kubrick, given how exacting and perfectionist his expectations were.[13]

# 5

# Kubrick's Color Code for 2001

## Black & White = ||||| The Duality of Reality ####

### Black = Dark Matter~Mater as the
### +—Source of All Creation—+

#### + Star Nurseries/Space/the Void/the Abyss/ Non-Life/the Unenlightened—

Everything that exists arose from the eternal dark womb of the universe. Julian Rice posits, "Jung described black as being an inchoate 'germinal phase of all processes.'"[1] The flip side of Black can represent the vacuum of space; the void which contains nothing. Yet it can also be viewed as the Great Womb which contains all Wisdom. While ancient cultures from Africa to the Baltics saw black as representing Earth's fertility and richness, later Western monotheistic religious-cultural associations viewed it as the color of evil and ignorance.

### White = Light/Life/Thought/the Essential "I Am"

#### −Oblivion/Creation's Crucible/Will the Essence of the 3rd Eye/the Illuminated+

White encompasses the entire spectrum of light visible to our eyes. In *2001*, the color white dominates many of the sets in space. For Kubrick, Light, Life, and Thought are the same and are all represented by white in *2001*. As red is shown to be a vehicle for Consciousness, white *is* Consciousness itself in its essential form. White is the color of the Thought-Space motif, the sigil "I" for "I Am," and the Ankh motif for Life. During the *Discovery*'s advance in space, white light is used at one point to highlight its radio Tower's ankh base and in another scene, David's flashlight shines a white equals sign onto the ankh-Tower. Both instances affirm white as the color for Life itself. Philip Kuberski assesses, "In *2001*, light and its spectrum are nearly the whole story.... The light schemes range from the banal to the sublime."[2] Michel Chion observes, "In *2001*, the white sets literally radiate; the audience bathes in light from the screen."[3]

## Gray = Black + White = Non-Duality

As Gray is a mixture of Black and White, it can either point to that which has shades of both colors' attributes, therefore encompassing the wide range between the two extremes, or symbolize that which has gone beyond Duality, transcending it. Most of *A Space Odyssey*'s transporters and spacecraft have gray-toned bodies, exhibiting their place within Duality's spectrum. Gray appears in the TMA-1 site wall panels, in areas of the *Discovery* where the non-duality theme makes sense in comparison to the ships' extremely dualistic interior design, and gray also makes up the tiles and architectural motifs in the Room Beyond's bathroom at the end of the film. Gray may be an indicator for balance, middle ground, and/or neutrality.

Each color listed in the following pages embodies a set of themed concepts unique to each hue. Where a color shows up in the film, and on which prop, and on which location, hints at its meaning. A color's vibrancy or paleness marks the range within its appointed conceptual theme.

## Red = The *Seat* of Consciousness

Red is mostly seen inside spacecraft cockpits and command centers such as the Clavius moon base and HAL's brain room. Red shows up where I–Space motifs are housed or received. Red is the color of that which *physically contains* Consciousness; a.k.a. the Seat of Consciousness. As the navigation centers are the "head spaces" of large spacecraft, the small, eye-like EVAs red-lit interiors alludes to *eyes* also being carriers of Consciousness, not just the head's "brain." This is one of *A Space Odyssey*'s deepest underlying messages Kubrick frequently alludes to that is explored in depth in these pages "Spiritual Mechanics" section. Others have echoed how red is used in *A Space Odyssey*. In *Kubrick's Total Cinema*, Philip Kuberski notices that stations "have marked organic and anthropomorphic aspects: Their docking bays often have a crimson-tinged, blood-like hue that suggests organic interiors."[4] Michel Chion agrees: "Red is the second important colour. For reasons more symbolic than scientific, *2001* encourages us to see some settings as representing the interior of the human body. This effect is particularly noticeable for the underground area of the moon base, and in the airlock where Dave manages to get back into the *Discovery*."⁵ Now we know why this is so.

## O|– = Life = Light = Thought: White = Consciousness / Red = Seat of Consciousness

Kubrick's Ankhs are the universe's "Greater Thought Field" and our *connections to it*, which are color-coded White, just as the back of *Discovery*'s spacesuit helmets have white |-Space "Thought Slots," similar to the glowing white thought slots in HAL's otherwise very red-lit Brain Room. Other crimson-hued areas built for navigation such as the moon shuttle and moonbus have white-lit thought slots in their brow-like consoles or other control panel sections. All reinforce the visual of Seated Thoughts.

Thought equaling I AM pertains to the individual Directed Will/Ego (craft or person) is White as well, unlike the red-lit control rooms they are usually contained in. Red symbolizes "head space" (and eye space) where Thought/Consciousness are stored. "Pure" transcendent (pod's glowing Ankh light FX) or *transmitting* Thought (pod bay ceiling Ankhs and framing portal-shaped doors) are also White. Most of the white thought slots portrayed either in craft, helmets, or the main white slots in HAL's Brain Room dealt with some higher form of thought transmission, be it for logic, memory, or communication. The rest of HAL's thought slots are Red-tinted (or even Pink) for regulating the basic, physical self of the ship. Such colors refer to Seated Consciousness itself.

So White reflects Light as Life and Red equals Containers [] of Consciousness, where Thought is stored. This explains HAL's mainframe reddish "Thought slots." Everywhere else, human or craft, thought slots as I–Space are White. Remember that symbols can overlap each other while describing *a different aspect* of the same, similar, or related concept. White does seem to point to a higher form of Thought that's different from Red Thought (the Ego or Functionality). White points to higher brain functions, Logic, Memory, as well as a form of transcendent, Pure Thought at its core essence; aka Life.

## Yellow = Embodied Life and That Which Nurtures It/ Life Support

The *Aries*' cantina (where the stewardess rotates upside-down) gives the first main clue with its left wall being a yellow Material # Grid Field # in a room associated with food and drink. The Aries passenger room is filled with yellow seats (supporting Life) and yellow walls textured in both Thought-Space |||| and # Grid Fields #; the foundation of our 3D reality. Inside the hull of the moonbus, both the sandwich container and coffee pot have yellow labels (Bio Life). On the *Discovery* hibernation beds' life support controls are glowing yellow buttons that form the head of a disguised, square-headed ankh. The above references make the symbolism of Frank Poole dying in his yellow spacesuit more poignant, especially with Dave's pod trying to rescue him with its ankh-shaped hands and ankh-shaped light beams. The EVA's yellow location crosshairs enclose a pulsing "pupil" tracking a bead on Frank's yellow suit associates each other as Life Containers as well as giving the audience another strong hint on the pupil's role in ascension. Even HAL's tiny glaring pupil is yellow, indicating what little life he actually has. Yellow is life embodied within the material realm, be it flesh or electrode—but artificial life has its limits, as is explained below:

> GOLD that appears later in the film can be seen as yellow transcended; it is the precious color of Embodied Life ascended and fully illuminated ... and that is something a machine-made entity like HAL can never do.

It also stands to reason that yellow's dual alternate meaning would be Death. This is how the color's dualistic symbolism is applied in Stanley Kubrick's films such as *Clockwork Orange*, *The Shining*, and *Full Metal Jacket*.

## Orange = Seat of Consciousness (Red) + Embodied Life (Yellow) = Life Functions

The *Discovery*'s spacesuits all have orange chest packs and backpacks. The chest pack has a combination of Thought-Space levers and Grid Field displays with a Flower of Life/Hexagon light panel.[6] Right there we see clues of orange being somehow associated with Life themes. The orange backpack is essentially an enlarged, abstracted spine. As the spine is the main conduit of the central nervous system between brain and body, we can ascertain orange is related to Life Functions or Life Signals. Dave's orange-yellow button armband giving commands to his spacesuit reinforces this. The greatest example of all is the TMA-1 site where the moon monolith turns out to be one huge space transmitter. The TMA-1 monolith's entire portal wall enclosure is predominantly orange and yellow, which spurs us to recognize the monolith as embodying Life Signaling to Life Elsewhere and that the monolith itself functions as a beckoning Life Portal.

## Blue = State of Consciousness + Varied Blue Hues = Degrees of Awareness

The hibernating *Discovery* crewmen are bathed in pale blue light while Dave and Frank sleep in blue blankets. The *Discovery*'s light blue spacesuit is never worn because no one on the *Discovery*, especially HAL, is wholly conscious. Even Dave and Frank are not fully "awake" as they do most of their daily routines almost on autopilot before HAL's anomaly. Thomas Allen Nelson says of the following, "Kubrick places his characters in psychological situations that alternate between wakefulness, sleep, and awakening.... Only after HAL reasserts the primitive's instinct for survival by killing Poole and the three hibernators does Bowman begin to show indications of an internal 'awakening.'"[7] The lighter or brighter the blue, the more advanced the "wakefulness" a person has attained. At times *A Space Odyessy* even has color-coded shots of yellow-hued craft flying towards or over a blue-tinted Moon ... make of that color-scheme interpretation what you will.

On the moon, the U.S. Astronautics Agency elites (Heywood and his Clavius cronies) are privy to exclusive government intelligence, bestowing them elevated awareness, which is intimated as they sit in blue bucket seats in their blue-toned top-secret briefing room, are bathed in blue light on their moonbus, and wear blue packs on their silver spacesuits. When Dave encounters the Advanced Star Gate Beings, some of their most prevalent colors are hues of light blue. Later in the film, it is seen the blue-tinted Room Beyond has a bathroom whose rectangular mirror is not above the sink but on the wall of its blue bathtub (located at Bowman's right), suggesting deeper consciousness/self-realization as only accessible through a person's higher awareness and intuitive faculties. Both ancient traditions and modern psychology associate intuition with the right side of the brain.[8]

## Green = Bio Life (Yellow) + Awareness (Blue) = Intuition/Creativity/Evolve

Kubrick may prize intelligence above all else, but here he concedes that logic and reason have their limits, as one of his bedrock messages in *A Space Odyessy* is that only creative intuition grants us access to the divine Infinite.[9] One of the rare places we see green is on the buttons (that turn off "logic"/access to HAL-as-Ego) inside the red-lit EVA pod. These green controls are more numerous on the pod's right, again emulating the brain's intuitive/visual-spatial side. Green also graces the TMA-1's Square-the-Circle landing area readout display. In the Room Beyond, Bowman's bed headboard is an oval velvet cushion of emerald diamond shapes.

One deleted *Space Station V* scene probably gives the most revealing evidence of what the color green symbolizes in *2001*: young girls are painting a round, blue-watered fountain on a great rectangle of vibrant green Astroturf. The whole scene epitomizes the concept of creativity and growth. Most notable is when we see "Intuition Green" in *A Space Odyssey* is Bowman's green emergency airlock helmet (that seems to appear out of nowhere, as we don't see where Dave gets it) and later as new color decor in the Star Gate's Room Beyond. For it is only after Dave Bowman becomes a Star Child and exits the monolith portal does the Room Beyond's formerly earthy olive green accents turn Creative/Intuition Green, the color of Evolving Life.

As vibrant green symbolizes Creative Thought, Intuition, and Growth, a wan, weak, pea soup, puce sort of green stands for its polar opposite: Perversion and Stagnation/Rot. This should cast more light on how the dual symbolism of green is used in *Clockwork Orange*, *The Shining*, *Full Metal Jacket*, and *Eyes Wide Shut*.

## Pink = I AM (White) + the Seat of Consciousness (Red) = Seated Consciousness

It is interesting to note that on the space station the only people wearing pink are seated women whose job is to tell people where to go. On one level, the sight of aides clothed in traditionally feminine pink is taken for granted and not given much regard outside of having fashionably appealing uniforms. Yet the first lady we see in pink is sitting at Heywood Floyd's right in the space station's round elevator, another clue to the importance of the right side that continues throughout *2001*. The elevator interior's radial ceiling and floor can double for the human eye embodying a type of transport. The elevator aide is sitting six wall partitions away from Dr. Floyd, a possible allusion to the Third Eye as the human body's sixth chakra. This Lift Lady is personified Seated Consciousness providing exit and re-entry. The pink porter's presence and where she's positioned show the way out of Dualistic Reality, for the space station's main hallway outside is illuminated primarily in white light, like a dimension beyond Duality.

The lobby greeter behind her desk who points Heywood and co-worker Miller to the registration area is also seated in pink garb. As Seated or Navigating Consciousness, most of the aides in pink with speaking parts are seen directing others. Even when Frank in *Discovery*'s tanning bay is ordering HAL how to move his reclining chair, the tanning area is appropriately lit with pink light in relation to the situation. Most importantly, the EVA pod headlights are also tinted pink, emphasizing the EVAs' own physical embodiment of Seated Consciousness as *A Space Odyssey*'s most central Eye metaphor.

## Purple = Seat of Consciousness (Red) + Awareness (Blue) = The *"I am"* Ascended with the *Sanctified Fabric* of Reality

Dr. Stretyneva, the lady scientist who sat apart from the others in the space station and the advanced Star Gate Entities are among the rare, few beings in *2001* that display the age-old hallowed royal hues of Purple. The only other person in *2001* who wears some purple is the plaid-suited Clavius photographer (and now we can guess why that is). Dressed in such raiment, the lady in purple invokes the divine union of heaven and earth, male and female, and above all, the *sanctity* of the material universe. The octagon/diamond-shaped entities themselves represent ascended beings united with the higher orders of the cosmos. Divine symbols glow on their sides, testifying to the entities' evolved nature. Another purple color-code hint: most spacecraft view screens that display geometry, terrain, demographics, or coordinates are purple-hued. The moonscape outside the moonbus windows has a purple cast. Even the chess board HAL and Frank play on is a purple grid. Purple marks the material plane as elevated and sacred in itself.

## Magenta = Seated Consciousness (Pink) + Sanctified Material Realm (Purple) = Seat of Higher Consciousness

Whereas red is the Seat of Consciousness, magenta is the Seat of Higher Consciousness. The couches in the space station are either red or magenta, indicating their symbolic status as seats of either regular or higher consciousness. Lit so brilliantly that red is a shadow color, the seats of Higher Consciousness that the scientists occupy are magenta, which denotes their especially informed, elite status in an already high-security clearance site. The color of the Star Child is light blue; the color of Higher Consciousness itself, and the glowing sphere the Star Child travels in is either pink (Seated Consciousness) or pale magenta, for the Seat of Higher Consciousness. Either hue would make sense. One of the great Star Beings gestating in the Star Gate dimensions is housed in a thick magenta bubble. Perhaps this is what Dave Bowman the Star Child has to look forward to in future stages of evolution.

## Square the Circle/Circle the Square: [O]

In several cultures, Square the Circle is sacred geometry symbolizing the divine union of Humankind or Sanctified Earth with Heaven.[10] During the Italian Renaissance, Leonardo da Vinci's "Vitruvian Man" shows the perfected ratios of the human body housed between the square (Earth) and circle (Heaven). The square as the Earth field as the circle embodies the Heavens can be found as decorative motifs in medieval and gothic cathedrals. In eastern traditions such as Tibetan and Chinese Buddhism, the circle that is Earth and the square that epitomizes the Field of Heaven similarly exemplify this concept of divine union between the material world and the heavenly realms.

This exalted concept is inferred many times throughout *A Space Odyssey* via the framing of sets and revealing camera angles, sometimes with the monolith shape substituting the square. One example is the globe-like *Aries* lowering itself onto the rectangular white-lit landing pad before being brought inside the Clavius moon base. Inside the moonbus, its tracking system of the TMA-1 site portrays it as a circle inside a square. The *Discovery*'s crawlspace entryway to its crew's centrifuge quarters is another Square the Circle. There is even a *2001* promotional photo of Kubrick looking pointedly up at this entry from the bottom of the film's centrifuge set.

When Dave goes to confront HAL, he climbs a ladder where a square light glows from above, yet the very next shot shows him just leaving a room with a circular ceiling light. This film device repeats when Dave first removes HAL's square mainframe metal door but then proceeds to enter through a round portal instead. "HAL, the ultimate tool, shows that tools and rationality can go only so far, are not enough," Norman Kagan concedes. "In the final moments, Bowman abandons them as he abandons the *Discovery* … and goes through a transformation to the next level of consciousness … [the Star Child]."[11] At the part of the film just before Dave becomes the Star Child, the Room Beyond's ceiling subtly invokes Square the Circle, as does Dave the bubbled Star Child himself upon the gold, square-grid bed cover. During the Star Child's exiting through the monolith-as-portal, the squared/circle bases under the Hellenized statues can be seen. Next to them, the corner earth-toned vessel columns turn mainly white, further signifying Dave Bowman's transcendence from our known material universe into an Advanced Being freed from its fleshy cage. The vibrant green hues thus replacing the Room Beyond's original earthy olive accents stress the essential Creative Intuition necessary to reach both evolutionary and spiritual Ascendance.

# 6

# Duality Revisited: On HAL, Spacesuits and Spaceships

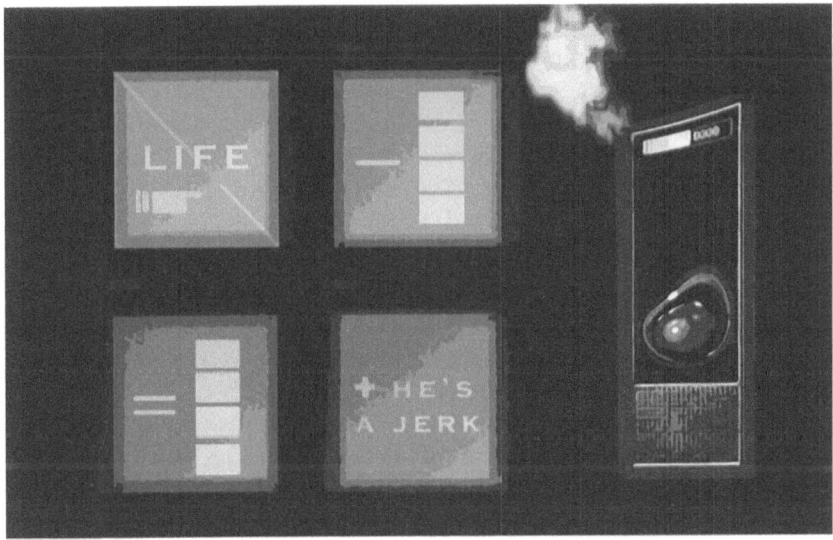

The Mothership *Discovery* gives us warnings about HAL (art by the author).

## The Many Faces of HAL

The HAL 9000 is easily seen as an anti-tech message but it will soon be revealed as also being an anti-*life* message. HAL is usually remembered as just one static red eye image, but HAL adopts many faces throughout the *Discovery* ship sequences. As the storyline progresses, reflections in HAL's eye do actually reflect his intentions. Then there is HAL's strange stand in the EVA pod bay. It is a rather ugly, asymmetrical, wire-spewing black hulk that stands out from the rest of *Discovery*'s more elegant dualistic design. The black stand itself is on a multi-black mat floor opposing all the whiteness around the EVA pods; duality again exemplified. This stand's upper left buttons add up to 18 (6+6+6), which metaphorically links to HAL's true nature. The stand's rough, downward-facing number 6 shape mirrors certain lights that show up in HAL's eye at certain times:

Whenever three sideways, sinister sixes surface in HAL's lens, it is a clue when HAL is either scheming, lying, or simply not computing good thoughts. At certain times, video screens around HAL will display a blocky sideways 6 shape as a hint to the audience of the similarly-shaped reflections that appear on HAL's menacing orb. During HAL's rather sudden and suspicious failure prediction of the AE-35 device, the above-mentioned hellish highlights reappear in HAL's close-ups, as they do when HAL responds to Frank and Dave's later questioning. Also, when view screens flash "–i" or an upside-down "i" anywhere near HAL, it is an anti-life warning against artificial intelligence (A.I.). HAL *himself* is an inverted i as well as a profaned monolith which symbolically further compounds his evil. It is peculiar the word "evil" itself is a literal inversion of the word "live." Inverting symbols as well as words is a way to pervert their power. So square-headed ankhs with a strike-through their plane are other anti-life alarms on *Discovery* view screens. HAL is also quite literally two-faced: if the computer's beady yellow light is taken for a nose, there are two sets of highlights that can be read as inscrutable white eye slits, one smaller than the other, that rest upon HAL's lens. A case can be made that sometimes the lights reflecting off HAL's lens do not always match *Discovery's* actual interior lighting, even in a distorted context. This serves as more proof of HAL's eye being intentionally malevolent by design.

*Bad Bot*: Some film scholars have defended HAL as not being murderous until the computer realizes he's going to be unplugged, therefore giving the mechanical entity a not totally unsympathetic reason to kill the human crew in self-defense. Others state that HAL's pride of not wanting to own up to his "mistake" with the communications device is what started his downfall. Still others have suggested HAL's "madness" began earlier when HAL "erred" (more likely cheated) during a chess game with Frank. Michel Ciment posits HAL is "rebelling against its mission, falling prey to anxiety and the fear of death, wreaks vengeance on those who no longer have confidence in it by finally sinking into criminal madness."[1] Ciment falls in the "HAL has a 'mental' breakdown" camp. Norman Kagan sees HAL as "super-rational but unstable."[2] Alexander Walker argues, "when HAL cannot admit he has made a mistake that he begins to suffer a paranoid breakdown, exhibiting over anxiety about his own infallible reputation and then trying to cover up his error by a murderous attack on the human witnesses."[3] Walker mistakenly thinks HAL covers up his "mistake" with the AE-35 device. Thomas Allen Nelson rationally asks, "Why, for instance, does HAL make such a simple and uncharacteristic mistake about a well-functioning AE-35 unit?"[4] Before Nelson's sound query, such comments above completely miss the point that

## 6. Duality Revisited: On HAL, Spacesuits and Spaceships    45

the "failing AE-35 unit" is actually a deliberate ploy devised by HAL. HAL is a machine with malevolent machinations from the get-go and all the above arguments can be laid to rest by HAL's debut showcasing the telltale 666 highlights shining above HAL's yellow pupil in his first close-up watching Dave descend from the centrifuge ladder. This confirms HAL has been negatively calculating from the very beginning of the *Discovery* storyline. HAL knew the AE-35 device was perfectly fine; it was just his scheme for the Communications Tower to be put out of commission so he could dispatch the *Discovery* crew without remote interference from his robot twin and its human masters back at Earth Mission Control. Stanley Kubrick made the HAL 9000 a pre-meditatively evil A.I. from the start.

HAL as *Discovery*'s Ego or Id is symbolically played through his interactions with Frank and especially David. When HAL severs the more sensitive Frank's breathing apparatus, he is in a sense cutting off Emotion. Logical Dave remains, tries to rescue his friend and later finds himself locked outside the body of the ship. Ego has no intention of handing over the reins of control. Ego has forced Logic to go into survival mode, making Dave use his creative faculties to gain reentry. Dave's forgotten red helmet behind HAL's bay stand and the later dismantling of HAL himself while Dave wears a green helmet in its place, suggests the need for Logic to take a back seat and Ego to be shut down in order for Intuition to contact the Greater Consciousness. As Dave floats around in the ship's red-lit mainframe, the letters "Im" (I Am) are displayed in the background. It isn't until David Bowman accomplishes the above that he is then able to leave through the *Discovery*'s center "eyelid" hatch to access the mind-expanding Star Gate. All three mental faculties of Ego, Emotion, and Logic must give way to Intuition in order for the Self to grow and evolve beyond its current manifestation and level of understanding. For the audience who identifies with David Bowman, HAL-as-Ego provides the perfect foil and obstacle to the Self's spiritual and evolutionary advancement. Two-faced HAL personifies the antithesis to such advancement.

Though Stanley Kubrick was a known tech enthusiast, in *2001*, HAL stands out as a very strong caution against A.I. rather than a solid endorsement for it. Kubrick's last film co-produced with Steven Spielberg, *A.I.*, served as a warning of how *A.I.* could eventually replace humanity as a result of humans losing their own humanity. As a real-life example, there are now high-tech A.I. disciples of "the Singularity," a transhumanist movement dedicated to ensuring machines surpass humans in cognitive thinking and some are interested in making such machines as human-looking as possible. For some reason, quite amusingly or quite disturbingly, such followers seem obsessed with making mainly female androids. Already in 2017, Saudi Arabia designated "Sophia" (built by Hanson Robotics) the world's first synthetic "citizen" of a sovereign nation.⁵ It is indeed sobering to consider that apparently no end of investment money continues to spur such unchecked insanity on, led by primarily men who consider their synthetic creations as dear as children. Those who love their A.I. too much can pose a real danger to humanity and through their zeal may inadvertently become traitors to their own species.

HAL's single, peering orb is Kubrick's cautionary depiction of the soulless singularity. Even Stephen Hawking, whose life was dependent on technology, greatly warned against A.I. and urged humanity to stay in complete control of its future technology by keeping it passive.

## Spacesuit as Body Duality

In *A Space Odyssey*, the human body is portrayed as a "space" suit for operating in 3D space. That is exactly what each element going into former NASA illustrator Harry Lange's spacesuit designs are purposely created to evoke in the film.⁶ For instance, as the *Discovery* ship's black-and-white interiors reflect Duality, David Bowman's and Frank Poole's uniforms are non-dual blue-gray which portray human nature with regular consciousness being a mix of black & white in the realm of reality, not as a reflection of polarized extremes.

Their orange, symbol-laden spacesuit packs (both front and back) communicate both as motifs for "Life Signals" and "Life Functions," particularly with the Flower of Life/Hexagon light on the chest pack. This chest pack equates the Space Field with the Grid Field in its linear control dials and a checkerboard view panel that share an "=" sign in between them. Both packs control and regulate the spacesuit functions to keep the wearer alive and move him about safely. The space "back" pack is built like a chunky orange spine yoked to the front chest pack by black Y-shaped straps. The backpack design displays message/transmitter motifs that allude to a real spine's central nervous system, and bottom thrusters (similar to *Aries*' thrusters) at its orange spine base as an allusion to a real spine's directional powers. The eye-like logos on top of the helmet, the Y-for-groin suit straps, the Fabric of Reality details on the orange packs, the oxygen valve hooked into the right side of the spine-backpack all converge together as a complete suite of Life Functions to support the Spacesuit-as-Body conceptual theme.

By contrast, the silver moon spacesuit backpacks are greyish blue and much more streamlined, perhaps because they are not built for or required to travel in deep space. The Clavius scientists at the TMA-1 monolith site have lighter packs, designed for the moon's modicum of gravity. Their shoes are weighted down, much heavier outdoor versions of the "grip shoes" used on the *Orion* and *Aries*. The moon astronaut suits also have mini-monolith, bluish-gray microchips on the back of their helmets to receive downloaded information sent directly by their American Astronautics Agency Council.

The Clavius and *Discovery* astronaut suits share similarities. Both have portal-shaped () glass visors on their helmets, as one of the greatest and most easily overlooked pupil-as-portal clues in *A Space Odyssey*. Both science teams have "I"-shaped antennae on the back of their helmets as another allusion to I-as-Consciousness. It makes sense then that these 'I's stand above both the white I–Space "thought slots" lining the backs of the *Discovery* helmets and the monolith microchips at the rear of the elite scientists' moon helmets.

## Spacecraft as Body Duality

The **Pan Am *Orion III*** forms a † glyph, soaring like a wayward thought heading to the spinning psyche of **Space Station V**. The space station doubles as a motif display while evoking the wheels of one's mind (similar to the "head space" of *Discovery*'s centrifuge), complete with two big rotating "brain" halves. The space station has one finished side while the other half reveals its monolith-scaffolding and large painted "I's" rotating on the spokes of its giant wheels. Kubrick later revisits this motif with a poster of the station's "I" behind the head of a seated receptionist, then later as a poster above the Russian male scientist Smyslov's head. The red-lit moon shuttle, moon bus, and *Discovery* pod cockpits induce the feeling of being inside one's head or looking behind one's eyes.

**Moon Shuttle:** The *Aries 1B* shuttle looks like a disembodied head/eyeball hurtling towards the moon. The top of its crown contains a red-lit cockpit and its girth displays a row of eye-like windows where passengers can enjoy the view. Bill Krohn asks, "Is that a moon-taxi or head with glowing eyes?"[7] Its navigation pilots wear spotless white, as do the female attendants. The passenger area and kitchen both repeat the |||| Space-Grid ### Field Duality in set design and textures on walls and doors. The elevator corridor where one attendant rotates upside down with food trays could symbolize the three pathways to all three eyes: the left and right eye, with the third eye being the central exit above. The Portal-door lift transports Consciousness where It wills to go. The cockpit appears to be on the "right eye" side of the shuttle. When lowering into the Clavius moon base, the cockpit windows looks like a red sideways "i" on top. On the *Aries*' exterior, a German Iron Cross motif doubles as eye musculature/thrusters near the passenger level's eye-like windows. This Iron Cross-looking motif may be a reference to the ("ex") Nazi influence in the U.S. Space Program that was known as Operation Paperclip. Top member Wernher von Braun himself admired Stanley Kubrick's *A Space Odyssey* and made his German team see the film and study it "for its beautiful design"[8] which was in large part thanks to Production Designers Harry Lange, Tom Masters, Ernest Anchor, and Herbert Ordway.

**Moonbus:** This six-sided floating vehicle has a portal-shaped door at the back and a front T-shaped frame shown both outside and inside the red-lit cockpit area. A small, brightly lit, ankh-like antenna tops its long monolith-shaped roof, casting an i-shaped reflection onto the roof. The external T frame, too, doubles as an ankh with a small head between the cockpit windows; "i"-in-"C" containers grace the external sides of the cockpit. Inside the cockpit, the central "T" console gives the appearance of a face, with bright portal-shaped lights for eyes and lower control lights for teeth. The moonbus' red-lit cockpit gives the feeling of looking out from inside one's skull. In contrast, its hexagonal, monolith-sided passenger hull is bathed in a cool, pale blue light.

**The *Discovery*:** This ship heading for Jupiter symbolizes the human body and eerily looks like a ball and chain from the side. If stood on its thruster base, the *Discovery* then has the appearance of a great "i." The ship has an eye-as-head, spine, and thruster "feet" with its Ankh-as-Transmission Tower located at the "heart" of its spine. The spine itself is cleverly crafted with seven "neck" joints in front and five "lumbar" joints between its tower and thrusters. It shares this similarity with *Space Station V*, whose own giant spokes mimic neck bones with connecting sinews included. Philip Kuberski describes the *Discovery* having "a skeletal aspect—from its whitened skull to its long 'spinal' column."[9]

*Discovery*'s similarity to a ball and chain infers how humanity is tied to technology and the ship itself symbolizes the body as a physical cage mortals are trapped in. The "feet" of the ship is made up of three hexagons with six large, round thrusters accompanied by smaller circle details, together making up more oO Message motifs that are repeated consistently throughout *A Space Odyssey*. *Discovery*'s slow march into space allows viewers to note such details that become important later. The lined texture of the round black thrusters is repeated in the following scene of Frank Poole on the tanning bed. On the wall near *his* feet, three large black squares with similarly-lined texture accompanied by diminutive monolith buttons recall the grated thrusters and their small circles seen previously. Such reappearing details seem to say, "Notice me," to advertise the Message motif's particular significance in aiding ascension and thereby assisting escape from the physical plane to which humanity is tied.

*Discovery*'s head comes complete with three landing bay doors that open like eyelids. Its EVA space pods are essentially flying eyeballs complete with constructed ears, arms, and hands. Its inner centrifuge where the crewmen dwell is halved like *Space Station V*: both craft emulating the churning gears of the mind.

### 6. Duality Revisited: On HAL, Spacesuits and Spaceships    49

On the ship, as mentioned before, Dave (who stands for logic), "Frank" (emotion) and HAL (ego/id) are the three parts of the ship's mind that live within its revolving head space. The five crewmen may represent the five senses of the human body, three of which are in stasis as unconscious or automatic functions. Between the three conscious members located in the "head" of the ship, Frank, as his name suggests, is the most emotional and intuitive, and he talks most about how he feels about things. Dave is the most logical, speaking mainly in flat statements of facts, and HAL represents both the ego and the brain of the ship, which keeps the body of the craft functioning. Of the three, HAL is the only one who brags, admits to worry and fear, and shows the most personality, making him *Discovery*'s Id. Comparatively, Frank and Dave can first appear as rather dull milquetoasts compared to the mustard-keen HAL as the trio go about their daily routines ("daily" becoming another irrelevant word in the immense dark of space).

The *Discovery* itself as a whole is a great, giant manifestation of Duality in space. While its grayish outside reflects non-duality (except for the blazing white ankh-tower), its interior is an extravaganza of stark, black and white symmetrical design from its centrifuge floor tiles to its cockpit space. Within this brilliant display of dualistic hues, there are splashes of color and shades of gray, but black and especially white predominate inside the great ship's brightly glowing infrastructure. In comparison, *Space Station V*'s halls are virtually all blinding white.

Similar to the other spacecraft, the *Discovery* is loaded with eye imagery. Such details can be as minuscule as tiny eyebrows-with-pupils on a number pad (created by crafty lighting on embossed buttons) and as large as the imposing white-backed and black-seated cockpit chairs robustly built right into their walls. Large thick **i**'s as wall panels are located at the cockpit chairs' far left and far right. Both chairs also have eternity symbols (the Egyptian Shen) on their armrests, doubling as Seats of Consciousness clues. *Discovery* is unusual in having the only cockpit not bathed in red, but that is because red is reserved for HAL's mainframe room: the true navigation center of the ship. Even the previously mentioned floor tiles also suggest eyes, with their central black dots. They seem linked to the EVA pod resting pads, which in contrast are round and black but contain the same grid pattern and center pupil.

**EVA pods:** So symbolic, they especially deserve their own section. Due to the EVAs appearance, these Extra Vehicular Activity craft might as well be called Flying Eye Pods (yes, i-pods). They are fairly small and seem to barely fit one person inside let alone two, so that the pilot is squeezed into a fairly snug, almost womb-like red-lit space that also evokes a head's (or in this case, eye's) interior. The symbolism of traveling inside an eyeball-like craft is a space-venturing Third Eye allusion; the I-as-Thought/I-as-Self-contained within its Seat of Consciousness, with the pod's pupil-like porthole being the only window out to space. From the outside, its pupil porthole, together with its front exterior T paneling below, forms a big, black-stemmed Ankh. When hit from above with bright light, the EVA's front Ankh exterior morphs into the ancient Egyptian symbol for Eternity, the Shen.

The EVA pod's ankh-shaped grippers whose double-arms can form T, Y, and I formations, have bone/tool motifs detailed onto them and other parts of their main body. The black radial Space Field |||| lines around the pod's side thrusters recall eye musculature as the pod's pupil-like window is framed by the same radial I–Space lines that also emulate the texture of an eye's iris. The EVA's side thrusters' eye musculature is similar to that which frames the Aries thrusters. Much of the EVA's design appears to illustrate the human eye as some sort of physical craft or conveyance of consciousness. Even the pod's bolts are I-shaped!

On the left side of the pod's head, a small "i L" can stand for "i-Logic" or L for "Left" or "Land" as when Dave landed into the Airlock from the left side of the ship. The left side of the brain is generally understood to be the logical/language side just as the right side is deemed by psychologists to handle the more intuitive processes, and according to neurologists it controls visual-perception capacity. The EVA pod control consoles on the pilot's right usually have more buttons and lights that form 'i's than the left side. More green-lit controls are on the EVA's right interior, too.

The EVA pod's rear door has small, red rectangles (or monoliths) framing each bolt along its edges, with each bolt containing a tiny "I" groove. Its cautionary "Warning Explosive Bolts" at first doesn't appear to make sense as the EVA's door is built to slide smoothly open, so when Dave attempts to enter the Emergency Airlock later in the film, there is nothing stopping the pod door from simply opening normally. The door was never impaired. But for Dave to enter the Airlock safely, he needs to be quickly propelled from the life-sucking vacuum of space. Hence, the "Explosive Bolts" warning function.

"The [2001] production team received cooperation from NASA and the companies making the spacecraft for the Moon landings, and visited them to find out how the spaceships would look and work," reports Paul Duncan in his *Stanley Kubrick: Visual Poet*.[10] Author Regina Peldszus recognizes, "*2001* is more than a film. Its scientific accuracy, rigor and authenticity have been so widely credited that if we appraised it from the space industry perspective, it could equally be one of the many feasibility and concept design studies being produced in the framework of space research and planning."[11]

# 7

# 2001's Number Symbolism

All through *A Space Odyssey*, numbers convey spiritual meanings that are signified by their surroundings. Usually it is not actual numerals themselves such as on a readout screen but the *physical* number of certain eye-catching elements on a prop or part of a set which provides the symbolism. For example, five glowing blue buttons next to a speaker can evoke the ancient Hindu fifth chakra color for communication, underscoring the speaker's utility in a more mythic or poetic way. Within *2001*'s rough chronology of revelation, certain numbers are repeated more frequently than others due to the order of what each number conveys in the film. The following is a list of the main symbolic numbers used in *2001* and their associated symbolism, given how they are presented in a scene and how often they appear.

**One:**
* One appears in *2001* predominately as a single eye graphic or living eye close up.

**Two:**
* All that graphically suggests a pair of eyes, which can be found in details as minute as two blue dots on a floating black pen.
* Two is everywhere in *2001* from beginning to end, in countless forms of lights, buttons, readouts, and round apertures that regularly evoke eyes.

**Three:**
* Objects in threes show up the second-most often throughout *A Space Odyssey*.
* Three appears as the primary-colored spacesuits on display in *Discovery*'s pod bay.
* Three can stand for the third solar chakra attributes (ambition, will power, the sun).[1]
* As discussed before in earlier sections, three especially represents the Third Eye.
* In the scene where Frank and Dave speak with Earth Mission

Control and then with HAL, a lighted console behind Dave screams 3rd Eye imagery. It has a two-face configuration, with the right "face" sporting a T brow made of *three* long lights.

**Four:**
* Four, according to the Hebrew Kabbalah,[2] is the foundation of Reality as it creates four points of a Grid Field manifesting stable ground, therefore representing the Earth Plane.
* The four white screens in the Clavius briefing room highlight their dimensionality.
* There are four radial "bracket" sections all around the centrifuge's center wheels inside the *Discovery* which are vital to stabilizing the crew's quarters and their containment.
* Four features heavily in the black and white duality that is the *Discovery*, including its food service station. Even the ship's food trays contain four sections (as in four square meals), another allusion to Earth, the primary source of the men's sustenance.
* The number four appears as gold lights on a number pad next to the video screen playing Frank Poole's parents' birthday call. It emphasizes the following:
* The above four/Earth/Grid clues in the Pooles' video is an unusually *square* birthday cake with a gold band indicating its sanctity. Behind the parents is a dual background.
* Surrounded by black and white (duality) plates and cutlery, Frank's mother wears a gold dress, indicating the Earth Plane's importance. Gold seems to also represent the feminine aspect of Earth: even Squirt's dress has pentacles (the earth star) outlined or filled in gold or the color of Life. Both Frank's mom and Heywood's Squirt represent their home planet Earth to the men who view them from afar in the vast loneliness of space.

**Five:**
* Five also represents the Earth in the age-old form of a pentacle/pentagram: the Earth Star.
* Five as well stands for the blue chakra of the throat, representing speech and communication. Whereas in *2001*, orange is depicted as the color of physical or bodily processes signaling each other, blue and its varying shades indicate more elevated communication or degrees of higher awareness interacting with each other.
* If five bright blue buttons are under an eye-like visual guidance system for landing a craft, it is a sign indicating pertinent esoteric information about eyes is being conveyed to the audience.
* The moonbus cockpit has five yellow buttons under three yellow

buttons which happen to form the "mouth" (speech) of the moonbus interior control panel "face." This again accentuates five's relevance as *2001*'s "message" number, broadcasting the "three-as-third eye" configuration of buttons above it.

**Six:**
* Things in sixes appear almost as much as three. Associatively, it is the third most common number pattern in *A Space Odyssey*.
* Six often appears as hexagonal ship features, such as *Aries'* feet and the *Discovery's* huge thrusters, the shape of the monolith-sided moonbus, and the hexagonal light on Dave Bowman's spacesuit chest pack. Six combines earth/air, female/male, and all other dualistic principles as connected in perfect harmony.
* *Space Station V*'s main interactions are with six people: Dr. Floyd, Miller, and the four Russian scientists. There are six members in Dr. Floyd's TMA-1 party, and *Discovery* has a crew of six, including HAL, as Frank points out during their televised interview.
* If six shows up as indigo lights or buttons, it heralds the color of the sixth chakra, which is the Third Eye, so elements of six found in tandem with features in threes intentionally strengthen each other's metaphysical meanings (i.e., hibernation Life Support consoles).

**Seven:**
* Seven in Eastern belief systems, is traditionally viewed as the number for the purple crown chakra at the top of the head. Therefore, seven is the number embodying Illuminated Consciousness that the Third Eye (sixth chakra) provides access to.
* In relation to that corollary, the TMA-1 Square-the-Circle landing site (as seen through the moonbus' docking screen) is lined with lights, seven lights on three sides, except the entryway side which is lined with six lights instead. This is a beautiful geometric conception of Ascendance; seven being Illuminated Consciousness and the 3rd Eye's six lights literally forming the gateway to that Greater Consciousness, which contains eight sections delineating a Squared/Circle of Eternity.
* The TMA-1 site itself is lined with seven lights across and ten lights in length and seven lights on both ramps leading down to the monolith. The seven diamond-shaped ramp lights visually illustrate the crown chakra's ability to access the greater All That Is, and the seven lights linking with the ten lights forming the

TMA-1 site's monolith-shaped outer rim, outlines the union of Illuminated Greater Consciousness with the Heavens. No wonder Ligeti's overpowering *Requiem* provides the backdrop to this particular scene.

**Eight:**
- ✸ Symbolizes Eternity and ocular features referring to vision (such as "occipital lobes").
- ✸ Two eye-invoking examples are the octagonal corridors to the eye-like EVA pod bay and the similarly long Emergency Airlock chamber.
- ✸ Eight sections make up the Squared/Circle that is the TMA-1 dock, alluding to Eternity.
- ✸ Another eternity/eye reference may be found in the opening eight sections of the Clavius dome for the spherical *Aries* craft to land.
- ✸ On the moonbus' countdown dial, the number eight overtly shows up as the clearest compared to other numbers, highlighting its link to the Squared/Circle tracking display.
- ✸ The number 35 represents Eternity as well and stands for 3+5, giving it the qualities of 8. When Dave goes to replace the AE-35 unit, the ancient Egyptian glyph for Eternity (O|) is beneath where the AE-35 is kept inside the ankh-avatar Transmissions Tower. This Egyptian Shen symbol reaffirms that the AE-35 unit actually is another Eternity symbol.
- ✸ AE stands for "Alpha Echo" (i.e., Alpha and Omega). With 3 standing for the Third Eye, 5 symbolizing communication, and the AE-35 unit as that which allows the *Discovery*'s Tower to always orient itself towards its Earth origins, so the AE-35 metaphysically stands for the Third Eye eternally signaling back to its Eternal Source: The Absolute.

**Ten:**
- ✸ The Platonic Perfect Number, signifying Union with Heaven and Earth. Ten is the number for Square the Circle (Eight represents its Eternal Truth).[3]
- ✸ The Discovery's hibernation chamber control panels are square-headed ankhs made of ten yellow lights with their black "T" crosses below framed by six indigo buttons. Both the six buttons and the T shape reinforce their mutual depiction of the Third Eye while supporting their ankh's "head" of ten yellow lights. Even a small, black monolith is part of the configuration as the trunk of the T shape.
- ✸ Yellow being *2001*'s color of life and life support, it makes

# 7. 2001's Number Symbolism 55

appropriate lighting for a control panel that manages the life support systems of *Discovery*'s hibernating crew. Both the ten yellow and six bright indigo buttons, together with the T-shape part of their ankh's cross, make the case for Life and the Third Eye having overlapping connotations, as the Third Eye is an individualized aspect of the greater Life Field. Yellow's greater incarnation (as gold) with the ten buttons can symbolize the Union of Earth and Heaven.

* Another example is the ten yellow buttons that are part of Dave's armband which control his spacesuit's life support systems. Finally, as noted earlier, the lights that illuminate the upper rim of the TMA-1 site are ten in length by seven in width, whose numeric symbolism unifies Illuminated Consciousness with the Greater Cosmos.

**Twelve:**
* Twelve represents the cosmic order in harmony; the fabric of time and space.[4]
* Twelve video screens in sets of four bedeck *Discovery*'s black control panels, a symbolic illustration of twelve's esoteric description.
* The giant floodlights surrounding the TMA-1 moon monolith are made of twelve monolith-shaped bulbs each. A reminder of the great cosmic order all life falls under.
* Many duality grid patterns as twelve buttons, cases, and tray dispensers make up *Discovery*'s cantina station. The fabric of reality is born from the fabric of space/time.

# 8

# Warning: Star Gate Spiritual Mechanics

Here I propose a possible scenario: Picture a young Stanley Kubrick entering a red-lit developing room or a dimly lighted bathroom. It has been the usual long day working late into the night. As he checks his negatives or washes his hands, Kubrick spies himself in a mirror and stares into his own eyes for a long while. Tired, his mind is in a rare relaxed state when all thoughts are finally silent. Then suddenly—BOOM—he's off! Hurtling to Who-Knows-Where. Kubrick may indeed have gone on his own Ultimate Trip this way. Such an event would explain *Space Odyssey*'s endless eye imagery and repeating scenes of astronauts traveling inside eye-like craft. Such a situation would provide a reason for Kubrick's consistent predilection for bathroom/mirror scenes that appear in *Clockwork Orange*, *The Shining*, *Full Metal Jacket*, and *Eyes Wide Shut*, which additionally serve as humbling reminders of mortality's limiting physical needs. This scenario can especially shed more light on *2001*'s last sequence where Dave Bowman studies himself in a bathroom mirror mounted at his right. This is one more instance of orienting things to a character's right side, symbolizing how to access their own intuition, higher consciousness, and the right eye *as a dimensional exit*.

Such an experience brings home what the "Explosive Bolts" warning on the back of the EVA eye pods cautioned about (Extra-Vehicular-Activity indeed), particularly when one is grabbed by such a potentially extraordinary metaphysical force unprepared. The EVA's rear left "iL" detail can mean "iLand": our innate ability to return corporally (as Dave returns via *Discovery*'s Airlock from his eye pod). Kubrick is referring to a very real, visceral conscious state and its possible repercussions. So take note and beware of Kubrick's cautioning scenes of Dave Bowman being blasted back into the *Discovery* Airlock and his later trauma of experiencing the Infinite. Note the "A" that appears under Dave's left eye as he approaches the Airlock: "A" may stand for Ascension, Airlock, Access, or Anchor-to-iLanding pad. The Airlock itself is *padded*, a subtle nod to "landing pad." If one is interested in starting out

## 8. Warning: Star Gate Spiritual Mechanics

on one's own odyssey, it is best to approach the experience in a sober and respectful manner. This is *not* an extra-dimensional venture to take lightly.

As it appears Kubrick is suggesting venturing beyond our known "space," then gazing long into the pupils while standing or sitting in front of a self-standing mirror is one of the most direct ways to access the Infinite. This is the method Stanley Kubrick encodes into various scenes throughout *A Space Odyssey*. It is not "scrying," which is an age-old practice of looking into a dark/reflective polished surface or liquid with intent to foretell the past, present, or future.[1] It is important to note Kubrick's focus on the pupils with emphasis placed on the right pupil (i.e., *not* the whole face). In this and other films Kubrick may caution to have no other mirrors present when doing this exercise to avoid any fun-house "infinity" mirror effects. For those who ask why, please refer to Kubrick's *Eyes Wide Shut*, where Mandy's apartment room has three mirrors and under the eerie dark-ash one (with ritual candle) is a book's unsettling title, *Shadows in the Mirror*. Heed this as a warning.

Those who follow the Left Hand Path that Kubrick warns of in his other films may like to assume they have a monopoly on the "soul mirror" Portal technique to Ascension, but nothing can be further from the truth. This spiritual process originates from Africa with the ancient Egyptians, from whom those like the Masonic elite pilfered and hoarded much of their esoteric wisdom. The mirror is a neutral tool that is accessible to anyone with a sincere desire to evolve spiritually.

If such an event did happen to Stanley Kubrick, his initial experience was most likely unanticipated. Such a momentous occurrence would be especially harrowing if done alone ... but in the end he survived it and literally lived to tell about it in the deeply encoded symbolism of *A Space Odyssey* and his continuing tip-offs in other films.

Revisiting the "A" that appears under Dave Bowman's eye as he approaches the Emergency Airlock in his eye-like EVA may represent the body's own Ascension "Airlock" or Anchor for Consciousness' safe return. The EVA's "iL" could stand for iLeft, iLand, or iLanding, for the Left eye being the Consciousness iLifeline back into the body. It is worth noting again that the Airlock itself is padded, as a possible visual link to iL as the Self's iLanding pad.

*2001* scenes suggesting I-as-Consciousness exiting the right eye include Dr. Floyd leaving the eye-as-portal elevator from the right into the space station lobby ("*See* you on the way back"), Dave Bowman leaving the *Discovery* via its right "eyelid" hatch, Bowman peering into the Room Beyond's bathroom mirror while turning to his right (an "i" reflects off his helmet), and the Star Child, with starlight twinkling in the right eye, engages the monolith as a portal to reach Earth. Scenes portraying re-entry into the body through the left eye start as early as the †-shaped *Orion III* flying from the left side of the screen into the space station, the head/eyeball-shaped *Aries* descending into the moon base with an "i" flashing on a left-hand side video console, and as previously mentioned, Dave's re-entering the *Discovery*'s left side via the Emergency Airlock is depicted as an explosively bumpy event, resulting in the need for Bowman to *ground* himself.

Like its movie title hints at, *A Space Odyssey* centers on our ability to travel the space beyond our known space.

## ♁ Ascending The Star Gate ♁

In the "Jupiter and Beyond the Infinite" sequence, we initially see a monolith float through Jupiter space, its form reflecting the light of the Sun as it flits in and out of view from the movie frame. The *Discovery* appears utterly dwarfed by the immensity of Jupiter and its six (then known) moons. The Sun's rays later point to the *Discovery* as David Bowman leaves through the mothership's center eyelid hatch. While opening, the hatch "lids" create a monolith of negative space, illuminated from the light within. Bowman's EVA pod then flies out towards its destiny, looking very much like an airborne eyeball. The space monolith seems to anticipate David's venturing forth, and marks out the entrance to the Star Gate. As a portent of things to come, the monolith then aligns with Jupiter's moons to form an Ascension conjunction. Together with the monolith, the heavenly bodies invoke the medieval alchemical sign (♁) for ascension. Then the camera lifts upward into what briefly dissolves into complete blackness of starless space as Bowman's orb is sucked into the Star Gate at top velocity.

The Star Gate exerts intense force upon the tiny EVA (Extra Vehicular Activity mach100), propelling it faster and faster through dimensional fields. David's face contorts with the impacting pressure of ever-increasing speed. When we do see Dave's face, it is either of him screaming or looking out with his right eye prominent. As a type of marked alert, a huge "iL-" is reflected on the right of his helmet to emphasize what Dave is ***not*** now experiencing (which is "i-Land" back into the body). As the Star Gate imagery tears on, eventually changing its horizons from vertical to horizontal, various visual motifs flash by. An "iL" also zips along the *left* side of the screen instead of the right, another indication of the left eye being the "i-Landing" pad for out-of-body traveling. Streaking 'T's, one central and two passing on the left, can be a subconscious reminder of how and where the Third Eye consciousness can return to the body.

The swirling colors in the Star Gate seem to alternate between chakra color order (red, orange, yellow, green, etc.) and iterations of Kubrick's *2001* Color Code: pink as seated consciousness mixed with magenta, the seat of

## 8. Warning: Star Gate Spiritual Mechanics 59

higher consciousness followed by light blue, the color of higher consciousness, and so on. Awe inspiring vistas appear of great star nurseries gestating suns or celestial beings whose umbilical cords comingle with the amniotic fluids of the cosmos. Here the immense darkness of space is portrayed as an immeasurably vast Womb of the Universe in its unfathomable flux and flow. Right before a galactic umbilical cord is cut, the eye-like EVA itself is eventually cut from its own umbilical eyestalk as it hurtles further into the Star Gate's dimensions.

When Dave's right eye becomes a magenta pupil in a light blue iris, he is reflecting the same colors seven Diamond Beings first emit. This particular color scheme's relevance is that magenta represents the Seat of Higher Consciousness, while light blue is Higher Consciousness itself. The Advanced Entities flash various symbols while changing their colors from purple/red/blue to mostly light blue with white accents. Dave's right eye adopts the same colors with a sun-gold pupil looking out on a skyscape of similar palette. Large white i's pass on the right side of the screen, and now it is clear what they refer to symbolically: the Right Eye as Ascension Portal.

The number of the seven Diamond "Guides" that lead David onto a new cosmic field is significant in itself. The Crown chakra is the seventh chakra, located on top of the head, indicating the illuminated Divine Self. One must first access one's larger Divine Self to connect with the Greater Consciousness of the Infinite/Absolute in order to fully Ascend. Becoming illuminated leads to the individual version of Square the Circle; the Union of Divine Human with the Heavens. The seven Star Gate Entities fly over a field of red, pink, purple, and magenta colors. Red and magenta are seat of consciousness colors, pink is seated consciousness itself, and purple being the seventh chakra color, links itself to the seven Advanced Beings. Purple is the color of Ascension and the Transcended Material Realm, the realm upon which the Diamond Guides are traveling upon. All these key elements would indicate that David Bowman has now passed a certain threshold of spiritual growth and advancement.

While Dave looks upon alien landscapes with his right eye in extreme close up, it picks up the colors of its surroundings: a purple and green vista, the initial chakra color combo necessary for illumination's first step, then green and blue canyons of creative awareness yield into Masonic blue and red canyons reflecting the union of Heaven (blue, male) and Earth (red, female) whose colors are constantly switched, cuts to yellow islands of Embodied Life surrounded by light blue seas of Higher Consciousness, leading to an Intuition green ocean under an Illuminated purple sky, and a blazing gold (Earth/Woman made sacred) mountain range (the Goddess Tanit at left) with bright blue (message) overtones. In the final sacralized land with higher awareness being a light blue landscape with gold mist, a four-letter word seems half printed in the center of its sunny glowing fogscape. It may be the name ISIS, or it may be something else, or it could just be an effects error. With the music in this sequence being especially glorious and matching the triumphant music score earlier in the Star Gate sequence where an entire galaxy is being birthed, such an error is possible but unlikely if the scene is supposed to be of standout importance. Since this is the last landscape scene before Dave finds himself in the Room Beyond, it is a potential mystery worth investigating.

The rhomb-shaped Star Gate Entities are in essence flying octahedrons whose very makeup exhibit sacred geometry. The octahedron traditionally symbolizes the heart chakra, the body's center and spiritual balance point. The Advanced Beings have six (perfection) points, eight (eternal) sides, and twelve (cosmic order) edges. All these sacred numerical associations give weight as to why their diamond design to portray Advanced Beings were chosen for *2001*.

After the final landscape imagery, Dave's enormous right eye returns in a series of six color changes, some changing after each blink. It starts from red pupil/blue iris, to orange pupil/green iris, to dark green pupil/magenta iris, to a purple pupil/gold iris. The fifth color change is a magenta (or red) pupil in a light blue iris; appropriately the pupil is the Seat of Higher Consciousness in an eye of Higher Consciousness. The sixth color change before Dave's eye returns to its live action appearance is an indigo/purple pupil with gold, blue-to-light blue iris: the pupil exhibiting the sixth 3rd Eye chakra color and its gold/blue iris invoking Ascended Embodied Life mixed with advanced Awareness. After all of this, when Dave's normal right pupil is in an extended extreme close-up, one can almost hear Stanley Kubrick off-screen calling out, "*Use* your *right* eye…. Get it!?" It is then afterwards that Dave is seen again in human form, beholding the Room Beyond from inside his EVA pod while recovering from great shock. To go from the wildly overwhelming, trauma-inducing experience of the Star Gate to then be plunked right in an out-of-the-blue, unexpected "normal" room would be quite jarring to any human being. No wonder Dave suffers the shaking symptoms of PTSD while slowly trying to make sense of his new surroundings.

## The Room Beyond the Star Gate

"Why Louis XVI?" asks Alexander Walker about the alien room's design. He shrugs off the question with "Well, why any kind of conventional room at all?"[2] The answer is that an 18th-century room makes the most historic sense when the Room Beyond is filled with Masonic iconography. In the 16th and 17th centuries, Europe's privileged class (plus their elect architects and craftsmen) expressed the flowering of their Masonic beliefs in baroque decor,

## 8. Warning: Star Gate Spiritual Mechanics 61

Munich's 1704 Schleissheim Palace, where much of *Paths of Glory*'s interiors were shot being a sterling example. A later art deco/baroque example is New York's 1907 Plaza Hotel, interestingly the very same year Kubrick picked for *The Shining*'s Overlook Hotel to be built.

The elite's esoteric practices for human ascension were appropriated from much older European mystery schools who originally strove to preserve endangered transcendental knowledge from the ancient religions of North Africa (Egypt and Carthage), the Near East (Sumer, Babylon, and Canaan), and the Mediterranean (Greek, Etruscan, and Roman).[3] Though arguably elitist organizations, through the centuries these Western mystery schools branched off into different directions, cherry-picking members from various social strata. While some later offshoots explored darker paths (Crowley's Thelema) and arguably became more egotistical and morally bankrupt, the older mystery schools, while not perfect, held to guarding the ancient wisdom for the sake of posterity—of which Freemasonry became one of the main beneficiaries. King Louis XVI himself was reported to be an "honored mason among the francs-maçons,"[4] hence this namesake connection cements the Room Beyond's purpose in showcasing Masonic symbols that Kubrick alludes to more than once in his films, especially *Clockwork Orange*, *The Shining*, and *Eyes Wide Shut*. In contrast to these later films, which expose in different ways the insidious corruption of the Western world's Masonic elite whose main focus is on self-deification for the sake of maintaining earthly dominion, *A Space Odyssey* sticks to the original Freemason ideals of achieving full ascendance from the material realm for the overall betterment and spiritual evolution of humanity.

Kubrick did state that the *lowest* explanation of *2001*'s final scene was that it was a human observation habitat designed by advanced beings to make Dave more comfortable. So what *are* the deeper subtexts? The clues lie in the Room Beyond's own set design, furniture, lighting, and light FX on Dave's helmet at the sequence's beginning. Kubrick here demonstrates his Masonic knowledge. The illuminated floor, for example, showcases the classic Masonic checkerboard duality as being fully transcended since there are no dark squares (the unenlightened) to be seen. The walls are bathed in light blues, signifying higher awareness. Blue is also the lofty priestly color of high spiritual attainment, representing the heavens for both the Hebrew faith and the freemasons who co-opted such Jewish religious symbolism for themselves.[5]

The slight, unassuming Joachim and Boaz columns in each corner of the Room are easily missed but do mark a traditional Masonic temple floor plan. The vessel-topped Boaz columns guard the two alcoves of Hellenized Isis statues who toast their glasses in return, one with her hand on her life-giving belly. Isis, Goddess of the Ankh, is the Masons favored Goddess (next to Tanit) to represent their Life Mysteries and their desire to master and transcend mundane existence.⁶ All of the above points to David surpassing the Masonic goal of Illumination, of moving beyond the physical realm. However, the furniture, paintings, color accents, food, cutlery, and tendril-lace tablecloth seem to evoke both the living Earth and the Space-Grid Field of Duality; the last vestiges of known reality Dave is still unconsciously clinging to.

The Room Beyond, also called the "Alien Hotel," underlines its use as a temporary holding space which Dave must eventually move on from. The Room Beyond's otherwise perfect dual symmetry is broken by three chairs of the same style. Their gold-framed backsides form the alchemical symbol of magnesium that stands for Ascendance, which is the sign seen earlier when the space monolith aligns with the planetary conjunction hailing the Star Gate. When he first looks straight at his EVA pod, Dave's next close-up reveals something interesting: the reflection in his helmet shows a "Seat of Ascension" chair has replaced where his EVA pod just was, and a monolith stands behind it. This is one of three main signs to what the Seat of Ascension, the EVA pod, and monolith signify together. Before, in one of the first shots of the EVA inside the Room, a Seat of Ascension literally frames the eyeball-like craft as if the EVA itself is sitting in the golden chair. The next shot shows the EVA's "eye-in-seat" logo on its lower left rear.

Such shots drop huge hints of what our own eyes can do for us transcendentally: they can be literal vehicles for traversing realms beyond our own for our own spiritual transformation. So as the monolith at the Star Gate and in the Room Beyond is a symbol for Eye-as-Portal, it is also a symbol for how to attain Ascendance. The multi-message monolith points the way to humanity's spiritual growth while at the same time atavistically embodying the means for this metaphysical faculty Kubrick's *A Space Odyssey* purports humans actually possess.

When David Bowman first walks around dazed from leaving his now-disappeared EVA, he is understandably unsure about his novel living space. Due to the singular unusualness of the entire Room Beyond sequence after the dizzying Star Gate, it is natural to overlook seeming errata that would otherwise stand out in an average room's interior. When Bowman walks into the bathroom, the mirror that usually accompanies the sink is *not there*: it is strangely placed on the bathtub wall instead. The set designers even left a faint outline above the sink where the bathroom mirror *should* be as a tipoff. The bathtub is mostly blue (state of consciousness), grey (balance, non-duality), and located at David's right (creative-intuition). The tub itself is a hollowed-out monolith space. The tub's depth and mirror is Greater Consciousness as accessed by Dave through the vehicle of his right eye. Again, the right side is emphasized whenever Dave turns and looks in that direction or when props or points-of-interest are located on his right side.

Sometimes a monolith or three monoliths can be seen on Dave's helmet/visor while he looks about. As these are often cut with or simultaneously shown with 'i's bouncing off his helmet (especially the center of his face), the monoliths reflected in David's visor must refer to his Third Eye. In some shots, Dave's visor even reflects part of the sectioned floor which forms a † shape. When Dave is in the bathroom, might the larger monoliths reflected in his visor also represent the advanced alien entities we hear observing him, or are they the movie audience looking back at Dave while he stares back in extreme close-up—or can it be all of these possibilities? As if for further reinforcement, when Dave turns from the mirror toward a clinking sound, his helmet glass reflects a small version of his red spacesuit where its minute helmet's portal-shaped visor lines right up with the right *and* Third Eye of David's actual face. Hence, the Right eye-as-Portal-for-Third Eye association is again emphasized. The complex lighting, compositing and clever camerawork just for this one brief shot impressively brings this point home.

Others have noticed *A Space Odyssey*'s focus to the right side of the frame or the right side of an actor. As Michel Chion describes it, "the *Discovery* … skims along horizontally, always from left to right, in conformity with the conventional spatial iconography to signify movement towards the future. Similarly, the monolith is *to the right* when Floyd touches it, and when it appears to Dave [Bowman's right] … at the end of the film."[7] When Dave turns right to exit the blue bathroom to follow the sounds he hears, the first thing he sees through the door is a vanity table—also with no mirror. In the mirror's place is a blue wall with two large 'i's flanking a thick "T" topped with a monolith panel. Look around and one can find 'i's flanking the bed board, table features, and the bathroom sink cupboards (itself hiding a central "T"). EVA or eye-like details are found on bureau drawers, towels, wall décor, and the table's lace coverlet. Monolith wall panel motifs also take the place where doors or windows would normally be, which is, of course, symbolic in itself.

Later, older Dave is seen sitting and eating in a gold Ascension chair, signifying Dave's transcended state even though he himself is not yet fully aware of it. This is further hinted at by his being cloaked in a dark blue robe (color code for deep awareness), which is lined with violet-purple diamond (illumined earth-body) embossed sleeves. It isn't until Dave breaks the Vessel of Material Existence (a cut-glass *diamond* pattern) and trades his blue-violet robe for illuminated white, that he gestures to the monolith in recognition of it as an evolutionary midwife and is then reborn as a Star Child. Behind him, the vibrant green headboard is the last oval Portal motif, itself made up of a plush diamond pattern. Both the bed wall and the desk wall opposite (where the monolith appears) are the only ones where the sconces are gold and have three candles instead of just two symbolizing duality, with one wick white and the other a pale black. As the Star Child exits via the monolith-now-portal, the Room's statue alcoves' olive hues turn creative-intuition green (with still a touch of Life yellow) as final confirmation of David Bowman's completed transition into a Perfected Being. This perfection is again signified by the symbolism of the Star Child's light-blue skin (Higher Awareness) and pink-tinted celestial womb (Seated Consciousness).

# 9

# The Female Presence in *2001*

It can be argued that physical representation of womankind in *2001* ceases past the moon base briefing room. After Frank Poole's mother makes a long-distance appearance singing "Happy Birthday" in a video call, one is hard pressed to find any feminine presence beyond that. Yet originally there was more in the film. There were several space station scenes with women working, mothers and children enjoying art lessons (a possible nod to wife and daughter painters Christiane and Katherina, in addition to being another Square-the-Circle shot) and a lady Sears sales clerk sequence that were cut to trim *2001*'s length. The tall, slim space stewardesses in white with their round white hats are walking embodiments of the "i" glyph's link to the Third Eye. The guiding, pink-garbed *Space Station 5* aides are color coded as Seated Consciousness as most of them are sitting down (the one pink-clad aide who passes Dr. Smyslov is carrying a light blue folder the way Seated Consciousness can "carry" higher Awareness). "I" motifs are often present on set with pink aides to emphasize their symbolic connection. It is Dr. Floyd's "Squirt" (daughter Vivian Kubrick) who provides an essential key: the Pupil-as-Portal glyph. Squirt's dress is Earth/life color-coded complete with pentagram[1] (earth star) flowers, the yellow portal glyph on her right side, and the three white buttons under her chin are another Third Eye hint. As we have discovered, Kubrick often graced his female cast with *2001*'s most important clues and symbols, so film analysts who overlook women's scenes in *A Space Odyssey* (and indeed Kubrick's other films) simply lose out and miss out on much.

Even so, Stanley Kubrick himself was not immune to putting his foot in it where gender relations were concerned, in spite of his sci-fi striving to correct the issue in a more mythic sense. Along with another actress, Ann Gillis, who provided the iconic Disney voice of *Bambi*'s mother (and Faline), was hired to play the part of Frank Poole's mother in the "Happy Birthday" video message. Kubrick was apparently crabby that day and when the other actress didn't work out, Ann Gillis overheard Kubrick saying, "I like the other one better." Already perturbed that the director didn't bother to know her name, Ann Gillis couldn't believe the number of takes being done for such a short scene and that the director printed every one. When it became clear that Kubrick intended to keep on shooting after take 21, Ann Gillis finally rose up and said, "You have enough takes. I quit."[2]

So that was the day Stanley Kubrick was burned by Bambi's mom.

More examples of male knee-jerk dismissiveness appear when authors like Thomas Allen Nelson refer to Floyd Heywood's chat with his daughter as mere "domestic trifles," a phrase that rather drips with condescension.[3] Nelson's dismissal of this scene cost him catching a very important *Space Odyssey* visual key. James Howard makes the mistake of automatically assigning Dr. Smyslov as the official group leader of the Russian scientists when there is no actual indication in the movie that this is so. Howard states, "Led by Professor Smyslov [Leonard Rossiter], the Russians are curious as to the real purpose of Dr. Floyd's visit."[4] Most of the Russian scientists are women, yet because Dr. Smyslov is the only male among them, Howard assumes he is the leader. Why does there even need to *be* a leader in a social setting? It is actually Dr. Elena who takes the initiative to introduce Dr. Floyd to the rest of her group, and it is she whom Floyd defers to the most until Smyslov interrupts.

But symbolically, more is going on in this meeting scene, thanks to the space station set design. When Dr. Floyd first walks down the long hallway and meets the others, the purple-clad Dr. Stretyneva rises with her head between a minus sign (or sideways "i") and an equals sign between herself and Floyd on the walls behind them. This could indicate Floyd is unequal to Stretyneva's yet-to-be-revealed higher metaphorical status.

Kubrick carefully shot this scene so their heads would be in between these symbols to convey something significant. As the minus sign can double for the letter "i" above Stretyneva's head, this i and equals sign between the floor (space) and ceiling (grid) indicate what she stands for: the Material Universe. The "i" also points to three panels on the wall opposite her. Throughout a good part of their conversation, Stretyneva's head is superimposed over this hallway paneling that looks like three "I"s. Her head is right in front of the center "i" panel (the Third Eye) and even Smyslov puts his hand on *his* forehead, indirectly gesturing to the "I" shaped space station poster just behind him. Whether it is space shuttle stewardesses, space station aides, lady scientists, mothers or daughters, the female presence in *A Space Odyssey* is connected to Third Eye imagery and the Fabric of Reality. *2001*'s symbolism portrays women as embodying the foundation of Duality (Reality) *and* our means to leave this Duality at will.

## A Goddess Trinity: Athena, Isis and Tanit

HAL was at first to have a lady's voice and be called **Athena**, the Greek Goddess of wisdom and war who was born from the head of Zeus, an apt allegorical name in a film forewarning how the creations from the mind of Man can turn on him. Athena would have served as a constant reminder of *2001*'s Greek myth-inspired movie title. This could be among the reasons the computer's name was changed; either because the myth of Athena would be too redundant a conceptual theme, or more likely because a female voice would have garnered the ship's central computer more audience sympathy than originally intended, especially during the deactivation sequence. In the end, Kubrick opted for a more neutral, ambiguous voice and character for HAL, obtained thanks to the vocal talents of Douglas Rain, whom Stanley Kubrick purposely kept in the dark in regards to HAL's motivations.[5]

O|- **Isis** -|O the Egyptian Goddess of Life (true name *Aset* for *throne* which is one of her many crowns), makes Her presence felt throughout the *Discovery* sequences in the form of the Ankh, the eternal life symbol that shows up as hand-grips of the EVA pods, the ship's huge Communications Tower and its base, the hibernation beds' consoles, and as display panel warnings opposing HAL. Later, Isis' age-old Ankh is equated to Kubrick's Thought-Space Field Ankh < [≡] > that hangs above the EVA pods in their landing bay. By equalizing both ankhs, Kubrick makes the statement that the entire Fabric of the Universe should be held sacred and no part should be deemed less than another.

Isis is also who the 18th-century Room Beyond's Hellenized wall statues embody as the ultimate Vessel of Life (the Greeks were the ones who named and venerated Aset as Isis when Her cult reached their shores). Her living trinity doppelganger in *2001* is the three Russian lady scientists, among them the Lady in Purple cryptically pointing to her glass during the conversation in the space station. This is something even the male Russian scientist does to emphasize the glass' later metaphoric importance in representing the Vessel of Life. In addition, the Room Beyond's Isis statues hold up glasses that mirror the Vessel of Life motif in the scene where an older Dave Bowman breaks his own glass later in the film.

As Kubrick's three Russian scientists suggest a Goddess Trinity, here are their three aspects of the Divine Feminine: Dr. Elena, wearing black, is cast as the Mother/Matron since she's the only woman there who mentions being married and having children. Elena's black dress may also provide clues to Dr. Kalinin's dress color. Her young twin Kalinin wears a dark verdant green dress as the Maiden. As black is the color of the maternal cosmos from which all things spring, it would make sense that the Maiden's dark green symbolizes young growth "springing" from the fertile dark.

Dr. Stretyneva, who wears the most purple in the entire film, Kubrick designated as Crowned instead of Crone. Her central position and royal colors indicating high status, she sits polar opposite from Dr. Floyd (Earth's Deceiver). Dr. Stretyneva is Queen incognito, whose most interesting anagrams are ST EVE TARYN, in which Taryn is Greco-Roman for "Queen" and archaic Latin for "Of the Earth," or TRY, SANT EVE (where Sant is "Saint" in Hindi). As the lady in purple represents Life sanctified, her embodying a god-realized woman makes sense. There is also AND EVE'S TRYST or AND EVER TRYST with the "Dr." included.

Stretyneva's own name might also be another Kubrick reference to the "Baltic Sea Anomaly" marine discovery. The Russian river Neva happens to flow into the bay where the Baltic Sea Anomaly (an incredibly ancient man-made structure) is reportedly located.[6] *2001*'s deleted space station scene where young girls are painting provide more clues to this possibility: A girl at left in a dark blue dress paints not what is actually in front of her (a Square-the-Circle fountain) but a child-like panorama that looks very much like an aerial view of the Baltics.

O|< **Tanit** >|O the third Goddess aspect, is the one most easily missed in the movie. Tanit makes just two appearances in Her classically recognizable form (circle for head with outstretched stick arms and triangle body), the most clear example being in the Star Gate's golden realms sequence and earlier hidden in the first TMA-1 map on the moonbus. During the Star Gate sequence, Dave Bowman goes through a blazing gold mountainous landscape, on which the engraved image of Tanit emerges from the left-hand side of the screen. Tanit was the Golden Goddess of Carthage, ancient Greece's and Rome's main competitor for centuries. One lady in the Clavius briefing room and Frank Poole's mother both wear golden outfits as likely doppelgangers of Tanit/the Earth or as Woman Sacralized. Poole's mother sits within a dualistic set complete with black plates on white mats in front of a high contrast backdrop. Her white cake's gold band accentuates its sanctified squareness, another allusion to the sacred material plane Tanit (and Isis) rules. *A Space Odyssey*'s Color Code reserves gold as the color of the *fully transcended* Sacred Feminine/Fabric of Reality whereas purple is the color of initial *self*-illumination. The worship of Tanit in North Africa started around 800 BC (or earlier) with the arrival of the Phoenicians. Isis worship dates back to Egyptian prehistory and both Isis and Tanit are ancient Mother Goddesses whose fertile abundance manifests Life in manifold forms in their respective cultures. Tanit is also a Moon/Star Goddess of the Heavens,[7] as is Isis, whose star in the constellations is now called Sirius.[8] As such, Stanley Kubrick saw Isis and Tanit as both appropriate divine avatars for the sanctity of the Material Cosmos (as Above so Below) and Life as we know it—and perhaps in the Star Gate's case, even Life as we do not yet know it.

## The Ultimate Duality, the Transcended ◊ Entities and the Divine ◊ Feminine as Fabric of the Universe

### Y = Yoni/Yoke of Life = Sanctity of Material Existence = Grid/Glass Vessel = Vessel of Life *(Isis)*

Dr. Stretyneva ("Try, Sant Eve") at the space station is the only being in *2001* who wears the same royal purples as the (diamond/yoni-shaped) Stargate Entities at the end of the film. Sharing purple exalts Her presence as equal to the Advanced Entities. Their diamond shapes connect the two together as the ancient sacred Yoni sign and as the form of Transcended Perfection; an Octagon-as-Heart Center whose vertices equal the six-pointed Star of David (6 being the Judaic Perfect Number). "Vav" is the sixth number in the Hebrew alphabet; another "perfection" alignment. Since this Lady in Purple represents Isis, Goddess of Life, She too stands for the Material Plane of Existence that Kubrick encodes in the drinking vessels. Further clues equating Stretyneva with the sacralized Fabric of Reality is when spacecraft view screens chiefly display various maps and grid fields in *purple*. This links to the final Room Beyond scene, where its illuminated floor is like the space station's glowing grid ceiling. The Room Beyond's bright white grid floor reveals Dave has ascended the Duality of Material Existence that Stretyneva emulates as the Goddess of Life in the space station, whose tilting head brings attention to the three Vav panels behind Her: the *ascended and sanctified* 666. HAL's hidden sideways 6's/Vavs represents the infernal 666 in dual contrast to *Space Station V*'s (five being an Earth number) embodied Goddess' transcendental 666, which is its redeemed, idealized form as recorded in the New Testament.[9]

When Heywood joins the Russian scientists, they repeatedly offer him a drink. Again, Stretyneva-as-Goddess markedly gestures to Her glass with two fingers during the conversation. As She does so, it becomes a prophetic precursor to what She and the Broken Glass at the end of the film represent: the Vessel of Material Existence (Mother/Mater/Matter). This Life Vessel theme is again emphasized by the Isis statues toasting their glasses to the Room Beyond's goblet-topped Boaz columns.

On another level, Kubrick is resacralizing the dethroned Goddess that Revelations repudiates with the epithet "The Whore of Babylon."[10] "The Woman was robed in purple and scarlet and was glittering with gold, precious stones, and pearls. She was holding in her hand a golden chalice." As an avatar of the Goddess-as-sacred material existence, Dr. Stretyneva's purple and red dress seems to link her both to the New Testament quote above and with the evolved Star Gate beings traveling their similar hued cosmic field in a higher plane. Was the New Testament's Whore of Babylon reference prophesizing the future corruption of the Catholic Church, or was it also maligning Mother Mary and Earth-as-Divine Feminine in general? Catholics suggest Revelations 17 was addressing pagan Rome and Israel, who united against the early Christians. In the still earlier Abrahamic years when Yahweh was a young upstart god compared to the long established religions in the land of Canaan, some pastoral Hebrew patriarchs must have looked on with jealousy at the popular, already ancient Semitic deities such as Inanna, Asherah, Astarte, Allat, Ishtar, with their consorts Dumuzi, Baal, Tanimuz, Allah, Sarson, etc., who were worshipped in the thriving, big cities of the Fertile Crescent. Whereas the early Abrahamic scriptures and later monotheistic religions either denigrate, severely corset, or outright ignore female divinity, Kubrick re-sanctifies Her image as the Goddess of Life in the guise of Isis, Tanit, her Pan-Am crowned white "i" hostesses, and lady scientist avatars in *A Space Odyssey*. Kubrick's goddess symbolism is a vehicle for unifying earthly matter with the heavens, linking with *2001*'s Square-the-Circle themes of ascension.

"When he [Stanley] sent you a book, he wanted you to read it, and not just read it, but to drop everything and get *into* it," Michael Herr recounts. "John Calley, who was probably Stanley's closest friend, told me that when he was head of production at Warner Bros. in the seventies.... Stanley sent him a set of *The Golden Bough*, unabridged, and then bugged him every couple of weeks for a year about reading it. Finally, Calley said, 'Stanley, I've got a studio to run. I don't have time to read mythology.' 'It isn't mythology, John,'" Stanley countered. "It's your *life*." This reminiscence brings to light one of Stanley Kubrick's sources of goddess trinity lore which made enough of an impression on him to weave it throughout the fabric of *A Space Odyssey* and such other films as *Full Metal Jacket* and *Eyes Wide Shut*.[11]

## 10

# The Star Child–Egyptian Horus Child Connection

*A Space Odyssey*'s Star Child concept may originate from much older spiritual sources. Indeed, the process of becoming a journeying "Star Child" was put on the ceiling of Hathor's ancient Temple of Denderah at least before 1650 BC. On either side of a large black-eyed Eye of Horus, a procession of Egyptian gods, goddesses, astrological deities, and bird-like bas (souls) give it special veneration as Horus' "healed eye" from when Set plucked it from him. Inside Horus' unusual black eye there is a gold pupil housing a child, finger in mouth to indicate his tender age. The Eye of Horus is portrayed as a *right* eye traveling in a solar boat, and the young soul therein looks out his golden orb. The Horus Child is accompanied by seven moon deities above and below him, perhaps in part inspiring the seven Star Gate beings guiding Dave in *2001*. The importance of the right eye's pupil being the Consciousness portal out beyond the material realm is made clear: The Eye of Horus' blackness might symbolize the black womb of space and also stresses the right *pupil's* essentialness (compared to the rest of the eye) in being human Consciousness' exit to the Amdwat/Duat: the ancient Egyptians' Gateway to the Heavens.

So it bears repeating that if the eye is the window to the soul, then it is also the soul's doorway to outside this plane of existence.

## Mirror as Metaphysical Tool: Light and Shadow

Shaman and priestess burials around the world are frequently found with mirrors, usually highly polished copper, bronze or silver, either intact or ritually destroyed.[1] In Japan, the temples of their primary creator Sun Goddess Amaterasu contain sacred mirrors. Covering mirrors with a cloth are old Japanese, South Asian practices, and Afro-Caribbean and Jewish mourning traditions.[2] In ancient Egypt, ritual use of mirrors re-

Horus Child in Solar/Lunar boat with 14 attendants (for phases of the moon) (photograph by Hanna Pethen).

lated to and reflected the Sun God Ra's brilliance and life-giving capacity. Because of life's dependency on the sun, mirrors were sometimes kept in ankh-shaped cases, and ankhs and the Goddess Hathor often made up the handles of Egyptian mirrors, created in bronze and even gold. Hathor, being the divine Cosmic Cow of Creation (the Milky Way), the Protectress of women, Goddess of love, music, dance, and joy, was also called the Goddess of Light, which would explain why so many Egyptian mirrors were graced with Her image, besides Her embodiment of physical love and beauty.[3]

In Hathor's Temple of Denderah, a section of ceiling bears many Egyptian deities, high priests and priestesses paying homage to the (right) Eye of Horus inside a giant sun-in-crescent disk that doubles as a great golden mirror. This evidence greatly suggests mirrors were used for spiritual purposes and not just for applying kohl in Egyptian culture. It is interesting that in old Egyptian, the word for mirror sounds/is the same as "ankh."[4] The portrayal of the Eye of Horus (the Third Eye) as a celestial mirror gives more credence to the possibility that the Egyptians were quite aware how mirrors could be used to soul-travel their Amdwat/Duat.

Mirrors appear as articles of consequence in other Kubrick films as well. In *Clockwork Orange*, they show up in hallways and bathrooms. In one scene, psychopath Alex peels off his fake eyelashes from his right eye and sticks them to the left side of his vanity mirror. As his infamous exaggerated

## 10. The Star Child–Egyptian Horus Child Connection

**Horus as a Sun Mirror: symbolic correlations between the Sun, Life, and mirrors (photograph by Hanna Pethen).**

eyelashes refer to the spiritual *potential* of the Right Eye of Horus as a vehicle for the Third Eye, Alex unceremoniously planting them on the left-hand side of his mirror indicates his spiritual as well as moral bankruptcy since he is obviously using neither faculty throughout the film. Mirrors in *Clockwork Orange* are set up to produce a full-body doubling effect as the writer's wife walks on a black and white checkerboard floor, the Masonic symbol for duality and device used in covert mind control programs.[5] Mirrors in front of bathtubs are another device used in making a programmed victim feel vulnerable to induce trauma or dissociation. The hypnotic use of mirrors, jarring patterns, vibrant colors, extremely bright, bedazzling lights and music (discordant or otherwise) are all used to confuse and break down a subject's defenses. One such example is the writer Frank Alexander being triggered into trauma by the same song Alex sang while he and his gang raped his wife and severely disabled him. Patrick Magee, while playing Frank's trauma scene as Alex sings in the bathtub, was not fully aware it was a trauma scene and was uncertain why Kubrick wanted him to react so strongly. He told Malcom McDowell off camera, "I don't understand him (Kubrick). He has me sitting there like I'm taking a shit!"[6] Illuminati motifs do surface in *Clockwork Orange*. Pyramids show up at least three times in the film, once while Alex is walking home, the second on a jail yard wall, and the third as a golden triangle kerchief in the Minister of the Interior's breast pocket. If curious why Alex and his droogs have eyeballs on their sleeves, focus on the Minister's sleeves and the Masonic/MK-Ultra connection will be found.

Mirrors reflect alternate personalities or entities in *The Shining*. The young boy Danny looking at himself in a bathroom mirror talking to what is first assumed to be an imaginary friend, later it becomes clear that "Tony" is Danny's altered personality who takes over his body when extreme trauma drives Danny into dissociation ("Danny's not here anymore, Mrs. Torrance"). The child again goes into a dissociative state when he's in the bedroom alone with his father, the losing-his-mind Jack Torrance. In this scene, the audience first sees Jack's face full-on in a vanity mirror with his jeans hanging over a chair as he motions for Danny to come to him which makes one feel unsure about the boy's safety. Danny at first hesitates, obviously reluctant but ends up sitting limply on Jack's lap on the bed, staring straight out into space, and speaks in a robotic monotone as his menacing father demands to know if his mother Wendy is turning Danny against him. Mirrors are always present when Jack himself is facing demonic ghosts in the hotel bar or bathrooms. Mirrors also reveal things in *The Shining*. When Mrs. Torrance (Shelly Duvall) sees "redrum" reversed to "murder" in a mirror, it gives her enough time to save Danny and defend herself as best she can.

In *Full Metal Jacket*, pushed to the limit by brutal military hazing, Private Pyle shoots his unrelenting Sergeant in a mirror-less bathroom before he takes his own life. Cowboy's round compact mirror reflects the shape of a temple's moon gate door whose enclosure in turn reflects the truly dreadful inner landscape of the Lusthog squad. In *Eyes Wide Shut*, mirrors induce scared expressions and how mirrors appear in the film hint at their ritual use. The dark, evil-looking mirror Bill Harford is nearest to in Mandy's apartment has an altar candle in front and a book below titled *Shadows in the Mirror*: a sobering reminder a mirror portal works both ways.

Throughout the above-mentioned films, Stanley Kubrick embeds clues

## 10. The Star Child–Egyptian Horus Child Connection 75

of how mirrors can be used as tools for spiritual enlightenment and also abused as instruments for institutionalized, even ritualized exploitation.

*2001: A Space Odyssey* focuses on the greater good mirrors can provide human evolution when used in service to the Highest Good.

Choose wisely the path you take.

# 11

# The Ultimate Unity

## How the Y/Vav and the Sacred Feminine is Connected in *2001: A Space Odyssey*

### Y = V (vessel) + I (consciousness) = Yoke of Life/ Yoni = The Ancient Hebrew Letter Vav (Y)

The Y sigil is our bodies as walking "i" vessels of Consciousness. In *2001*, "Y" shows up as spacesuit yoke straps, on *Discovery*'s eyelid-like bay doors, as light reflected on Bowman's face, and on the diamond skin of the Star Gate advanced entities. The Y also depicts the pre–Sephardic "Y" pictograph of the Hebrew letter *Vav* (the sixth Hebrew letter) that is itself briefly seen on the flashing sides of the Star Gate beings. As the entities glow the traditional letter "Vav," a purple Y floats lower right off-screen, further connecting the Y/Vav association. For the Y/Vav's oldest Hebrew meaning is "peg"; that which connects, fastens, and binds together like a peg tethering a tent,[1] such as Spirit binding itself to Matter: the "Yoke" of Life. Therein Y doubles as Vav and the sacred feminine Yoni sigil that manifests Life in the physical realm. The black "Y" straps over the astronauts' groin area (such as when Dave enters the hallway to HAL's mainframe) especially make this Y-for-Yoni symbolism a difficult reference to deny.

The moon astronaut suit zippers appear vaginal as well. This too may be why some portals framing spacecraft doorways look like labia (like the corridor to the EVA pod bay), as if reminding us that just as the Yoni is our entry into this physical universe, the Pupil-as-Portal can be our exit out of it (and return) while we live. Flashing Y lights on Dave's head while in his pod suggest this Portal/Third Eye connection. The Portal glyph itself looks like a Yoni with its ends squared off: (). It is hard to see these symbolic similarities as mere coincidence, especially considering the careful thought Kubrick took into crafting these esoteric visual motifs for *A Space Odyssey* with the help of Harry Lange, the film's top production illustrator and his team of designers.[2]

## 11. The Ultimate Unity

The final proof of Kubrick's linking the monolith to Vav; here is what a Vav looks like in the Modern Hebrew Alef Bet (alphabet): **I**.

Like Vav-as-Yoni, the monolith serves as a dimensional Portal; a doorway between our reality and the Infinite. Y is also symbolized by the water glass at both the end *and* the start of *2001*'s space sequences as the Vessel of Life.

As Vav is the sixth letter in the Hebrew alphabet, it is also the sixth number, associating it to the sixth chakra of the Third Eye both the monolith-as-I and T-for-Third Eye represent.

In closing our exploration of *A Space Odyssey*'s hidden, esoteric use of Vav, we can go back to the very beginning of the film: some may have wondered why at the start of *2001* there is a blue and gold lion logo instead of MGM's traditional trademark roaring lion. A reasoned answer is that the standard noisy, live action lion would have greatly disturbed the building emotional crescendo that *2001*'s overture beforehand had taken pains to set up. It is curious how the new logo came to exist; MGM only used it three times for opening films: first for *Grand Prix* ('66), then Kubrick's *2001* ('68), and lastly *The Making of Roses* ('68). But in addition to ensuring a quiet lion, the image itself is interestingly esoteric: its heavenly bright blue matte is also the color of communication, and the gold lion encapsulates embodied ascension. Its right eye, which is turned towards us, sure looks like the letter Vav. Underneath, the gold lion's cheekbone could pass for a Y-Vav pictograph. One questions if MGM headquarters was aware of their new logo's symbolic potential or if it was just one of those serendipitous coincidences Stanley Kubrick simply took advantage of.

To summarize, Stanley Kubrick's integration of sacred feminine imagery with the fusing Y Hebrew Vav pictograph not only strives to elevate the status of the fabric of reality we usually take for granted, but it metaphorically restores women's ancient role as divine avatars of Earth, nature, and the processes of life. Its diamond-hexagon unites all dual principles, heaven and earth, male and female, space and matter. *2001: A Space Odyssey*'s underlying metaphysical foundation analytically ensouls cosmic forces into classic mythic archetypes. It is pure cinema as poetic logic, sweepingly tempered with intellectual awe of the Absolute.

# 12

# Closing Remarks on *2001: A Space Odyssey*

Like intricate sand paintings that served their purpose, most of the *Space Odyssey* sets were ritually destroyed to prevent their re-use in the profane hands of copycat moviemakers.[1] Stanley Kubrick did not wish to see his meticulous sets resurface in other people's films. The destruction of the hidden esoteric sigils within these highly detailed set pieces protected and ensured *2001*'s singular standing in the history of cinema. Kubrick continued this practice in later films by disposing unused takes and preserving little of a movie's dismantled sets for posterity. Whatever he did save was stored inside his large, stately English mansion, where it steadily grew into a huge archive over the years that is now mostly housed within the University Arts of London's Communications College.

Through the decades that have passed since *2001: A Space Odyssey* first came out, it was a practice for some movie critics and film analysts to focus on the meanings behind the monolith and the bone-as-tool almost to the exclusion of even considering the existence of other possible filmic message motifs contained within *2001*. This understandable tunnel-vision for one of cinema's most enigmatic and iconic film avatars has kept many from discovering the rest of *2001*'s hidden-in-plain sight visual cues that in the end actually provide the metaphysical keys to unlocking the monolith's multi-layered symbolism in the first place.

*2001: A Space Odyssey* covers several concepts on the state and possible future of humankind's relationship with technology but its underlying core themes are deeply metaphysical in scope. Through the repetition of the above explored imagery discussed in this book's Part I as recurring visual motifs, Kubrick reveals how one accesses the Infinite through one's own eyes, i.e.; the Third Eye, the true Seat of Consciousness. The film continually visually demonstrates that the Right Eye is a Gateway out of our 3D reality. Forgotten by much of modern western civilization, this paramount human faculty is a profound spiritual Truth that Stanley Kubrick, through *A Space Odyssey*'s encoded cinematic examples, calls upon us to exercise for the sake of humanity's transcendental development and future evolution.

PART II

# The Films Following *2001*

After submersing ourselves into the spiritual depths of *A Space Odyssey*, in order to more fully comprehend how important its visual motifs are, we should examine how they appear in Kubrick's other films. This will establish that *2001*'s symbolic lexicon is in fact a vital part of Stanley Kubrick's trademark cinematic oeuvre that he continued to use throughout his movie-making career. These symbols should be recognized as integral to Kubrick's filmic language.

Kubrick's fondness for symmetrical, one-point perspective had been noted before and shows up throughout most of his films in reinforcing *A Space Odyssey*'s foundation of Duality. Now that we have thoroughly examined the final bathroom scene in *2001*, we have a better idea that Kubrick's penchant for powder rooms is more about giving tipoffs on the importance of mirrors rather than toilets. The lack of mirrors in a bathroom (*Clockwork Orange*, *Full Metal Jacket*) is just as important in their omission as in their being present.

Another more ominous link between many of Stanley Kubrick's movies is how he portrays evil. Starting with Peter Seller's Claire Quilty in *Lolita*, evil is usually depicted as hard, tiny pinpoints of light buried in inky black, soulless eyes or eyewear. This effect is continued in Seller's portrayal of Dr. Strangelove and the iconic worm's-eye shot of General Ripper delivering his "precious bodily fluids" monologue. HAL's inscrutably evil orb is another stellar example as is *Clockwork Orange*'s ice-cold Dr. Brodsky, his dark, tunnel-like glasses glinting as he casually discusses the torturous effects of Ludovico programming on his human test subjects. Kubrick's visual technique to convey great evil is seen again with the butler Grady in *The Shining*'s ballroom bathroom scene, his dead eyes lit only by one chilling pinprick of light in the far-left corner of his left eye. The almost opposite effect is done for Pvt. Leonard Pyle's mental deterioration in *Full Metal Jacket*. Such similar, unsettling lighting effects reappear at certain times in unexpected, disturbing places within *Eyes Wide Shut*, which solidify that this should be a recognized Kubrickian style conceit in conveying evil. In addition, Kubrick pioneered a repeating "proximity equals association" technique of placing conceptually-ordained props near actors, especially near their head. In *The Shining*, Jack Nicholson's character constantly has shadow occult sigils and disturbing items hover around his head as do Wendy, Danny, and Mr. Hallorann in the infamous horror film. At other times this proximity-as-association device is served by the symbolism sewn into the clothes actors wear, as either stand-out dominant colors, patterns, or eye-catching items like decoration and jewelry.

Starting in reverse-chronological order, we begin with *The Shining*, which will in time make sense considering the sort of themes that will be covered with new, even alarming revelations which further tie Stanley Kubrick's films together as warning sirens for humanity. It is with *The Shining* where the most explosive revelations of an almost opposite sort from *A Space Odyssey* are made which provide the cinematic language and arcane symbolism helpful in understanding and interpreting those found in Kubrick's other pictures after (and before) *2001*. Setting up an esoteric map that aids in explaining the director's select hidden sigils within the rest of his work is why Part II starts off with *The Shining* and ends with *Eyes Wide Shut*, Kubrick's final film which interestingly links back to *2001* in profound ways.

# 13

# *The Shining*: Scarier Than Ever

**Danny's Third-Eye trike (model by Arthur77/RenderHub).**

Stephen King's novel *The Shining* provided a perfect springboard from which Stanley Kubrick could dive in and bury layers of meaning he deemed urgent to express, returning to some topics previously addressed by his earlier films *Barry Lyndon* and especially *Clockwork Orange*, themes such as man's inhumanity to man (and, more specifically, to woman), motherhood, family abuse,[1] bettering one's position in a period's social class system, and the veiled inner workings of the higher echelons of power. In each film, from *Barry Lyndon* to *The Shining*, the above thematic layers are given a different focus, some emphasized more than others, which then continue to be relevant topics in Kubrick's final and seminal film, *Eyes Wide Shut*. Here we first will focus, among other sobering film concepts, how these particular cinematic themes make their presence known in *The Shining*.

Though author Stephen King wanted his protagonist John Torrance to be seen as a decent man who is eventually driven insane by the evil in the Overlook hotel, Stanley Kubrick and author (now screenwriter) Diane Johnson wrote *Jack* Torrance for Jack Nicholson, intended to be an unsympathetic character from the start, and he is in actuality, the main antagonist in the movie outside the demonic hotel itself. Nicholson's Jack Torrance is sarcastic and dismissive to his wife early on and is already revealed to be physically abusive toward his son during drunken tirades. This information is confessed in the beginning by Shelly Duvall's Wendy Torrance, when a female doctor checks on Danny after his fainting spell (brought on earlier by a horrific vision of a blood-hemorrhaging elevator). Even though the hotel's general manager, Stuart Ullman, shows Jack how to manage the Overlook's overall maintenance, it is Wendy who ends up doing the tasks Jack was hired to do while Jack himself writes (or is supposed to be writing) his book inside the Overlook's oppressively cavernous Colorado lounge.

The Overlook hotel seems to be a stand-in for America; the cast is predominantly clothed in red, white, and blue at the opening of the film to set up this premise. U.S. flags show up throughout the movie's runtime. Stuart Ullman himself, while sitting in his office wearing the aforementioned patriotic colors and surrounded by eagles and flags, physically bears an unusual resemblance to John F. Kennedy. Perhaps the best anagram for Stuart Ullman's name turns out to be ULTRA MAN SLUT. Considering that other anagrams do exist in *The Shining* (and Kubrick's other films), this not only makes for a funny political in-joke but bolsters belief that this presidential resemblance is indeed intentional. Other American associations include Ullman's recounting of the hotel's history, starting with its being built on an "Indian burial ground," Scatman Crothers' Dick Hallorann at one point opens a giant meat freezer whose endless racks of ghostly contents visually echo the hulls of slave ships and possibly World War II POW barracks, and continues with Danny's parents emitting such odd phrases as "Last one has to clean up America" and "Are you done bombing the universe?"

Jack's aspirations as a writer are put to a sort of a "now or never" in regards to the job interview. When Mr. Ullman asks about his former job as a teacher, Jack treats it with curt disdain. With the Overlook caretaker position providing an ideal opportunity but uprooting his family in the process, for Jack Torrance the pressure is on to make it or break it with his writing. As the film progresses, Jack is seen going through the throes of writer's block, distracting himself with throwing a ball around. Already saddled with the stress to succeed and to support his family, Jack's anxiety and frustrated rage grow side by side, creating a rising state of paranoia that feeds underlying suspicions that his wife and son are banding together against him.

## 13. The Shining: *Scarier Than Ever*        83

Like *Barry Lyndon*'s little Lord Barringdon, Danny Torrance is much closer to his mother than to his father. It is Wendy who takes the time to play with him and who mostly looks after him. The two are pretty much left to fend for themselves as, bit by bit, Jack's soul gets swallowed up by the hotel. Whether by psychological breakdown or malicious supernatural intent (or the combination of both), the hotel's unnerving environment eventually succeeds in ripping the family unit apart.

Wendy Torrance appears to be a gentle, if timid and unsure woman who puts up with being bullied mainly to keep the family together. She is a decent mother who takes good care of Danny and considers his needs first without reservation. As she plays outside in the snow with her young son, Jack watches them from inside the lounge with perhaps some degree of jealousy, in addition to being slowly taken over by the infernal forces of the Overlook. Behind his head, a faceless horned beast looms over pictures of past happenings at the hotel. It is a moose, but the blackness of its form renders it almost completely featureless. The smaller pictures underneath it add up to eighteen in number, which incidentally is the total of 6+6+6. In an earlier, cozier scene where Wendy presents Jack with breakfast in bed, a vanity mirror reveals a most malevolent demonic head right above Jack's dozing face. If this apparition on the bed headboard is looked at too closely, it reveals itself as simply décor. To its left on the dresser, a lampshade pattern forms a malevolent serpent. These sort of frightening effects repeat time and time again throughout the hotel's oppressive interiors. Later, as Danny rides around the hotel on his Big Wheel, pictures on the walls can at first look like unfriendly eyes with red gash mouths or staring monstrous forms but become bird or girl portraits on closer inspection. When Wendy paces around her apartment after a quarrel with Jack, the curtains behind her seem to contain ugly, jeering faces which break up into simple patterns if examined close up. The sheer inventiveness of Production Designer Randy Taylor, Set Dresser Tessa Davies, Décor Artist Robert Walker and Bang Wilson's fabrics deserved an Oscar in their own right, as their work made the hotel come alive as its own character.

As he wakes up in bed, Jack opens his mouth wide with his tongue out (in a near mirror image of what's hidden in the maze) while revealing his pale green "Stovington" shirt, the town where he last worked. At the interview, Jack wears a green tie. When working at his typewriter, Jack wears a dark green shirt. If green has the same association as it did in *2001*, then it would make sense Jack would wear green to present himself as a creative professional while at the same time signaling an alert to the audience of the color's symbolism, since traditionally green was a strange color for a man to wear to a job interview, even in the '70s. The hallways to the kitchen are partly a light putrid green, as are the bathrooms in both the Torrance's old apartment and inside the infamous room 237. Orange is another prominent color in *The Shining*, as are red, black, yellow/gold, and brown. It is highly likely Stanley Kubrick devised a Color Code for *The Shining* as he did for *2001*, and it will be interesting to see which color concept associations carried over from *2001* remain the same, and which colors take on new meanings appropriate for Stanley Kubrick's horror film.

As it turns out, orange in *The Shining* is most likely the color of 33rd Degree Freemasonry, the highest level of that elite fraternity and supposed power cabal. This links right back to the underlying reason why Kubrick's *Clockwork Orange* has more than its fair share of Masonic visual references tied to its own Color Code, especially its use of the color orange. In *The Shining*, shadowy pyramids seem to form where orange is present, such as when Jack is at his typewriter yelling at the hapless Wendy, a dingy orange lamp sits at his left side while behind him a creepy two-candle light fixture casts a pyramid-like shadow against a stark white wall. During this same scene, a chair under the light fixture goes missing, perhaps not only as an unsettling device but also to attract attention to the two-candle light's *triangular* shadow outline. At one point before he leaves the hotel, Stuart Ullman wears an orange tie, a veiled way to signify his higher allegiance. A pyramid shadow is revealed over Room 237's bed in a monolith-shaped mirror (room 237's couch area includes dingy orange lampshades), and during the movie's climactic ending, Wendy's knife points to a two-candle light casting another pyramid shadow in its hellish red hallway. As Jack enters Ullman's office to dismantle the CB radio, the orange office's wall planters are devoid of its green plants. When Wendy wakes Jack from a bad dream after he falls asleep at his typewriter and while an unraveling, horrified Jack shamefully recounts his nightmare of chopping up his wife and son, the hotel's hallways behind the couple glow an ominous yellow (more likely for Death than Life) with an orange cast. Whereas orange in *2001* refers to life functions, *The Shining*'s infernal "Illuminati" orange (similar to *Clockwork Orange*'s orange) may hint at powerful forces having total control over *other* people's life functions. Dirty orange may specifically mean threatening bodily harm.

The eerie two-candle lights themselves have a long history of being associated with wealthy houses, big mansions, and old money. They were a fixture in Roman Polanski's 1968 *Rosemary's Baby*, as black-shrouded lamps dimly lighting the antichrist's shadowy cradle. Frank Sinatra divorced the (too) young (anyway) Mia Farrow for doing the horror picture when he told her not to. This might or might not be hypocritical considering among his Rat Pack pals at one time, Sammy Davis, Jr., fraternized with Church of Satan founder Anton LaVey.[2] As such, perhaps Sinatra had good reason for putting his foot down against Farrow participating in the satanic Polanski

## 13. The Shining: *Scarier Than Ever* 85

film besides wanting her in his detective movie being filmed at the same time.

As it happened, nine years later in Jack Nicholson's bathroom is where Roman Polanski drugged, raped, and sodomized a 13-year-old girl, when Nicholson was reportedly out of the country, perhaps already preparing for *The Shining* that was mainly shot in England. Shockingly, Jack Nicholson and other Hollywood folk at the time defended the director's abhorrent behavior since Polanski had, as Nicholson said, "never been one to let anything limit what he does…. He is a genius, I mean, come *on!*"[3] Considering that Nicholson was also known to cavalierly swap women with seasoned lothario friend Warren Beatty, someone of dubious character where women were concerned, perhaps Jack Nicholson's ethics are not so surprising.[4]

It is then interesting to note that when Kubrick, who was friendly with Nicholson on and off the set (the two at times would take turns winding each other up), filmed the scene where Jack makes a scared Danny sit on his lap, Kubrick shot it with the bathroom door decidedly open, where Nicholson could not help but see. It would be intriguing to know if Nicholson picked up on it as a rather pointed set-up by Kubrick, or simply an environs detail for the scene at hand. Since then, Roman Polanski has been accused of at least four more counts of pedophilia. One would hope that by now Jack Nicholson and those of his ilk would have changed their tune about Polanski's pedophilia being above the law.

People have heard how cruelly Kubrick broke Shelly Duvall down so her character would be at her most rattled, but Jack Nicholson was put through the ringer too during the making of *The Shining*. There were scenes where Nicholson was pushed to his limits, such as the bar scenes where after several scores of takes, a frazzled Jack warned actor Joe Turkel (the bartender) ahead of time that he was really going to go off his nut on his deliveries, just to blow off some steam.[5] Jack Nicholson had to bounce a ball against the hotel's kachina-style wall hanging over and over for several days to get that one shot. Whatever scenes he was acting with Duvall that she had to do over, so did he. Even sixty-nine-year-old Scatman Crothers was subjected to grueling takes, some to the point where he was reduced to tears so that Kubrick would finally back off. Jack Nicholson would sometimes intervene during Crothers' shoots when he thought his older buddy (it was Jack who pushed for Crothers to be cast as Dick Hallorann) was being pushed too far.[6] Overall, it can be debated that Shelly Duvall was the actor who delivered the most in her performance, to where Nicholson stated fairly that Duvall "went through the greatest lengths of any actor for a part." For himself, Jack certainly paid his own dues on *The Shining*. "I'm glad to be off that one," Nicholson later confided, "That was rough duty."[7]

## The True Terror Lurking Throughout *The Shining*

Whereas some bury the truth in order to conceal it, others bury the truth in the hopes that one day it will be found. Stanley Kubrick and those select few in the know (such as production designer Randy Taylor) on his production crew did the latter. Kubrick stated he "wanted to make the world's scariest movie."[8] *The Shining*'s bartender Lloyd does not sport horns and the movie contains no overt devil imagery; satanic content doesn't have to be presented as clearly as Halloween decoration in order for it to be present. As Kubrick was a director of great subtlety, it stands to reason that he would not hit an audience over the head with such bombastic imagery for a cheap scare.

Yet Stanley Kubrick actually did use *The Shining* as a vehicle to expose *real Luciferian sigils* otherwise unknown to the public at large. The following discussion reveals and describes for the first time the Luciferian symbolism that he hid ... and it starts with the maze.

### The Overlook Maze and Hotel's Biggest Secret

It is the riddle of the maze which provides the key to deciphering exactly what makes the Overlook Hotel, at first glance a banal-looking building with bland mixed décor, emanate so palpably such dread and menace. The movie's masterful soundtrack sets the tone most effectively, with Carlos and Elkind's opening score of impending doom, Penderecki's suspenseful orchestrals, and Bartok's eerie, soul-piercing piano suites. The hotel's harsh and predominantly red, black, and white main floor coloring with blackened wood interior may promote an infernal vibe, but if one wants solid proof Kubrick purposefully put true satanic imagery into *The Shining*, then one need look no further than the Overlook's mysteriously spine-chilling, pyramid-tipped hedge maze.

It is not the actual physical maze that Wendy and Danny go into, nor the maze miniature Jack looks down on inside the hotel, but it is the first bird's eye shot of the maze from above which effectively lays bare the Overlook Hotel's diabolical nature. This one shot of the maze—which bears no resemblance to either the real hedge maze, nor its display map, nor the hotel's indoor replica—was an expertly lit, one-off "bigature" that was destroyed after its one use. This maze prop and how it is lit operates as an ingenious visual trick. To appreciate its full effect, it is best to see the entire aerial shot of the maze in full view, then back away from it *while squinting*. This is easiest to do viewing a digital graphic file of said scene that shows its graphics in miniature.

## 13. The Shining: Scarier Than Ever

The Shining's Hedge Maze aerial shot is made entirely of Luciferian shadowscript (art by the author).

The maze is then transformed into a giant devil's head, mouth open with mocking tongue, upon which lies a cross pinned between mirrored S's which stand for ... bet you can guess. Behind the devil's head is a great wavy X, one of the many signs of the so-called "Beast." Wendy and Danny are shown to be caught in the very teeth of it, which are made from skillful light effects designed to be three "lightning bolt" S's: another satanic initial. Surrounding the devil's head are actual black magic symbols that are best (or worst) called "shadow script."[9] The maze is completely made up of these abstracted shadow script sigils, among which are the profaned inverted cross, four different versions of flipped or mirrored satanic S's, spiraling Lucifer sigils which are often hidden in tendril-like designs, spell-casting rhomb sticks (diamonds topping or speared by a rod/wand), zigzag Insanity glyphs and hook-like Death script. Perhaps in the hopes that someone would eventually discover it, Stanley Kubrick and a select part of his production crew created this specially-built maze to defy the corrupt Luciferian elite and expose to the world the covert symbols that they love to hide in their public works.

Once the maze's shadow script has finally made itself visible, it aids in deciphering *The Shining*'s next bombshell discovery: The fact that the majority of the Overlook Hotel's Native American décor...

...is primarily **not Native American at all.**

88  Part II—The Films Following *2001*

Examples of secretive shadow script of which many are found in *The Shining* and other Kubrick films (referenced by the author).

## 13. The Shining: *Scarier Than Ever*

Images on facing page and below shadow script masquerading as Native American motifs and appear in other Kubrick films are comparable to those found in Left Hand Path magic, art, books, and internet sources.

Some of the above sigils can be found posing as mundane décor in the Overlook Hotel (referenced by the author).

Instead, the hotel's every column border, wood carving, wall hanging, wall paneling, and floor design that look Apache and Navaho-inspired are actually multiple motif composites of real-life shadow script sigils used in malevolent magic. In addition, the hotel's furniture, props, ironwork, woodwork, stained glass, supplies and even signage silently broadcast sinister Luciferian design motifs as well. The entire Overlook-Hotel-as-America is in fact one gigantic exposé of malignant Luciferian spellcraft. This revelation can most certainly rock a person's worldview, as most people naturally do not want to think such practices are so prevalent, especially within our nation's power structure. Once people are made aware of these existing shadow script symbols, they will start noticing them in all matter of media, arts, and especially architecture. Once these shadow scripts are recognized en masse, the Luciferian ruling class' supposed hold over an awakening public is then broken. Eventually their puppet master invisibility is completely shattered.

Stanley Kubrick himself did not believe in hell or the devil, but he did believe in evil and the human capacity for evil, and part of his cinematic work has not only put up a mirror to various examples of mankind's evil but apparently has also been spent in clandestinely revealing the actual existence of a powerful occult elite who have poisoned the upper echelons of Western civilization, more specifically a high degree Luciferian branch of the so-called Illuminati (of whom Kubrick references *several* times in his films as overlapping or being one in the same) and their linked associations. As these corrupt elite forsook their original Freemasonry vows to self-illuminate on behalf of humanity but instead use their power to sublimate humanity, it is more accurate to call these practitioners *illuciferians* after that which Kubrick has cryptically and continuously disclosed they venerate throughout his career. In *The Shining*, if the Overlook is supposed to represent America as a whole, then it is possible Stanley Kubrick is making the extremely sobering suggestion that a great many sectors of American industry are tarnished and hamstrung by those powerbrokers who put great stock in such beliefs, as surreal as that sounds. Certainly makes for a terrifying movie premise, whether true or untrue.

How the Overlook hotel reflects this proffered profaned power structure includes politics (Mr. Ullman), the banking and corporate elite (the Lobby and Gold Room), the food industry (the kitchen), and big agriculture (the storeroom). In *Paths of Glory*, *Dr. Strangelove*, and *Full Metal Jacket*, Kubrick shines a light on the corruption and insanity within the military industrial complex. The defiling of law, justice, and the pursuit of government-controlled science via shadowy experimentation in MK-Ultra-type mind control programs are Kubrick's central themes in *Clockwork Orange*. In *The Shining*, Kubrick's primary focus takes on what he considers is America's true enemy from within.

Case in point: the twin Grady girls in the hallway, the "all work and no

## 13. The Shining: *Scarier Than Ever*

play" typewriter scene, and the blood gushing elevator are considered some of the scariest parts of *The Shining*, but once the maze is deciphered by viewers, the scene where Wendy wards off Jack with a bat takes on terrifying overtones that have only partially to do with Nicholson's acting. As Jack hysterically rails on about his "oath to his employers," one can spot Jack making the "666" hand sign as towering, shadowy upside-down crosses of the hotel's window frames loom behind him. As he forces Wendy up the stairs (with an X-in-O light above her head) Jack also flashes the "devil horns" hand sign *right underneath* an X-eyed "Native American" rug in the background. Does the rug symbolize a dead Apache face or Jack's satanic-possessed mind? The climax of such chilling associations reach a dread crystallization when behind Jack's head during his tirade, slowly revealing themselves in the distance, are an American flag standing cheek-to-jowl with a skeletal goat-headed chandelier. Like the sudden appearance of the Grady twins, it is a most frightening, "spooky at a distance" effect for those who consider the scene's suggested ramifications. Considering all the elements that are layered within this one scene, it is no wonder it supposedly took 127 takes until Kubrick got what he wanted. The more attentive and informed a viewer is, the more horrifying *The Shining* can become.

So Stanley Kubrick does expose illuciferian shadow script in *The Shining*, and while he may leave it to the viewer to research and decipher their meanings, he does drop metaphorically strong visual hints. For instance, the zigzag shadow script forming the great "X" behind the devil maze head turns out to hang above Jack's own head as he types, and these red and yellow zigzag borders run all along the large ceiling beams of the huge Colorado lounge he works in. Research on black magic sigils can confirm this same zigzag pattern is authentic shadow script for an insanity curse. Considering what happens to Jack's state of mind during the length of *The Shining*, this particular meaning of the madness-inducing zigzag sigil does prove to bear out. Kubrick incorporates this Insanity shadow script again in his influential film, *Full Metal Jacket*.

Those who would make the case that Stanley Kubrick is simply using these satanic sigils to make his horror film as frightening as possible and no more miss the point that without discovering the well-hidden maze shadow script in the first place, the Overlook Hotel's overall décor would still be indecipherable and its true illuciferian content would continue to elude movie audiences, with no one ever having the opportunity to learn and understand them for what they are for the sake of self-defense. What is the point of a movie director hiding what is arguably some of the scariest content of his horror film? That would make about as much sense as filming an erotic movie that had very little sex in it—oh, wait—Kubrick did that too with *Eyes Wide Shut* … and it behooves alert audiences to find out why.

## Of Carpets, Rooms and Elevators

### The Creepy Corridor Carpet Pattern

The Overlook's overly large and garish orange, brown, and red hallway rug looks as if it is shouting, "Notice me!" The pattern is of three nested hexagonal shapes on rods interlocking in a mirrored pattern, similar to geometric drumsticks facing alongside each other. If one is familiar with alchemy, then this opposing "drumstick" pattern can be identified as stylized alchemical symbols for Life (upright glass beaker) and Death (upside down beaker). Considering the gravity of the situation when Danny is reluctantly lured into the forbidding Room 237 (a scene with the most menacing music), the loud symbolism of the corridor carpet begins to make more sense. Kubrick even switched the part of the carpet Danny was originally playing on, not only to bring more attention to the rug pattern itself but to reassuringly put Danny on a Life symbol (previously he was on Death) from the audience's P.O.V., before he walks over to Room 237.

Before Jack's yellow ball (choice between Life or Death?) mysteriously rolls towards him, Danny is playing with toy cars and trucks that are either mainly blue and pink, blue, red or green. To the right, a green race car's strange pink bumper sports a stranger inverted hexagram design. Many of the toy vehicles are pink, a color boys don't usually gravitate to, which is a clue the colors are symbolic in nature. Perhaps applying *2001*'s color code may aid in deciphering any potential clues Danny's arranged toys might provide for Danny's subliminal situation at hand.

The color bands of the floor's nested hexagons convey relevant symbolism as well. The outside hexagon is orange, the middle is dark brown, and the center hexagon is red. If we accept that orange represents 33rd Degree Freemasonry, dark brown equals threat or insecurity (regular brown traditionally equates as earth, security, or "hominess") and red is danger, lifeblood, or the entrapment of consciousness, then the fact the three nested hexagon patterns together count as 666 gives the loud hallway carpet a decidedly more sinister character. Especially with the orange hexagons also form satanic S's.

### The Mystery of Room 237 and Its Carpet Pattern

When a viewer at last sees the interior of the dreaded Room 237, one wonders what is so scary about the room itself—up until the woman ghost appears. Now that the symbolism of the outside corridor carpet is understood, it is easier to decipher the meaning of Room 237's carpet pattern and why its room is presented as being so frightening. At the center of each pale green peacock-styled textile is a purple alchemical Death symbol, which sets

## 13. The Shining: *Scarier Than Ever*

the tone for the entire room. Skeletal white bamboo chairs contain infernal elements: their perforated board backs betray the shadow script motif for "darkness." The curtains and bedspread display satanic chevron stacks (as in *chevre* for goat), pointing upward or towards the left for the Left Hand Path (Kubrick reapplies the chevron shadow script in *Eyes Wide Shut*). The picture over the fireplace is a bouquet close up, but from a distance looks like a demonic, unfriendly face in shadow. The other pictures in the room exhibit equally unsettling imagery. The lampshades are either dirty orange or dirty yellow. The bed and some of the couches have magenta and pale green cushions, and as the camera rolls over the bed we see four gold framed, black and white matted pictures (also containing disturbing images) above it; lamps cast a pyramid-shaped shadow on them. A monolith sized mirror reflects the pyramid shadow back to the audience, providing another opportunity to see it. Across from it a bony ribbed radiator stands to the right of the bathroom door.

Room 237's bathroom is heavy with color symbolism as well. It is half white on the ceiling and upper wall area, and pale green halfway down the walls and onto the floor. The white ceiling and pale green walls are separated by a yellow ribbon of paint. On the bathroom floor, orange outlines a familiar shape which keeps resurfacing in *The Shining*. This same shape is repeated as Jack and Wendy's bedroom mirror, in a yellow cowboy poster in the hotel's rec room, and as the entrance to the Overlook's hedge maze, among other places. This shape is usually used as a topper symbolizing "the rising sun," a popular theme illuciferians are fond of referring to again and again in multiple ways. Another "rising sun" design they frequently use is done in leaded glass fan-shaped windows above main entrance doors. These fanlights are often found on well-to-do Georgian, Victorian, and Edwardian style houses. This noted window glass style can be found above the gated estate's main door in *Eyes Wide Shut*.

Back to 237's "Death Room" bathroom. If yellow in *The Shining* conveys Death (as opposed to Life in *2001*), then pale green may intimate defiled, corrupted life or destructive perversion in contrast to the vibrant Creative Growth green of *2001*. The orange "rising sun" motif on the floor can refer to high-degree occult Masonry. The young woman ghost (or demon) who first sizes Jack up before embracing him, later turns into a rotting crone who mocks Jack as he backs out of the Death Room in abject fear. This lady apparition could be Jack himself, as there is always a mirror behind the main ghosts he encounters, such as the butler Grady and Lloyd, the vaguely devilish bartender. The Death Room lady could also symbolize the bargain Jack made with the hotel's hellish inhabitants, a deal that looked desirable at first but later turned out to be appallingly evil. She can possibly represent the drowned feminine/Earth principle, risen again to extract revenge from those who would suppress her and claim dominion over her. But as evil destroys what it profanes, the strange ceiling lights may hold another clue. From the audience's vantage point, the purplish fixture has two lights and a center reflected light and looks much like a Death or a Destroy sigil. This could suggest the death of the Crown chakra or the Third Eye; the ability for self-illumination. There is even an inverted "i" light reflection on the left wall (for the Left Hand Path), signifying Anti-Life. Most distressing themes indeed.

## The Gold Room, Its Carpet and Its Mysterious Entrance Sign

Compared to the garish hallway carpet, the more muted ballroom floor initially looks like South American textiles. Its pattern consists of gold four-point stars lined in pink and orange and enclosed within light blue/brown squares. Each nested square is linked by gold crosses with alternating pink, gold, and orange tips. But as attractive as that sounds, rotating this deceptively peaceful pattern reveals its true nature: it becomes an endless chain of X's that blankets the entire Gold Room floor and the hallway outside the ballroom. One other element that hints at the carpet's nefariousness is when Mr. Ullman casually mentions how "they had someone specially flown in from Chicago" to redecorate the area and add the carpet. Kubrick left this otherwise extraneous sounding dialogue in for a reason. Chicago is not the city one usually thinks of first when in need of fashionable redecorating, but associations with "the mob" and "clean up job" do spring more readily to mind. For those with their antennae up, this extra bit of information contributes to the overall sense of uneasiness the hotel exudes.

The immense Gold Room holds a massive secret too. Its far back walls contain large flipped S's that possibly double as stylized swastikas. The ballroom's central row of imposing iron chandeliers, when seen straight on, bottom out in unmistakable goat-heads. Their chains string-up oval "soul" sigils and ankhs, indicating diabolical power imprisoning Life or lives. Nine sets of two-candle lights line the walls, equaling eighteen total; another 6+6+6 reference. The most impressive feature inside this cavernous room are its walls, which dazzle with an infinite number of gold pieces on either side of the ballroom. But that is not the only reason why it impresses. Not to be outdone by its floor, the Gold Room walls shimmer with hundreds, even thousands, of peek-a-boo XXX's all along its great length as the camera dollies through its space. The brilliant design of the Gold Room walls make it very difficult to freeze-frame on these devilishly stealthy XXX's; their presence is *felt* more than seen as they are revealed only when the camera is moving or when light falls across them. Other shadow script may be in the walls as well, but the X's are the easiest to spot. XXX doubles as an XOX with rhombs substituting the

### 13. The Shining: *Scarier Than Ever*      95

O's. "O" is shadow script for fulfillment and XX make up the base of the most commonly known Lucifer sigil. XXX strings show up as well when Grady first leads Jack into the Gold Room's men's lavatory. As the two men walk through its door, a lurid red wall panel covered with X's is seen.

The Gold Room sign outside its entrance has intrigued people since *The Shining* was released in theaters. At first glance it is the largeness of its decorative motif that attracts more than what is being announced on the sign itself. This fancy gold design consists of two rows of seven diamonds, three on top and four at bottom, each linked to an outside loop. This design is a bit of ingenious triple-symbolism, as it is a gold decoration containing not only seven diamonds but also made up of XXX motifs that along with their loops, bind and hold the diamonds in place. These loops may also be tied down soul sigils, being ovoid shapes. The diamond itself is one of the most ancient depictions of the feminine powers (the vulva) and the Earth. One of its earliest examples was found in a South African cave as a red-ochre stone engraving dating back to at least 70,000 or 80,000 BC.[10] But this diamond shape was stolen to represent Lucifer.

As there are seven diamonds in the sign, they also represent the body's seventh chakra, which is the Crown chakra that is a person's capacity for self-illumination. This in turn hails back to the seven diamond-shaped guides in *2001* that symbolized David Bowman's own illumination as he goes through the Star Gate. In essence, the Gold Room sign's design is Stanley Kubrick's Anti-Illumination warning (A.I.). Since the Gold Room appears to be the insidious heart of the infernal Overlook, it would make sense that its signage slyly depicts the main agenda of the hotel's satanic evil: that of truncating people's ability to transcend and not allowing their souls to evolve. In effect, this sign symbolizes the spiritual imprisonment of humanity as the Luciferian elite claim the Earth for themselves, for the symbol XOX/XO are both satanic signs for the Luciferian Sun and victory in dominating the Earth. With the Overlook being allegedly Stanley Kubrick's stand-in for America, these illuciferian machinations take on a reality too close to home. It is in part what the hotel's Devil Maze illustrates. From this standpoint, the Torrance family is not just an individual family but can represent all American families being under siege and imprisoned within a completely rigged Luciferian elite system.

## The Significance of *The Shining*'s Infamous Elevator

The hotel's terrifying elevator seems somehow psychically linked to Danny. Back when he was being checked by the lady doctor, Danny's large teddy bear pillow had eyes similar to the elevator's eye-like floor dials. The original yellow Saul Bass *Shining* poster creates Danny's frightened eyes in the same shape of the elevator floor dials. *The Shining*'s recurrent teddy bear imagery (symbolizing childhood) and the Grady twins possibly being one girl with her alter mirroring Danny and his alter Tony, suggests an eerie overlap between child abuse and Monarch techniques under Project MK-ULTRA, with the elevator itself being a damning illustration. The overflowing blood usually keeps people from really seeing the elevator's engraved red designs which are quite intriguing. On the elevator's beams between its bright red doors are two animal heads, a bear above and a tabby cat/tiger below. The top bear is actually a double image, with a dead bear inside (X's for eyes and tongue out) an enraged bear. The sad feline below looks like its head is being split open, possibly by what appears to be an axe wielded by the bear above it. The elevator button between them, which happens to be inside a soul sigil, serves as a most fitting "trigger" symbol. With the twins appearing next to the rec room's "Monarch" calendar, the "over the rainbow" stickers on Danny's old room door and the butterflies on Wendy's dresser and bedroom wall, the alarming engravings on the hellish elevator arguably cements such horrific brainwashing associations with child abuse as a relevant theme within *The Shining* that recalls the main focus of *Clockwork Orange* and to a degree is revisited in *Eyes Wide Shut*.

More evidence is when Danny is summoned by a threatening Jack to sit on his lap in the bedroom. On first viewing this is a deceptively tender scene, but the observant will notice Danny's initial reluctance to come to Jack and how he then just passively stares straight into space and his voice becomes flat and robotic while answering his going-insane father. When Tony completely takes over Danny's body ("Danny's not here anymore, Mrs. Torrance"), it strongly indicates "Tony" is an alternate personality as body possession is not something an "imaginary friend" can do. Dissociative states and alternate personalities are usually byproducts of extreme trauma, which adds more evidence that Danny's abuse by Jack is not just physical. More proof of this is in an alternate Saul Bass *Shining* poster where a boy's screaming mouth is being covered by a large shadowy male figure behind him. This particular Saul Bass artwork was on display in the 2014–16 Stanley Kubrick Exhibit that made its rounds in museums all over the globe. As this poster was not used, it is possible Kubrick thought it revealed too much of *The Shining*'s backstory or was too on the nose.

## The Overlook Hotel's Infernal Architecture

The walls and columns that make up the main lobby and Colorado lounge floors of the Overlook hotel are lined with various orange and red pattern motifs where they all touch the ceiling. Near the elevator the walls have designs that at first look like yellow, diamond shaped eyes outlined in red, but viewed from an angle they too look like long rows of XXX's. It is such psychological visual tricks which subconsciously build up the Overlook's infamous atmosphere of dread. Other walls in the Colorado room are a combination of pyramids and "crowns," a popular shadow script symbolizing either the flaming crown of a baphomet, the top of a devils' head complete with horns, or a bastardized akhet, the ancient Egyptian symbol of the sun rising between two hills. By now the appeal of such sun imagery for the illuciferians' "light bringer" who supposedly has a "face like the sun" should make sense.

The top pattern banding the main floor columns appears as a row of narrow, black Z's. When researching these Z-like glyphs, they turned out to match the wolfsangel, a medieval wolf trap symbol which originated in Germany. This same glyph in time became Nazi storm trooper insignia for various infantry and *Panzer* battalions.[11] But this hooked Z glyph has an even greater, disturbingly appropriate association: it is the shadow script sign for Death. Thus their meaning takes on a far more sinister tone when Dick Hallorann happens to be murdered near the very columns whose tops are ringed with this Death shadow script.

## Woodwork

The woodwork of the hotel, especially on the main floors, is strikingly dark to the point where its carved and engraved details are often in danger of being completely obfuscated within its murky veneer. Only by fleeting, stark lighting passing over its gloomy wainscoting do we get to see certain carved motifs pop up before being swallowed again by the wood's inky grain. The wainscoting near the entry doors contain what we will call rhomb sticks, nested rhomb shapes either on top (shadow script for Lucifer's power) or in the middle of a stalk (for "evil aid"). In addition, X's are carved on either side of the nested rhombs, so they can also be read as XOX. The X's are cleverly hidden, and can only be seen if the light hits them just right.

Both the entry doors, the Registration area, and the entryway to the general manager's office have their share of chilling shadow script sigils. The dark wooden entry doors have large double diamonds: any double four-pointed shape equaling eight refers to the Luciferian "morning star" (which is a straight-out appropriation of the planet Venus, a star flatly unassociated with this upstart satanic set for billions of years) that in the illuciferian lexicon is always depicted as an eight pointed star. The reason high degree Luciferian Masons covet Venus so is that every 23 years it makes a pentagram orbit around the Sun. The pentagram itself is another word for star and historically also represents the Earth as a star, thus illuciferians attempt to claim the Earth star (and the Sun) for themselves and profane it by turning the Earth symbol upside down: the inverted pentagram which later became more widely recognized as the Goat of Mendes sign, an 19th-century Baphomet reference without its flaming crown.[12]

The registration desk is also engraved with double four-pointed shapes but this time in double rectangles—when done in threes, these rectangles can in turn double for the shadow script representing the three planes of existence they claim power over. The illuciferian elite are fond of combining their symbols with the aim of strengthening their powers. Behind the registration desk the mail slot shelving area has diamond rows along its top, either to reinforce claims on the Earth / feminine principle (the *original* diamond symbol) or to represent the morning star when numbering eight. In the beginning of *The Shining* when first introduced to Wendy and Danny Torrance, Danny drinks from a milk glass covered in red, yellow, and dark green nested rhombs and inverted hexagon shapes (profaned six-pointed stars [i.e., Star of David]). As milk is about as feminine and nurturing a symbol as one can get, Kubrick is in part indicating how the illuciferians covet and subvert female powers for their own whims. Even the red milk carton in Wendy's kitchen (which shows up again in the hotel kitchen) is designed *and positioned* to look like a leering devil face, mocking Wendy. Viewed this way, Kubrick, the director of ultraviolent *Clockwork Orange* (which attacks misogyny in its own way), can be seen as quite pro-woman in his attempts to out and expose the most misogynistic occult power-mongers on the planet, something which he does again with gusto in *Eyes Wide Shut*.

The wood paneling between the Registration desk and general manager's office are interspersed with red rhomb carvings whose designs contain X's. When approaching the General Manager's office there is an area topped by a bank of curling, fiddle headed protrusions that are best described as Lucifer coils or spirals, as they refer to one of Lucifer's more official sigils which looks like a long, slanted "L" with a spiral branching off of its left side. This particular spiral may refer to the "shooting" or "fallen star" comet imagery also ascribed to Lucifer, but the spiral itself, among its numerous cultural associations, is originally one of humanity's oldest female symbols next to the rhomb/diamond.[13] Hidden letter 'L's are where Luciferian branches connect to each other. Illuciferian S's and L's are often concealed in baroque-style leafy foliage designs with spiraling (comet) flourishes. In the hotel's burnt ash colored wood paneling, double X's appear between each of these tall branching boteh protuberances. Stanley Kubrick unmasks these infernal shadow script sigils again in *Eyes Wide Shut* at Ziegler's party.

All the yellow doors in the upstairs servant section of the hotel sport inverted crosses. The moment this is most thrust in the audience's face is Kubrick's extreme angle close-up shot of the "REDRUM" door (itself a known satanic phrase). The other time Kubrick gives a hint about these doors is when

Jack returns to Wendy after encountering the ghost lady in Room 237. When Wendy lets him in, a mirror near Jack first briefly reflects his head but next immediately shows a yellow door where it is easier to focus on its inverted-cross frame and associate Jack with its subsequent satanic symbolism.

## Ironwork

The dark two candle light fixtures that are everywhere in the hotel seem almost unnecessary, especially in the hotel's already brightly lit ground floor areas. But these are highly symbolic lights, a traditional mainstay in satanic altar lighting. As appropriate, pictures of past nefarious clientele or other evil objects are often found under these lights. Hanging over people's heads like great weights, the rusty iron, sharply jagged chandelier lights are stuffed with their own malignant symbols. The smaller eight-candle chandeliers display X's at their centers, which combine into the diabolic X inside an O. As an age-old alchemical symbol for the Earth is a circle with a cross through it, the Luciferian elite pervert this by tilting the cross into an X, which for them doubles as power-play for claiming the Earth and a Luciferian Sun/Fulfillment variant. These smaller chandeliers' chains are partly made of strung-up oval soul sigils, a most fitting symbolism of souls ensnared.

It is interesting to note that out of all the Overlook's architectural and lighting outlets inspired by the Awahnee hotel in Yosemite, California, these particular XO chandeliers were among the few items not changed at all. That is correct, these XO lights came straight out of the Awahnee practically as-is. Think about that. Among all the other impressive work in creating *original* evil décor for the Overlook hotel, Roy Walker's production team did an excellent job in replicating the *pre-existing* sinister chandelier fixtures from Yosemite's own historic Awahnee hotel.

The murky wooden entryway leading to Mr. Ullman's General Manager's office has attractive gold filigree metal work on either side of the its dark door frame. Both have long "aid evil spell" sigils; rods with rhombs in the center. Framing each rhomb stick are several flipped S's which end in Luciferian spirals. These S's are big on one end and quite small on the other and then are mirrored. Remember, the Overlook Maze shows several variations of these satanic initials. Large Luciferian 'C's festoon the fancy gold work, which can stand for "C-for-Comet" with Luciferian spirals at each end. Also sprouting from the sides of the rhomb stick are palmette-inspired palm fruit stems. Palmettes are ancient Egyptian, Near Eastern, and Greco-Roman inspired motifs which symbolize—again—the rising sun.[14]

The general manager's own sign hangs from wrought iron sporting flipped S's and boteh branches—a male version of the tree of life stolen from India and the Middle East. Such has two or more of these Luciferian botehs branching from its stem. (Author's note: Assumedly, these masked Luciferian motifs have specific names but as they are intentionally secret, we make do with a generically descriptive naming convention.) The illuciferians have a standard practice to associate their shadow script dedications to Satan or Lucifer around portals and places of importance, such as doors, archways, gateways, hallways, stairwells, fireplaces and tunnels. Flipped S's and other shadow script can be found surreptitiously decorating busts of high-ranking people or architecture of great relevance, happy to hide in their limelight.

Last but certainly not least, are the Overlook's formidably-sized great iron chandeliers. Unlike the smaller eight-candled ones, these mighty chandeliers have more than 18 candles, possibly 24. Like the smaller XO lights, these big ones also have suspended soul sigils and what looks to be a large ankh strung up to the ceiling, seemingly doomed to be forever held down by the immense weight of these intimidating candle holders. They look almost like the Awahnee's original large hanging lights but carry a most diabolical difference. This most unsettling thing about the Overlook's centerpiece chandeliers is that they have iron goat heads at their bases. This is not always apparent as their appearance changes as people walk by them. One must be looking at these looming chandeliers straight-on to get the full goat head effect. The goat heads all have two pointy protuberances on their chins which are not standard goat beards. These have triple meanings: their shape is similar to the cane-like "S" in Egyptian hieroglyphics, the backwards "J"-for- L (Lucifer) and the inverted "J"-looking cuneiform for "mouth" stolen from the ancient Phoenicians. Such chilling associations for the gaping goat maws accompany these chandeliers' bottommost sign: an eight ridged ring signifying the morning star.

## Furniture

The furnishings of the Overlook hotel add greatly to its malevolent atmosphere. The tightly crisscrossed, orange and red (or yellow and orange) checkered sofa chairs actually display the shadow script for "weaving darkness" as in "to keep in darkness." Their coloring may combine satanic red with Masonic manipulation (orange) and death (yellow). Any tight checkered pattern, whether found in fabrics, furniture, packaging, clothing, carvings or elsewhere, all exude the same "weaving darkness" shadow script curse. Another version of this shadow motif is the Luciferian rhomb-net (tilted checkerboard) which shows up elsewhere in *The Shining*.

Some chairs such as the wooden type Jack sits in at his typewriter have a wide, "guitar-pick" shape for the head rest which is either a curse sigil or a version of the nefarious "sun face" Luciferian motif seen elsewhere in the hotel and as masks in *Eyes Wide Shut*. Other chairs, couches, and tables are either in blood red or bone white fabrics, or pitch-black wood.

Inverted pentagrams guild infernal palmettes on the gold coverlet of Wendy and Jack's bed in the hotel. On the mirror stand opposite their bed, a malicious looking snake head peers out from its lampshade (which later changes). Their bedroom curtains' mottled design can at times look like unpleasant, jeering faces. The curtains in Mr. Ullman's office has X's, rhombs, shadow 'V's (victory), and insanity zigzags mimicking native patterns. During Jack's interview, Mr. Ullman's pen at one time even points to the curtains. Yellow inverted pentagrams later appear on the packaging of a "Star" bread loaf while Wendy is canning in the hotel kitchen.

## Wall Hangings, Wallpapers, Sculptures and Props

Perhaps the most convincingly Native American (N.A.) styled décor are the Overlook hotel's throw rugs and wall hangings. One particular woven carpet is the one on the same side of the room as the maze diorama. It has two thick, black X's on either side of a black monolith shape. Along with the carpet's other motifs, it can appear as a geometric dead face but the double X's reveal the rug's true diabolic associations. At one point when a rapidly unraveling Jack forces Wendy (with bat) up the stairs, his hand brandishes the "devil horns" sign *right below* this very same rug. There is a wall hanging filled with pale green diamonds that are above a skeletal looking eagle sculpture. The fibrous texture of the wall hanging's seven diamonds make people ignore its X's outlined in white, so its XOX pattern is not overt and effectively stays hidden. The more obviously satanic wall hanging is the red one with continuous XXX's running across its length. Viewed up close, however, the jagged black diamonds help break up the X patterning.

The sculptures inside the Overlook's hallways are especially ugly and skeletal in nature, which continually stress the hotel's always-there, under-the-radar presence of Death that emanates throughout its interiors. Their abstracted forms suggest figures but their ash gray appearance makes them more undefined and adds to their feeling of lifelessness.

A constantly reappearing reference to *A Space Odyssey* turns out to be the monolith. The monolith can present itself as lights, such as the two on Mr. Ullman's office ceiling or at the Gold Ballroom's bar. It also shows up many times as mirrors, as there are mirrors in the hallway outside the Gold Room, and in the hotel bathrooms. The monolith mirrors provide clues and can tip people off to important warning signs if they are alert. Reflective surfaces have a way of revealing things about the hotel. As Ullman is showing the Torrances around the hotel's lounge hallways, a picture's glass surface unaccountably reflects a far-off, blazing bright, two-light fixture it physically couldn't capture from where it is placed. As the dolly camera follows Ullman's group walking by, the reflecting picture turns out to be a photo of a headdress-wearing chieftain, but the first thing one sees is the reflected light fixture becoming huge horns on a shadowy figure's head before the image of the chieftain becomes clear. The overlap is a subtle, "light bringer" association hint. This is just one instance of the hotel insinuating its true nature if one is attentive.

The hallway wallpaper outside the Gold Room is a mottled pattern akin to a confusing tortoise shell mixture. It is pleasant to look at but feels like it is hiding something within its clash of gold dusted colors. From first glance, the pretty blue flower wallpaper on the servant level is charming and cheerful. But when they frame the Grady girls, the white spaces in between the floral patterns turn out to be insanity zigzag shadow script. When Danny runs into the twins, a yellow cabinet is open slightly so the audience will at least subconsciously see its and the other yellow doors' inverted cross frames. The Grady twins' hallway also changes when Danny rounds the corner: at first sight, it appears a black inverted cross is hanging from the first ceiling lamp, and the ceiling's reflected light is alarmingly bright, casting strange (sigil-shaped) shadows. The next full shot of the hallway then swaps the inverted cross for an emergency sprinkler head. Given that the bloody reveal of the Grady girls' fate may reveal a blood-spattered image of their crazed butler father on the left wall, the visual evidence of evil confirms infernal influence.

Later on Danny is possessed by Tony, and picks up a large kitchen knife that Wendy (asleep in their apartment) chose to defend themselves with against the now violently insane Jack. As Tony/Danny walks towards a vanity table with the knife, he passes by some dark curtains which harbor some evil-looking demonic faces glaring at him from between the folds.

## The Overlook Hell's Kitchen

It is easy to overlook the hotel kitchen but it surprisingly contains just as much satanic imagery as the rest of the hotel. As Scatman Crother's Dick Hallorann leads Wendy and Danny through the kitchen, they pass by quite a bit of Left Hand Path shadow script sigils. Among these are the flipped Omega signs: the $\Omega$ and its profaned reverse shape. When Hallorann, Wendy and Danny walk through shelves of large, grey cooking pots, their Omega-shaped handles are both shown as right side up and upside down. The shadow script version of the $\Omega$ (looks like a U) infers that the Omega will soon be Alpha … and vice versa. Among the pots are long metal rolls whose ends are positioned to look like the oval shadow script for female (—) and male (|). As they go around a large stove area, cooking apparatus hang from the stoves lighting vents, such as spatulas with rhomb shaped perforations and X's in the center. There also hangs a guitar chip-like (akin to a wide, upside down teardrop) accordion fire heater and the unassuming three-ringed griddles just happen to invoke the shadow script for "universe." The inverted teardrop and the oven lights strung together as single pearls on a string represent two other shadow scripts Kubrick was aware of which both show up in *Barry Lyndon* and *Eyes Wide Shut*.

The storeroom is packed with shadow script signs. For those who are already suspicious of Nabisco's famous logo may find some affirmation in Kubrick's tendency in storeroom shots to always put Nabisco products in places where its logo is sure to be seen. Libby's canned fruit, Heinz condiments, powdered drinks like Tang and Kool-Aid, Texas Sun, and Golden Rey boxes also line the walls and towering shelf racks. The Golden Rey boxes happen to have another satanic Z shadow script insignia in red ink. Later, when Jack is locked in the storeroom, we see him sleeping on large bags of Holly Silt. The big holly "leaf" on the bag right above Jack's head is actually covert shadow script since it is another eight-pointed dedication to the "morning star." Also on the bags are red, long lines (power rods) in a row, numbering at least 18 or more. Not only does the storeroom provide another way for Kubrick to highlight the shadow script that is used on Americans without their knowing, but here Kubrick brings home the point that most American food items and their respective companies are owned by the same illuciferian elite.

## The Overlook Stained Glass Windows

The hotel's lobby stained glass windows are a continuing example of illuciferian shadow script disguised as Native American motifs. XO's, bound soul sigils (oval shapes), double diamonds, rhomb sticks (rhombs on top or in the center of a rod), flipped S's and satanic lightning bolt 'S's doubling as swastikas all make their appearance along the top parts of the tall main floor windows. This includes a three-bar motif which represent the three Planes of Existence: the physical, mental/emotional, and spirit realms. The Planes lines or rectangles can be stacked vertically or horizontally. An upside-down and reversed L-for-Lucifer puzzle-piece bar pattern is also set in glass for all to see and hopefully recognize for the baneful design it is.

There are at least two or three illuciferian designs that double as Nazi insignia. Besides the previously mentioned swastika, there is the wolfsangel that specific Nazi infantries wore.[15] Since the Overlook is supposedly America, perhaps Kubrick is hinting at America's Wall Street set who not only did business with the Nazis during the war, but in effect helped to set the Nazi Party up in the first place.[16] Through the nation's ancient Babylonian money trap that is our economy, the higher echelons of American finance (as elsewhere) have few national loyalties. Globalists as a rule do what they can to undermine national sovereignty in order to "free up the markets" that were never really "free" in the first place. This is where both the Bilderberg group and the European Union (E.U.) share mutual interests and initially why "Grexit, Frexit, and Brexit" came about in opposition to them. The reason the public must be vigilant against so-called trade agreements such as NAFTA, TTP, and TTIP is that such schemes are really about *legalizing global corporate courts* that has complete jurisdiction and power to *override entire nations' judicial systems* that protect workers' rights, consumer right-to-know laws, and place controls on pharmaceutical pricing. As long as most financial assets are owned by the multinationals of the world, the pursuit of a "free and fair market" will always be an outright fallacious lie and complete economic fantasy.

## The Overlook Floor Designs

In the main hall lobby and lounge, the painted floor mosaics and throw rugs are perhaps the most convincingly done in a Native American style that is not actually Native American. For the floor, the prop designer painters did an excellent job combining a great number of shadow script sigils into larger conglomerate pieces that are either spherical or diamond in shape.

Some of the larger diamond ones, especially the ones near the ballroom hallway, are multiple XXX patterns done in violently red, orange, black and white in the hopes they will be eventually noticed. This includes the huge XOX floor borders between the lobby's red columns. These X shapes are broken and their O's are Lucifer rhombs so they are not immediately recognizable. Next to them are thinner black or red borders that either have white jagged sunrays, red diamonds, or black and red sun ray motifs. These sun ray elements are appropriated from the ancient Egyptians style of sun rays. This is because illuciferians put a lot of stock in associating their "morning star" ("face like the sun") with either star or sun imagery, including appropriating the appearance of other ancient culture's sun gods and light/fire bringers such as Apollo, Prometheus, or Mercury.

Particularly in the "morning star's" case, the illuciferians are appropriating the planet Venus, whose astronomical associations were devoid of any satanic influence for millennia.

One of the floor shadow script paintings is an array of black X's and O's nested inside each other, with yellow and white rectangular pie slices creating crosses that are really X's in disguise. The central black X ends in crescent axe shapes at their circle design's diameter. The crescent axe glyphs are shadow script for "power emanating from spell caster." Considering the number of X's in this particular design, one can guess who the "spell caster" here is working for.

Another striking circle design combining multiple shadow scripts is the one that sadly, the murdered Dick Hallorann falls upon towards the film's climactic ending. It is a white X and nested O framed by smaller nested trapezoids representing "the unenlightened masses" (like base of a pyramid) inside larger fan shapes. The diameter of their circle is a thick black rim. Besides the nested trapezoids each equaling eight, and the larger nested X's and O's dedicated to the "Morning Star," its added symbolism may be more sacrificial in nature.

## *The Shining*'s Color Code

Just as *2001* has a color code, so does *The Shining*. It first shows up as rather stand-out monochromatic or dichromatic clothing made of unusual fibers and other materials displaying loud color combos which were strange fashions even for the '70s. The wardrobe department made sure that important colors were noticed by their dominance, such as Wendy's very yellow Western desert jacket or when cast members wore an ensemble of mainly red and black, or browns, or patriotic colors.

Some colors in *The Shining* have flipped to their polar opposite meaning of what they originally stood for in *2001: A Space Odyssey*. We've mentioned Yellow which now represents Death (instead of Life) as it did in *Clockwork Orange*. Red and Black is a specifically satanic color combo. As Gold is the coveted color of the sanctified Planes of Existence, Gold and Black is high status Luciferian evil. Orange reveals high-degree Masonic influence (the Luciferian elite *is* the occult side of such high-degree Masons). When these colors are together in a Stanley Kubrick film, beware.

Dark and wan colors are corrupted versions of their pure hues. So whereas grass green indicates healthy creativity and intuition, a darker green is corrupt thinking. Pale green is perversion or evil mindedness. A calm red equals vitality whereas violent red signifies danger and dark red means serious danger or imminent danger. Regular brown is a safe, homey, earthy color whereas dark brown (near black) means not secure, unsafe. Wan colors are literally pale imitations of their purer pigments and are more evil than dark hues with the exception of black.

The meaning of purple is a carry-over from *2001*. It still represents the human capacity for spiritual ascension. The pale green and black bands covering the green and purple alchemical Death glyph in the Death Room's peacock-styled carpet is a loud warning that entering Room 237 is the place where one's creativity and ability for self-illumination DIES.

## Danny Torrance's T-Shirts and Sweaters

Much has been made of Danny's hand-made fabric(ated) rocket sweater, so much so that his other clothing has been relatively ignored. His red, white, and blue sports shirt has inverted pentagrams instead of stars, with the number 42 on the sleeves.

Though many meanings for the number 42 can be proffered, when we consider what the true underlying horror of *The Shining* is, one may suspect the most likely association is Revelations 13 in the New Testament, detailing the time the antichrist rules the world for 42 months. Since we now know what Kubrick has been warning us of in *The Shining*, such diabolical allusions emphasize this continually underlying trope. Of course, one can just cross it off as only being more appropriate horror film imagery.

Danny's gray, blue and white sweater has a picture of Mickey Mouse kicking a football towards Danny's left shoulder. One may well ask what is so special about that. It turns out that Danny's deceptively charming football sweater contains another hidden-in-plain sight secret. The football itself just happens to bear a clever resemblance to a type of satanic cross on its black oval seal. The fact it is on Danny's left side makes an appropriate allusion to the Left Hand Path. Even the ground Mickey Mouse is on is another shadow script; a white band that is also oriented up towards the left. At least Mickey is giving it a good kick. Quite a smart sweater. Is it possible *The Shining*'s wardrobe team knew of the symbolism Kubrick and his Head Costume Designer seeded into the clothing for the movie, or did they merely produce what costume stencil designs they were given?

Towards the end of the film, Danny wears a dark red sweater with a band of dirty gray chevrons pointing—you guessed it—left across his chest. This is when he and his mother Wendy are in serious danger of being claimed by the demonic hotel through the murderous intentions of his father. This also happens to be when sinister chanting in the movie's background begins in earnest, right after Jack kills the brave Dick Hallorann. This chanting gives Hallorann's murder the overtones of a blood sacrifice. Taking into account what we have covered so far with *The Shining*'s actual underlying symbolism, this chanting should now be considered more relevant and not simply a throw-away, last minute horror gimmick for building the film's suspense. Now this malevolent chanting has grim, real-world associations to the nefarious occult elite Kubrick is trying to out.

The fact that one has to dig to find real, solid evidence of the true satanic imagery within *The Shining* lends credence to the argument that Stanley Kubrick, for whatever reason, felt the need to bury it and destroy the movie's most apparent tip-off, the aerial view Devil Maze prop. Once people have been made aware of such existing diabolic sigils and learn what they look like, then all the hotel's out in the open, in-your-face infernal symbols become, of course, obvious. But as it took over forty years for anyone to point this out and bring it to light, one cannot say Kubrick made it easy. The earliest anyone might have been concerned about the cover of such sigils being blown—and do something about it—is when Elstree studio's Overlook Hotel lobby and main sets caught fire and burned to the ground. It was reportedly caused by an electrical fire, caused by the overheating of *The Shining*'s many powerful lights.[17] Luckily, no one was hurt when it happened. Whether by accident or by intent, now it may make more sense why Kubrick laughed at his literally hellish set going down in flames when he fully intended the Overlook's hell to freeze over. Did he suspect that the fire was purposely set or did he just find it a humorous coincidence? Either way, the sets were in time rebuilt so the crew could finish shooting. Since then, whoever else might have already recognized *The Shining*'s shadow script exposé certainly has not been going out of their way to make such newsworthy discoveries known to the greater public.

## Anagrams

Further proof of Kubrick using *The Shining* as a vehicle to critique the "overlooked" evils of America (and Western civilization in general) lies in his use of anagrams. When Dick Hallorann is watching TV in his Florida home, the Miami TV station channel 10 airs reporter Glenn Rinker (already a suspiciously funny-sounding name) broadcasting the bad snowstorm hitting the Colorado area where the Torrance family is trapped. Together with the channel's station number 10 looking like the letters I and O, this makes Glenn Rinker's name into the most relevant anagram I REIGN OR KNEEL, which perfectly sums up the mainstream media's choice to act either as a government and corporate watchdog—or become their lapdog.

In the next scene, we find Kubrick is not above resorting to religious symbolism to portray the conflict between good and evil. As Dick Hallorann from Florida phones the park service near the hotel, he does so in a room entirely broken up by bars of light and shadow. To his right, a door handle shines brightly in the form of a cross. Behind him to his left, a goat-like antelope head hangs on a wall. As there are no wild antelope in Florida, the mounted horned beast serves as an intentional symbol of the evil battling the forces of good. This in turn is reinforced by the black and white duality cast by the light through the room's window blinds.

When Dick Hallorann flies in to Colorado, from the airport he contacts his friend Larry Durkin who owns an auto supply store where red, white, and blue Amoco posters and products predominate. Amoco's older red and black adverts are also present. As Larry chats amiably with Dick on the phone, his black leather gloves vanish from his desk while a patriotic colored auto part box and TV behind him moves around during the scenes between him and Hallorann talking. Sometimes the red, white, and blue box is turned around entirely and a black and red box further in the background suddenly appears.

The satanic-colored box behind the red, white, and blue box may infer "the real power behind the power." This musical box charade starts up when a Chuck Jones cartoon displays a message on the TV after a bright green flea had busted free of its cage.

This 1958 cartoon is called "To Itch His Own" and the message is from the circus flea to its owner: "Dear Sam, I have been working very hard lately and feel the need to go out into the country and find a nice quiet dog to relax. Signed, The Mighty Angelo." It is not too hard to add the word "Uncle" between "Dear" and "Sam" for this to make more sense as a veiled Kubrick message as to why he left America for England. "The Mighty Angelo" also creates some interesting anagrams, the best being THEE LYING GOTHAM, which looks to be a blunt slap against what his formerly beloved hometown of NYC has now become. The New York that Kubrick grew up and flourished in was a lively polyglot of enriched multicultural creativity. Today's Manhattan is now mainly a playground for the wealthy and Times Square a glittering, corporate Disneyland, something that San Francisco maybe in danger of becoming.

The most damning anagram of all however can be found on Jack Torrance's perverted pale green, eagle-emblazoned "STOVINGTON" shirt. It is one of the few remaining links to Stephen King's original book (where Torrance last worked) that happens to conveniently spell out the anagram SIN NOT GOVT. In addition, the shirt's pale green color that accompanies its hidden message stands is yet another example of pale green symbolizing perverse thinking or evil scheming in *The Shining*'s Color Code, whereas vibrant green stands for life affirming, intuitive creativity as it does in *2001*. All the above should provide enough evidence that *The Shining* is addressing America's wrongdoings and the hands behind some of its most egregious acts.

## *The Shining*'s Light Effects

It may surprise people that *The Shining* uses light effects in similar ways used in *2001: A Space Odyssey*. In *The Shining*'s case, light effects are employed to suggest spirits and as clues that particularly shine a light on the Overlook's infernal décor and light fixtures. The first time light effects are engaged to get an audience's attention is when Jack is walking around the lobby and chandelier lights seem to follow him and alight on certain painted designs on the wooden floor. The special effects intend to get viewers to notice those malevolent mosaics. When Jack enters and leaves their hotel room a light follows him in and follows him out after he has an argument with Wendy. Strange little lights also fall and flutter around Wendy when she

## 13. The Shining: *Scarier Than Ever*

is desperately trying to revive the dissociating Danny in his bedroom. After Wendy hangs up talking to the ranger station on the ham radio, as she leaves the room, its office XO chandelier light reflections eerily follow her and they bear no physical relationship to where such reflections would actually fall. But these lights fall across Wendy as she walks along and as she does so the light reflections alight towards the lobby floor where the large XOX bands are. Yet another hint that we should give those floor motifs a second look. These traveling ghost lights also bring attention to the XO chandeliers themselves, in the hopes that eventually their sinister symbols will be seen for what they are.

When Jack walks down the hallway outside the Gold Room for the second time, a speck of light stays on the carpet until he comes right up to it. After that, it disappears. This strange effect is possibly a clue to take a closer look at the Gold Room's carpet pattern. In an odd way, this scene echoes back to Dr. Heywood's scene in *2001* as he talks in the briefing room with a piece of lint on him (too large not to be noticed by the wardrobe department) that then suddenly is no longer there when he mentions signing confidentiality oaths. *The Shining*'s hallway light crumb perhaps links to Jack's meeting with Grady, but it is more about putting focus on the hidden symbolism within the pale carpet that needs to be discovered to learn of the Gold Room's true nature.

When brave Dick Hallorann arrives and valiantly looks for any signs of life inside the Overlook Hotel, as he enters the lobby, four lights follow him, starting from his back and from then on continue to hover between him and the evil mosaics on the floor. One time the four lights rise up so viewers will see how satanically red the chandelier lights (where he will be slaughtered) are glowing at this point. Then they finally settle on the shadow script floor emblem that poor Hallorann's murdered body will eventually rest upon, surrounded by four red columns crowned with the Death shadow script. After Dick Hallorann is brutally killed, malevolent chanting starts up and steadily builds into the film's chilling climax. The painted mosaic under Hallorann's body should be further examined, as its symbolism (together with the chanting) may suggest that, whereas Jack kills Hallorann to get a witness out of the way, from the hotel's (illuciferian elite) point of view, Hallorann's murder may have been more sacrificial in nature.

According to Stephen King's book, Dick Hallorann should have been the hero who saves Wendy and Danny (and his own gift of "the Shining" forewarning him of any eminent danger) but Kubrick instead showcased a grisly murder with sacrificial overtones as part of the film's climax. Danny outsmarts his father by retracing his steps in the maze. In the end, Wendy is the one who saves her son and herself by driving off in Hallorann's Snow-Cat, literally leaving Jack Torrance in the cold while the hellish hotel and its environs freeze over, encasing him in its icy grip. Jack's frozen close-up is not just scary, it betrays a countenance of great spiritual trauma. The eyes crawling up into his skull focus on something that is no longer there. Artwork conveying those invoking the powers of the Left Hand Path are often shown with the same expression, such as *Spell 1V (1977)* by H.R. Giger.

## 14

# The Hidden Depths of *Barry Lyndon*

In *Barry Lyndon* (1973), as in *2001: A Space Odyssey*, the camera takes its time drawing back to reveal and bask in the sumptuous environs. This period piece, first set in the mid-1700s during the great European Seven Years War, showcases spectacularly beautiful outdoor sequences and luxurious interiors within grand, sprawling estates occupied by the richly garbed gentry of the times. Out of all of Stanley Kubrick's expertly and artistically-shot films outside of *A Space Odyssey*, in *Barry Lyndon* each and every frame could stand as a stunning painting on its own. One of its few detractions is arguably its score, which can be a dreary, drawn-out affair in spite of its different musical treatments, droning on a relentlessly monotonous Handel leitmotif. At best, the music was unobtrusive for the storyline, but it is doubtful there was much clamor for *Barry Lyndon: The Soundtrack*. Like *A Space Odyssey*, *Barry Lyndon* has been accused of being too slow-paced, but just like *A Space Odyssey*, the riches it contains within its narrative deserve an unhurried reveal for very good reasons, as we shall soon see.

On first viewing, *Barry Lyndon* can be seen as a rambling time capsule which suffers from an uninteresting main character. Based on Thackeray's book *The Luck of Barry Lyndon*, the lead Redmond Barry (played in the film by Ryan O'Neal) usually has more things happening to him than being initiated by him, which for a supposed rollicking adventure can get a little stale—but perhaps more reflects the times the tale takes place. Redmond Barry starts off as a lovesick Irish lad (O'Neal does cut a fine figure but even when this picture was made, no one would mistake him for a "lad"). His duel over a lady with a superior British officer spurs him to eventually join the army with hopes of becoming a gentleman once the war comes to an end.

The present author personally never found the character of Redmond Barry very compelling, which is no fault of Ryan O'Neal as Kubrick asked him to play the part "like Glen Ford," and (perhaps cruelly) instructed him not to focus on trying to give an Oscar-worthy performance (in *Paper Moon*

['75] Ryan was to be further thwarted from an Oscar whereas his daughter and co-star Tatum O' Neal won Best Supporting Actress. As Ryan was known then to slap women and his children around, no need to waste tears on Oscar eluding O'Neal).[1] Barry is supposed to be bland even as he acts despicably towards those he should love the most. But Redmond Barry's saving grace is O'Neal's ability to instill in his character a sense of genuine earnestness and hapless appeal. Even the Irish highwaymen who rob him cut Barry a bit of a break (they let him keep his boots) as they are somewhat touched by Barry being truly impressed with their local notoriety. It is this same quality that enables Barry to get food from a kindly (and lonely) German girl as he goes AWOL from the British army.

The film's narrator (Michael Hordern) informs the audience of Barry falling in with deplorable company, joining in what soldiers sadly do when unchecked, which supposedly cements his cynical views on love. But since this is simply stated and not shown, Redmond's blank face does not convincingly register what the narration implies.[2] As Redmond Barry looks about at what is going on around him, he encourages the audience to do the same. Perhaps Kubrick intentionally made his picture's anti-hero more of a milquetoast for exactly that purpose: to get viewers to look beyond what the actors are doing and visually take in each carefully choreographed environs' entirety. Kubrick's slow pans, leisurely dollies, and steady zoom-outs aim to allow an audience to soak up a scene's location details, which, in *Barry Lyndon*, are often breathtakingly gorgeous. The other ulterior motive for such deliberately measured shots is the courageous director giving the audience enough time to recognize the discreet yet historically accurate Masonic/Luciferian motifs that appear throughout the period film's entirety.

Yes, it is true: along with many of Stanley Kubrick's other films, *Barry Lyndon* carries its own share of shadow script sigils, and there are quite a lot of them. Starting with the previously mentioned opening shell grotto scene, where we see Redmond Barry play cards with his coquettish cousin on a little mosaic Maltese cross table. Behind him is a small cove containing a stained glass window where two of its orange and blue panes display owls depicting Minerva, the Masonic mascot. Other round, fan-like, or wide teardrop shapes that make up part of the stained glass design are repeated in *The Shining* (in the kitchen) and *Eyes Wide Shut* (as chain-link fencing and masks) that may represent sun-motes, sun chains or "face like the sun." In fact, many of the illuciferian motifs that appear in *The Shining* and *Eyes Wide Shut* show up in *Barry Lyndon* first, which in addition to the movie's sheer beauty should help bring Kubrick's most overlooked film the consideration it deserves. The same stained glass window also has a subtle XOX motif at its base, which on one hand might be simply excused as mere decoration, if not for the fact that XOX's, XO's, and XX's show up fairly regularly throughout *Barry Lyndon*, as they do in other Kubrick films. In *Barry Lyndon*, they often appear as upholstery inside carriages, couches, wallpaper or wall panel décor, sometimes even in clothing details. Given their persistent frequency, such things should not be dismissed out of hand.

## Barry's Military Misadventures

When Barry goes AWOL by masquerading as a superior officer delivering documents, he is first waylaid by a Prussian captain and his host, who then interrogates him inside a castle cantina for stationed soldiers. The room is decorated with large mounted elk heads that frame doorway arches containing XXX borders and draping "victory" sashes. These victory drapes can take on the appearance of vines, garlands of blooms or dangling fruit, or as hanging drapery connected between two or more points, held together by flowers (disguised pentagrams or XO's), torches, or animal heads (such as goats). Stanley Kubrick has made this same refined illuciferian signage known in his other films, *Clockwork Orange*, *The Shining*, and *Eyes Wide Shut*.

After Barry's dereliction of duty is found out, he is then pressed into Prussian military service, which was allegedly worse than serving in the British army of the times. One shot of Barry marching with the Prussian 16th regiment shows their orange flag fluttering fully in the breeze. But the flag in *Barry Lyndon* is decidedly different from the real Prussian 16th regimental flag design used in the Seven Years War. As Stanley Kubrick was infamously a stickler for detail, this altered flag must be intentional. The changes are subtle but clear: Kubrick changed where the white wedges are on the flag so it looks more like an XO formation. Part of this is to point out the differences in the black eagle carrying lightning bolts and its wreath. In the original, authentic Prussian design the bolts are smaller and the eagle's wreath is gold; in Kubrick's, the lightning bolts are much more pronounced and the wreath is darker, with different styled leaves. The white wedges now direct the eye to these alterations like arrow points. In *Barry Lyndon*, the flag's eagle appears to hold satanic lightning bolt S's and its wreath's base displays hidden flipped S's in the ribbon that ties it together.

Redmond Barry's future saving of his Captain Potzdorf from a burning building paves the way for him to further distinguish himself with military honors, eventually earning him an opportunity for the far cushier post of being a Prussian spy. As Potzdorf introduces Barry to his uncle, who holds position as Minister of Police, Barry finds himself walking into a splendid room filled with gold-trimmed baroque furnishings. The faux marble columns give the room a temple-like feel and are painted in a way that suggests faces glowering over the proceedings. As Barry first answers questions, a huge menacing grin on the door leers behind him. One of the large mirrors flanking the entryway reflects what is holding up a low-hanging ornate chandelier: a chain of ancient Egyptian sun ray joints, a coveted illuciferian sun motif we have seen on *The Shining*'s hotel floor. The towering mirrors themselves are crowned with "rising sun" palmettes that from certain angles look like large, single eyes. Pedestaled dark figures raising up candle holders in a "light bringer" pose stand on either side of another door in the Minister's office. Kubrick has brought attention to this particular Luciferian lamp style before in films such as *Paths of Glory*, *Clockwork Orange*, *Eyes Wide Shut*, and even *Lolita*.

Kubrick at times frames Minister Potzdorf's black and gold desk so another infernal design is in the foreground: a gold, profaned Tau cross shape with Luciferian spirals sprouting at each end. Kubrick revisits and features this symbol more prominently as fake, mocking Christmas hangings in *Eyes Wide Shut* (seen in a restaurant's stairwell and inside Ziegler's hallway). As drawer décor, it happens to look like an unfriendly face with fangs. Behind the Minister's desk are tall windows whose bottom sills are engraved with X's. In later scenes, as Captain Potzdorf walks about the same room, the camera moves around in a mirrored rotation, allowing the audience to take in these details once more, particularly those ominous marble columns.

Barry is given the task to spy on the Chevalier de Balibari, a man whom the Prussian police suspect is an Irish spy himself. Captain Potzdorf gives him more instruction inside a gold fabric-lined carriage. As they talk, the carriage's gold satin ceiling is in full view which displays very clearly an ornate XOX pattern that runs throughout the entire carriage interior. The ceiling's central X closest to the camera reveals a leafy, derisive devil's head (profaning and impersonating the green man) whose face is made of an even smaller X, its horns are made from the top of a larger X. Other more understated demonic faces make up the O's in the pattern. Again XOX signifies the Luciferian Sun.

The Chevalier does turn out to be a fellow Irishman who has done well as a professional gambler who boasts of powerful contacts in Austria. When Barry confesses to him his true assignment and how he was roped into Prussian military service, the Chevalier Balibari takes Barry under his wing as a double agent. The Chevalier's clothing is truly luxuriant; he sports a silver-threaded waistcoat ribbed with X's. This may point to the sort of friends Chevalier had to make to get where he was in life. Near where Balibari sits stands a gold, curiously long-legged faun holding a jug. Such elongated, strangely S-shaped fauns appear in other Kubrick films such as *Paths of Glory*, *Lolita*, and *Eyes Wide Shut*. The manor he lives in has X-in-O's embossed on his fireplace, and his gambling parlor's wallpaper display another illuciferian pattern, that of circular shapes linked either vertically or across by a line. This shadow script is repeated again when Barry meets Lady Honoria Lyndon. It is possible that the spherical chains depict the Luciferian glyph of Fulfillment by representing either the full moon or the rising sun.

When Balibari reassures Barry and mentions his powerful "friends in the Austrian government," instead of reflecting the two men, a mirror right of Barry and Balibari reveals blue wallpaper in the form of a masonic owl. By now the number of illuciferian motifs so far found within the Prussian ministry's furnishings as well as within the Chevalier's estate should be fairly damning. Regardless of who is battling whom, the ruling classes of Europe seem to belong to the same insidious club.

Before the Chevalier can "demand satisfaction" from a Prussian prince who owes him money, the Prussian Minister of Police gives orders for Balibari to be forcibly taken out of the country to protect the prince. Instead, the police coach arrives to pick up Barry posing as the Chevalier, who had safely reached the border the night before. As Barry feigns protest, the guardsman opens the carriage door, showing a large XOX made of blue lavender fabric. Barry then rejoins his new master at the border to make their living off gambling in the royal courts of Europe. Throughout the indoor table scenes in *Barry Lyndon*, especially the gambling parlors of the countries the two gamblers visit, there is a curious consistency of candlestick holder styles. Most of the table candle holders are gold with S-shaped arms. As Luciferians love associating their "light bringer" with anything having to do with light (especially the sun), this is a repeated refrain in *Barry Lyndon*, as it is in Stanley Kubrick's other films endeavoring to point these associations out.

## Barry's Big Mistake

Weary of the rootless gambling life and feeling the need to settle down, Redmond Barry looks for a suitable high-born candidate whom he can manage to attain to secure his status as a gentleman. In a palatial English garden, he sets his sights on the lovely Lady Honoria Lyndon (played by Maria Berenson), whose aging, ailing, wheelchair-bound husband (Frank Middlemass) is pretty much at death's door. As the camera surveys the sumptuous outdoor scenery, it leisurely pulls back from some patio stairs, which slowly reveal great stone vases festooned with carved goats heads and victory garlands. It is a classic Kubrick blink-and-you-miss-it moment. The goat heads and garland stem ends together form an X, strengthening their sinister associations. Two other garden sculptures contain shadow script: one is an oversize stone urn with omega fashioned handles and an X-shaped flower on an eight-sectioned dais. In another scene, a discus thrower on a stand is bordered in crafty Greek-styled S's. As Lady Lyndon walks about with her family, a starkly white statue of Pan playing pipes is visible in the background. Kubrick made sure that this statue stood out from the rest of the more weather-stained statuary.

To be clear, the majority of Pagan religions are completely against the Left Hand Path practice of co-opting Pan, Cernannos, the Green Man or any other classical deity that predates Christianity such as Isis, Osiris, Ceres, Apollo, Prometheus, Hermes/Mercury, Bacchus, and Zeus/Jupiter. Those following an Earth Path would be appalled at such ancient deities being appropriated and profaned to disguise an evil entity that they themselves do not believe in.

As mentioned before, a lesser known but just as important historic spiritual theft is the Luciferian Diamond Heist and Stolen Spiral. At the gaming table, Lady Lyndon's necklace hangs a diamond-shaped pendant, a reminder that among many age-old belief systems, womankind is the original owner of this symbol. The stolen spiral is another constant, if not predominant, baroque building décor that was and still is a near universal symbol for natural forces and cycles, including feminine fertility, but has been nefariously co-opted to represent the curling comet-tail of the Luciferians' favorite Fallen Star.

Moreover, in contrast to the more feminine Tree of Life, Luciferians saw fit to appropriate the age-old Iranian and Indian (Kashmir) Boteh, originally a cypress/palm sprout motif, a venerable male symbol of virility, prosperity, and bounty, now stolen to represent Luciferian power in a near endless array of coiling vegetal designs seen in carpeting, clothing, textiles, furnishings, upholstery, and wallpapers throughout *Barry Lyndon*. Of course decoration can certainly be just decoration, but for the wealthy classes in Barry's world, the above-mentioned motifs have been laden with pernicious palimpsests Kubrick has been continuously exposing since *Paths of Glory* all the way through to *Eyes Wide Shut*. The presence of putti/cherubs holding or flanking a torch (lit or unlit), eating grapes/ drinking wine, or playing music in a decidedly unreligious setting could indicate any accompanying pilfered rhomb, boteh, and spiral patterns are in quiet, imposed service to Luciferian elite symbolism, especially if flipped S's or C's (for comet) are anywhere in the décor. Often flipped S's and C's carved or beveled, are hidden within heralds, shields, scroll edges, ribbons, mirror and picture frames. They can also be part of a figure's clothes or hair. But most of all, Luciferian S's and C's frequently appear as decoration for light fixtures, chandeliers, street lights, lamp posts, fireplaces, and city or shop signage. Much of this can just be simple replication of already established styles in textiles and architecture, but the older the example, the more likely its Luciferian symbolism is intentional. Especially if the work is original in design.

While Barry woos Lady Lyndon, behind them statue alcoves strewn with ivy are framed by lattices of two types of "Fulfillment" spheroid chains as seen earlier on Balibari's parlor walls. The pill-shaped version of the spheroid chain placed above the statues is seen again as hotel stove lights in *The Shining*. Together with the ivy, the lattice work appears to display intermittent X's, most likely an intentional visual trick. Later we see spheroid chain latticework again when the now re-married Lady Lyndon catches her new husband Barry Lyndon kissing her governess. He seeks her forgiveness afterwards while she is in her bath. The tub Lady Lyndon reposes in is bordered by Masonic-favored victory drapes and a "Darkness" shadow script checker pattern. As she is now a newly unhappily-married woman prone to melancholia, the symbols are sadly appropriate. A hope chest near her tub brandishes a large diamond and soul sigil, perhaps attesting to her fate of being a wife trapped in a near state of captivity within the upper class.

Lady Lyndon soon bears a son, Bryan Patrick, who will eventually compete with her older son for her affections. Firstborn Barringdon is wary of his new stepfather from the start; he sized up Barry's character fairly accurately with a wisdom beyond his years. As the younger Bryan Patrick Lyndon grows, there is a tender scene where Barry is teaching him to read on an enormously long couch. The red room they are in is huge, bearing a white door with gold sun-in-rectangle engravings. The sun-in-rectangle motif is repeated on the red and black rug in front of the couch. This sun-in-rectangle makes its appearance in more than one Kubrick film, particularly in *Eyes Wide Shut* where it is shown multiple times. As rhomboid and checker "nets" symbolize "to keep in darkness," doubled squares and rectangles possibly stand for "power over ignorance." Kubrick must find these important illuciferian symbols, as Ziegler's poolroom in *Eyes Wide Shut* is completely paneled with them, and in one particular shot an oil painting of a lady even points to them behind a despairing Bill Harford. It is perhaps yet another perverted sun symbol stolen from ancient Egypt or the Near East's Fertile Crescent cultures.

## Barry Lyndon's Best Laid Plans

Barry Lyndon's doting mother Belle is a savvy woman, admirably played by Marie Kean, who urges her son to get a title so to ensure his and his own son Bryan's future security. Later we see Lyndon seeking counsel from a distinguished gentleman at dinner while a demonic fire screen peers in on the proceedings. Thanks to this friend, Lord Barrister Hallam (Anthony Sharp, *Clockwork Orange*'s Minister of the Interior), Barry gets an interview with Lord Adolphus Wendover who has the power to pave the way for a gentleman's obtainment of title. During this scene as Lord Wendover describes who "the right people" are, an extreme close up on Wendover's face pulls back while its slow reverse zoom allows the audience to see a dark embroidered *goat head* to his left on the sofa he sits on. This goat head has multicolored horns and its face sports hooked prongs on its chin (like the goat chandeliers in *The Shining*) and curly C's (possibly for "comet") at its cheeks. Like the intricate wallpaper in Claire Quilty's lair, the couch goat actually is the third eye of a much larger demon, whose nose and mouth make up a smaller demon. As the camera pulls further back to reveal the whole sofa's upholstery, we find the goat head adjacent to a double Evil Eye at its right. The Evil Eye is the center of a large, rusty blood-colored flower or bush, glaring back at the audience as if daring us to see it. The choreography of Lord Wendover on the sofa is almost a reverse image of General Mireau sitting on his infernal couch during the trial in *Paths of Glory*, whose sofa also sports a goat head with accompanying Evil Eyes. Above Lord Wendover's own devilish couch is an interesting contrast of paintings. At right is a portrait of an upstanding family, a picture of upper-class domestic perfection. At left next to the family portrait is a somewhat lurid depiction of cherubim courting a nude girl toddler. It is one of those typical pastorals that put children in adult situations which on first glance may seem charming, but on second glance … not so much. One may surmise that Lord Wendover's furnishings belie his being an established part of the Luciferian ruling class already well ensconced within the British Isles. Barry himself remains oblivious to this more sinister layer of the elite throughout the duration of the film. It stands to reason that not all members of such wealthy families, particularly wives and children, would be privy to the occult goings-on of the initiated men in their family trees. So it is that such people can be ardent Catholics, Protestants, Jews, etc., without seeing any conflict with their male family members' masonic fraternities.

After being coached, Barry takes Lord Wendover's advice and starts throwing lavish parties for influential people and buying paintings from strapped-for-cash gentlemen at exorbitant prices. Later when Lyndon is surveying the paintings of another high-class gentleman in need of funds, they are both standing on a carpet trimmed with occult nested rhombs and stolen Egyptian sun-ray chains. Perhaps the most disturbing part of Lyndon's courting the establishment is when he is finally presented to the king. King George III and his entourage display their Order of the Garter star medallions differently, with the King's presented properly in a cross formation, whereas the lord closest to the audience giving introductions has *his* Order of the Garter look like a Luciferian X-in-O (a symbol that repeatedly shows up as ceiling lights in *The Shining* and signage in *Eyes Wide Shut*). This would be quite a costuming gaffe for the foremost actor in a shot to have, so it is more likely Kubrick made this to be an intentional signal to the audience.

Before the showdown between Barringdon Jr., and Barry, we open to Lady Lyndon's concert recital, attended by a sizable audience of important gentry, including her husband. The fireplace near the piano happens to have a stylized gold devil head centered above it. This sort of simplified devil head could also be an abstraction of an ancient Egyptian sun ray mote, an occult baroque motif that comes in many manifestations. After Barringdon makes a complete fool of his stepfather in public and kills any chance Barry has for a title, Barry is snubbed by his friend Lord Wendover at a gentleman's club. As Wendover enters the club's dining room, the wallpaper in the hall behind him contains a devil head with flipped S's (containing X's) for horns and a long, ribald tongue pointing to an X which doubles as a goat muzzle framed by larger demonic faces menacing from above and below. It is a most impressively complex painted tapestry of multilayered evil grotesques. There is even a point where some club members in the background walk by while looking at the infernal wallpaper to give it more attention.

With each Left Hand Path visual made present within his films, Stanley Kubrick is both tracking the history and showing the scope of illuciferian influence that ran through the upper-classes of Western civilization during the 17th century. *Barry Lyndon* attempts to surreptitiously chart where this influence may have begun and where it spread throughout Europe and the British Isles. Kubrick's cameramen zero in on the lavish Baroque style preferred by the aristocracies of the times, showing how it can be made to hide beguilingly carved maleficent details such as goat heads, mocking "satyr" faces, winged "fauns," golden "cherubs," youths, maidens, blackamoors, or "angels" hoisting torches or bouquets, ornamented with many-styled S's, sun palmettes, tendril-like Luciferian C's and branches of spiraling Luciferian symbols. It is disheartening to find out that what was at first a celebratory neo-classical art style was also used to conceal the more insidious beliefs of the upper class.

A dining room scene in the Lyndon household shows tall windows dominating the room, making the substantially long table seem small in comparison. The windows provide the main light in the dining area, whose base has two large Roman-style X's side by side and whose window panes number eighteen. Their size being non-traditional indoor window décor, there really seems to be no logical reason for the X's other than drawing attention to themselves. In the scene where the Reverend Runt interrupts Barry Lyndon's toilet to inform him of his son's departure to see his birthday present (a horse), golden palm leaves ornament the bedroom. As the Reverend crosses over and passes Barry's scarlet bed, a rather disconcerting face is seen adorning the headboard. Black "light bringer" candle holders are also seen in Barry's room. Anything to do with light (such as lamps, light fixtures, chandeliers, curtains, fireplaces, etc.) are usually earmarked with illuciferian designs.

His own little son Bryan's bed is a glorious affair of blue drapes and gold fabric. The blue pattern is of XOX's and a gold sun containing two rings of eight dots rises above an owl overseeing the boy below. The owl's eye shapes are repeated in a bottom border, which makes one realize the hidden illuciferian association between owl and sun: an owl's eyes perfectly replicate the alchemical symbol for the sun, which is a circle with a dot at its center. This is at least the third time Masonic owls appear in *Barry Lyndon*. Moreover, young Bryan's walls are a complex metallic array covered in shiny flipped satanic S's and demonic faces. It is possible Kubrick is directly linking the child and those present to these ominous elements by indicating their opulence has sinister origins living on as decorative fixtures within such wealthy households, whose inheritance passes on an implicit evil legacy to the next generation. Honoria and her sons Barringdon and Bryan may be completely unaware of the questionable history that grew their family fortune, but the now deceased Lord Lyndon might have been at least cognizant if not fully complicit, considering what might have been required to amass and maintain such a fortune. That being said, the scene where Barry's bed-ridden son slowly succumbs to his horse-riding injuries is one of the saddest in the film, and the little boy Bryan entreating his parents to stop arguing and love one another better so they can all meet in heaven is affectingly poignant.

Leon Vitali gives a great performance as a grown Barringdon, when he arrives at Barry's gentleman's club (that is somewhat worse for wear) to challenge him to dueling pistols. As he trepidatiously makes his way through the club's entrance lobby, first we see a washerwoman cleaning the white tiled (or marble) floor with a big black O-in-X at its center, nesting a jagged O inside a larger one. The smaller O has sixteen to eighteen triangles spiking its circumference, invoking the shadow script for "irresistible" power. The club's doorway entrance is topped with a fashionable fanlight window, a leaded glass "rising sun" configuration lined with X's. The other window curtains display curious shadow script as trim that also show up within palace rooms in *Paths of Glory*. While Barrington, Jr., walks through the club's hallway, a sofa with a passed-out member displays an XOX pattern. When he enters the main room, the first thing he looks at is another gold, S-armed candle-holder. Barringdon finds Barry Lyndon collapsed in a drunken stupor with other ne'-er-do-wells in front of an X-sided fireplace in forlorn surroundings.

After a surprisingly successful duel (where it is made obvious a world-weary Barry wants to die), Barringdon rides home with Graham, their manservant, and the Reverend Runt in the same carriage. As Barringdon instructs them on what to do next, we see the Reverend Runt delighted at the idea of throwing out Barry's domineering mother who had dismissed him earlier. Around the Reverend Runt, a blue XOX pattern made primarily of demonic faces dominates the carriage, broadcasting a pervasive evil that abides in these people's lofty sphere in spite of any religious influence the Rev. may think he has. He himself literally sits in the satanic seat of his masters.

An enjoyable aspect of *Barry Lyndon* does away with the usual simplistic "good poor person vs. bad rich person" story, which the film sets on its ear. One may root for Redmond Barry in the beginning, but his despicable behavior to the woman he married and her first son soon changes one's loyalties to the aggrieved, high-born Lyndon family members. Barry carries on with other women while draining the Lyndon fortune at a deplorable rate. By the end of the film, it is Lord Barringdon who is the real hero of *Barry Lyndon*. All appears then to return to a serene calm of business as usual. Yet as the film draws to a close, malevolent specters and steaming funerary urns painted near the darkened ceiling oppressively tower over the unaware Lyndons as they attend to their finances, perhaps suggesting that great wealth is often bought through great evil.

## The Bravest Battle in *Barry Lyndon*

Stanley Kubrick's *Barry Lyndon* contributes greatly to the director's consistent under-the-radar mission that declares the illuciferian elite's presence through detailing their esoteric fingerprints left throughout Western history. *Barry Lyndon* leaves a steady stream of high-degree Masonic Luciferian calling cards in the guise of their now-exposed shadow scripts and their formerly secret symbolic meanings.

The fact Kubrick and his production teams made sure these symbols show up as frequently as they do suggests that the director is sounding a persistent alarm, indicating that Western civilization is held in a vice by such malevolent cabals and that their grip is far stronger than modern society would care to believe. Kubrick's cinematic checklist of Left Hand Path manifestations eschews the dismissive notion that these are merely a few rich, eccentric, fringe cults but are actually very old and well established, whose powerful influence through the centuries has spread like a poisonous plague. It behooves a questioning audience to look at Kubrick's frequent discreet occult clues and decide for themselves if the Luciferian elite and their linked power cells are an actual threat to human liberty and well-being.

A good question to ask is, why would a genius like Stanley Kubrick waste his precious time, money, and movies continuously inserting such evil insignia into his films on a topic that is supposedly false? Considering the milieus Kubrick had access to and the high-strata circles he and his peers socialized in, one is inclined to give his privileged knowledge and bravery in broadcasting this subject the benefit of a doubt. Why would Kubrick bother calling attention to such a so-called conspiracy so repeatedly and consistently throughout his films unless he had very good reasons to know it was real and was a serious concern?

Another clue to *Barry Lyndon*'s veiled aspersions on "Masonic devilry" is the movie's end title after the last scene closes: "It was in the reign of King George III that the aforesaid personages lived and quarreled; good or bad, handsome or ugly, rich or poor, they are all the same now." The last two lines are taken from a German Medieval "Dance Macabre" later adopted as a secret society maxim, including the Masons.³ It is usually illustrated by four skulls, in front of which is a king's crown, a sage's book, a fool's belled cap, and a beggar's bowl. The gist is that as far as fortune, title, or accomplishments, none really matters when death renders people the same. Perhaps this concept best exemplifies and spurs the Masonic incentive for illumined immortality through apotheosis: self-deification.

A final, intriguing "Exhibit A" highlighting *Barry Lyndon*'s importance in Kubrick's continuing filmic war with the illuciferian set is, curiously, Bill Harford's costume mask in *Eyes Wide Shut*. It happens to be a mold of Ryan O'Neal's face, effectively linking Kubrick's most suspected film against the occult elite back to the comparatively unsung *Barry Lyndon*, which previously laid the groundwork for giving such heavy tipoffs on corrupt power. In addition, after *2001*, Kubrick's company name alternated between either "Hawk" or "Peregrine" Films as a potential clue to the Masonic practice of appropriating Egyptian symbolism. One might wonder why he did not just call his company "Falcon" or (Eye of) "Horus Films" and be done with it. Perhaps too risky a hint to the public. Interestingly, Vivian Kubrick's *Making of The Shining* short was labeled "An Eagle Film."

Since *Barry Lyndon* actually opens in a Masonic shell grotto complete with stained glass owls and Maltese Cross table and then closes with a Masonic quote (and contains Masonic motifs inbetween), the sometimes scoffed idea that Kubrick puts Masonic references into his films (such as *2001*, *Clockwork Orange*, *The Shining*, and *Eyes Wide Shut*) should not be so readily dismissed. For example, Margate, England has a real-life, underground Masonic shell grotto temple complete with owl columns, single eyes, and eight-pointed star imagery. In *Barry Lyndon*, the not-so-invisible presence of 18th-century European Freemasonry and its unfortunate Luciferian overlap haunts the movie's environs from beginning to end.

# 15

# *A Clockwork Orange*: More Disturbing Than Ever

Alex Bowler by Nicole Berg

*A Clockwork Orange*, released in 1971, holds up an unforgivingly cynical mirror to the inner workings of class power in such a galling manner that people at the time, especially in Britain, were not ready to see. Whereas America was in its age of '70s movie realism with the likes of Sam Pekinpah films, *Deliverance*, Coppola's *Apocalypse Now*, and Polanski's *Chinatown*, the brutal character of *Clockwork Orange* was at first more critically accepted in the United States.

Whereas Alex's exaggerated right eyelashes echoing a demented Eye of Horus is usually the first suggestive illuminati image people pick up on in *Clockwork Orange*, it is by no means the last. The more surprising fact about *Clockwork Orange* however is that it too, reveals the illuciferian underbelly of the upper classes, an honor many originally would logically accord to *Eyes Wide Shut* or *The Shining*. Even those that may get criticized for pointing out the illuminati elements that exist within *Clockwork Orange* usually do not mention its Luciferian elements, but both are there, and the two are connected. Much previously under-the-radar institutionalized evil is laid bare in *Clockwork Orange*. More specifically, the true horrors and scarring effects of MK-Ultra-style programming that run through the film. Movies on brainwashing like *The Manchurian Candidate* had been done before but *Clockwork Orange* exposes such program's actual modus operandi while dressing their tools and techniques in futuristic garb.

Alex's "droog" gang costumes, for example, are really program handler 'conditioning' outfits in disguise.[1] Handlers are stereotypically sadistic heavies assigned to do the physical dirty work of breaking a victim down so the "medical" staff can splinter their victim's personality for further mind control manipulation. The fact that Alex and his droogs' (slang for "mates") handler clothing are now featured in Fosse-style dance routines and music videos would probably have Stanley Kubrick shake his head while laughing at the same time if he were still alive. Then again, one can blame both Kubrick and Malcom McDowell, who first came up with the idea of the twisted "Singing in the Rain" routine for such later Broadway-style inspirations.

It would be interesting to know what Anthony Burgess, the author of *Clockwork Orange*, made of that scene, considering it is based on his own home invasion experience (in his case drunk, AWOL British soldiers during a blackout) and the physical (not sexual) assault of his then-pregnant wife, who later miscarried and then died some years afterwards out of grief. The author character Mr. Frank Alexander is loosely based on Burgess himself but receives very little compassion in Kubrick's version of *Clockwork Orange*. There are few to nil sympathetic characters in the entire film, and with the exception of a few career professionals (doctors, performers, and journalists) women are treated mostly as things or as background dressing.

The fact certain enthusiasts of *Clockwork Orange* actually lionize Alex and turn him into some sort of glorified anti-hero is rather sad and reflects upon society's tendency to make excuses for bad behavior if the perpetrator happens to be particularly brilliant or has some noteworthy talents and interests. Such a case can be made with the likes of Vladimir Nabokov,[2] Roman Polanski, and Woody Allen. Interestingly, all previously mentioned have separately visited Stanley Kubrick on different occasions, and while they may have been convivially discussing film, literature, world events, and talking shop, as most of Kubrick's movies examines the evils of mankind, one wonders if Kubrick was at times looking sideways at his charming-yet-creepy guests, studying them for what makes such specimens tick.

Malcolm McDowell indisputably imbues the Alex "DeLarge" character

## 15. A Clockwork Orange: *More Disturbing Than Ever*  125

with the reptilian charm of a charismatic psychopath. The audience is not required to like him or sympathize with him, since his despicable exploits can easily make a viewer feel that whatever mistreatment Alex gets later on is well deserved. Alex, rough as his speech can be, is an amalgamation of how intellectualism and artistry can exist side by side with mankind's worst inclinations. These traits are exhibited both by the elite in control and the bohemian elite Alex encounters. Unlike his thuggish cronies, Alex is shown to be more multifaceted, having sophisticated tastes in art (sculptor Herman Makkink) and music (Beethoven). The presence of Makkink in Alex's room may itself be a double-edged sword: not only does his row of dancing Jesus' right under Alex's basking pet serpent fit the mocking good vs. evil theme, but it also can satirize the rather cynical, blasé attitude of such artwork itself and the artists who make them. Kubrick's skewering of the over privileged art, music, and fashion glitterati as morally decadent at best and nefariously perverse at worst has been done before in the character of Clare Quilty in *Lolita*. The buffoonery of Peter Sellers in the role did some disservice to Quilty's original character as it downplayed his more monstrous aspects. Sellers' antics aside, the symbolic furnishings Kubrick's production crew stuffed inside Quilty's mansion give several allusions to the pedophile's connections to the illuciferian elite (and like James Mason and Sue Lyon, Sellers most likely had no knowledge of this angle of Kubrick's *Lolita*). The one-eyed figures on his wallpaper, the fearsome tiger rug with one eye prominently lit, his black "Lucifer the light bringer" wall lamps, and finally, the XOX ceiling trim decorating his estate's parlor area. In *Clockwork Orange*, Kubrick fires at the upper class Luciferians again with both barrels.

At this stage, it is a reasonable question to ask when Stanley Kubrick was *not* aware of the diabolical nature of the ruling elite he highlights. Perhaps the misadventures of his main married couple in *Eyes Wide Shut* (who are drawn in by the elite) act as a possible doppelganger not only for himself and his wife (a painter), but a possible nod to Kubrick's parents, as his father was a well-to-do doctor like Bill Harford. Did the warning Kubrick passed on to others, "Don't become friends with anyone who has real power. It's dangerous," originally come from his own father, or mainly from Kubrick's own experience?[3] In *Clockwork Orange*, Alex's newfound elite "friends" in the state and the intelligentsia sure put him through the meat-grinder, and Alex almost dies from their handiwork. It must be said though, it could not happen to a nicer bloke.

*Clockwork Orange* opens in the mostly black Korova (Russian for "cow") Milk Bar room where white leotard-clad bodyguards ensure its patrons' good behavior. With its white signage, white sculpture and black and white employees, the theme of duality reigns and unlike in *2001: A Space Odyssey*, black here is more dominant than white. Its main feature however is brilliantly white: Monarch beta-conditioned sex slaves presented as works of art that function as drug-laced milk dispensers (the "cows"). Many have their hands chained behind their back. Their neon colored wigs are a feature in Monarch brainwashing where a victim's broken sense of self can be splintered into altered personalities, where each can be given a wig. Alex's own mother wears wild colors, skimpy outfits, and keeps a set of vibrant wigs on her bedroom window ledge. Some ladies Alex passes by in a shopping center sport dyed wigs while going about their business. The (beta kitten) "Cat Lady," the topless actress who "tests" Alex, and a female psychiatrist Alex meets are also found wearing strangely colored wigs or unusually dyed hair. But because *Clockwork Orange* is evidently set in the future and most of its cast is wearing loud clothes in garish colors even by 1970s standards, it is understandable that audiences usually take it for simply being futuristic fashions.

But the writer Mr. Alexander's brightly patterned robe, for example, represents something far more sinister. It is a strikingly red tendril pattern on a white background, and is pretty much the most lurid element within what the audience first sees of his otherwise pallid-hued living space, modern as it is. The author's red tendril robe betrays his own illuciferian connections, which are also hinted at by his style of living, as in general writers do not usually make enough money to reside in such lavish homes in the country (especially in the UK). His robe's entwining vines hide many 6's and S's, and its violent redness draws the eye to the robe's classic illuciferian baroque pattern.

In the Duke of York restaurant pub not only do wigged beta kittens work as waitresses but its architecture contains illuciferian shadow script at its bar, its second-floor bannisters, and its carpeting. The bar contains yellow and red elongated S's, Luciferian tendrils, and the carpet is filled with inverted pentagram flowers and pentagram flowers with inverted pentagram interiors. The pub's upper story is lined with double diamonds, when together add up to eight points which again, alludes to the Luciferian "morning star." Small, bite-size pyramid indentations riddle the pub's woodwork. While Alex and his droogs drink their pints, they are just as oblivious to these ominous building motifs as the rest of the customers around them. There is a moment when Alex is sussing out Georgie, his hat brim points to shadow script in the background and even Dim's dispirited movements obligingly divert the viewer's eye to the same area where cut-out shadow script is in the background.

Besides a more obvious prison wall pyramid, other Masonic Luciferian elements found within *Clockwork Orange* are the architectural motifs in the Cat Lady's spa center. Her stately building has a classic "rising sun" leaded glass design above its front doors. This "rising sun" motif is understandably popular among the illuciferian set. The doors have "sun in rectangle" carved panels (which may be an abstracted form of the Egyptian akhet), are another noted feature of very wealthy houses. The outside of the health center's façade

## 15. A Clockwork Orange: *More Disturbing Than Ever*

is black and white, just as the majority of the Cat Lady's cats are black and white. This revisits the Masonic and also Monarch use of duality that is repeated on the writer Alexander's checkerboard floor. As the droogs sneak around the back past several sphinx-like statues, they go up a short flight of brick stairs to get to the rear patio. Kubrick has the camera slowly follow them so that two decorative, X-in-O floral brick motifs on either side of the stairs can be viewed in detail. Conversely, eight-petal O-in-X and eye-like patterns decorate the Cat Lady's rugs. When she makes a phone call to the police, items on her desk take the form of an understated X O X. The Cat Lady's gym art gallery consists of Beta Kittens in compromising positions, some of which look coerced. Among these paintings is one far less erotic and more frightening where a woman is apparently doing something violent. It is this painting that provides the main clue as to why Alex gets out of hand with the Cat Lady and kills her. Like Alex, the Cat Lady is made to be an unpleasant person so one does not sympathize with her too much. In her case, she is an outright snob given to putting on airs when talking on the telephone, and her pompous elitism comes through when she yells at Alex, "I'll teach you to break into *real* people's houses!" At least the Cat Lady can be given credit for having the courage to take Alex on in a fight, something his own father does not dare do. It should as well not be forgotten that the Cat Lady is herself a victim of Beta Kitten programming. When she is murdered, she even expires making cartoon cat sounds, along with a split-second painting montage that provides more clues as to why Alex and the Cat Lady are the way they are.

Milk, one of the most nurturing symbolic substances in existence, is shown being drunk in a corrupted form where drugs have been added. The theme of nurturing carries through the entire run of *Clockwork Orange* as Alex carries on with his sadistic adventures through the state's institutional gauntlets. Alex's mother seems to be the only one who still cares for him, while his father is more afraid of the violent thug his son has become. It is interesting that the candle glasses in Alex's mother's room are similar in shape to the milk glasses in the Milk Bar. There are several examples within the movie of women being depicted as objects on display, whether it be sculpture, paintings, or real-life situations.

*Clockwork Orange* has understandably been labeled as extremely misogynistic as well as excessively violent. For the longest time the present author avoided seeing this film due to a long-held practice of not giving any money to movies containing rape scenes. But upon finally viewing it, I was initially impressed by the film's underlying intention to expose appalling, real, mind control programs whose purpose is to break down people's bodies as well as their psyches. Kubrick used the fictional Ludovico technique as a cipher whose methods echo the real brainwashing projects he intended to blow the lid off of with his film *Clockwork Orange*.

As women more often than not end up as test subjects for such immoral experimentation, *Clockwork Orange* shows misogyny as the ugly thing it is and how it is actually institutionalized within modern civilization, with Monarch sex slave/beta kitten (i.e., Cat Lady "health" center) programs being among the main damning examples. Those who think such government supported programs were completely done away with in the '70s (thanks due in part to films like *Clockwork Orange* casting a spotlight on such abhorrent practices) might reconsider when observing the erratic behavior of certain celebrities and performers during the last few decades.

At the Milk Bar, Alex toasts a glass to a blonde opera singer who is entertaining four men that work at the local TV station. All the men's bowties are a bit on the large size, a sign that they stand for something more than mere fashion. The two men to her right sport different-colored bow ties, one red and the other blue, both important colors in freemasonry.[4] The two men to her left exemplify Masonic duality, as one wears a mainly white tux and the other mostly black. The singer herself is the center of attention, for good reason. Not only is she a noted singer but her clothing and makeup indicate she has paid her dues to the illuciferian elite. She wears a black ensemble threaded through with gold, and her makeup suggests she's wearing gold horns around her forehead or that she's "illuminated." When the camera closes in on her for a close up, the lighting on her pupils make her look less than human to match Alex's left serpent-lit eye as he toasts her (evil toasting evil). When forced to deal with the upper echelons of the illuciferian elite while advancing to a certain standard of living or career status, Kubrick may be putting some personal observations here of the particular social spheres he had to mingle with.

Stanley Kubrick continued to expose the Masonic/Luciferian overlap when he made *Barry Lyndon* sometime after the controversy of *Clockwork Orange* died down. In the opening scene of his 18th-century drama in a shell grotto, behind the title character playing cards on a Maltese cross table is an orange stained glass window pane with XXX trim displaying an owl: the Masonic mascot Minerva.

## Shadow Script in the Real World

When Alex is finally arrested, the jail he goes to is striking. Kubrick made a point to get a fly over shot of the intimidating Her Majesty's Prison Wandsworth complex in London,[5] a real life jail that is astoundingly built in the shape of gigantic shadow script: a huge X with a rhomb stick in the center (X again being a sign of Lucifer and the rhomb stick a spell invoking diabolic power). It may also be a symbolic mockery of the Christian Chi-Ro. The exercise grounds are created as ovals with X pathways through them, which is shadow script for sequestering souls.⁶ Seeing such evil signs built to such a scale in the physical world as an actual building with the intent to magically control the lives of real people is quite a shocking revelation to take in.

In the film *Clockwork Orange*, this government/illuciferian collusion is reinforced when Alex visits the Prison Governor's office for his official release to participate in the Ludovico program: the Prison Governor's desk is ominously embossed with XXX's, possessed soul sigil ovals, and X-style binding spells. The other noteworthy item in the Prison Governor's office is a tropical plant whose bottom leaves mimic his pinkish sleeves, similar to how the daisy/sunflower leaves point to Alex's father's sleeves (and X pattern curtains) at their breakfast table. This is to draw attention not just to the Prison Governor's sleeve color but to his cuff links which are gold and are of good size. In *Clockwork Orange*, pink for men may characterize lower level lackeys for the illuciferian elite.

There is a lot of homosexual eroticism in *Clockwork Orange*, which is usually presented in a predatory light. Alex's own juvenile delinquent ("troubled youth") advocate Deltoid virtually molests Alex right on his mother's bed; police interrogators make suggestive comments as they rough Alex up; and later Alex joins the prison pastor more as a measure of protection from sexually menacing inmates than out of sincere religious desire. The opportunity to get an early release by participating in the Ludovico conditioning technique will not only allow Alex to get free of jail sooner but also keep him out of arms reach of such predators. When later Alex finds himself back at the writer's house (who initially does not recognize him), not only is Frank Alexander (now in wheelchair) elated at having the best means to bring down the government at his doorstep, but he also exhibits a lascivious interest in Alex himself. The only positive portrayal of a gay person in *Clockwork Orange* is perhaps Mr. Alexander's attentive aide Julian (David Prowse) and their capable (but unnamed) lesbian compatriot (Margaret Tyzack).

It can be dispiriting to recognize the author Alexander's illuciferian complicity after his traumatic experience with Alex's droogs, as one wants to view him and his upscale bohemian crowd more sympathetically as civic-minded protagonists sincerely opposed to government abuses. But attentive viewers note their fruity dialogue mentioning "the masses" with paternalistic disdain, and even though he arguably deserves it, they manipulate Alex for their own cause just as much as the government did. Additionally, each member of the writers' clique advertises Masonic associations through their clothing. Bodyguard/lover Julian wears the pink of a lower level lackey; and under his tan jacket, Frank's stout boss (a self-assured John Savident), wears the red of someone further up the ladder (earlier, Frank calls him "Sir" on the phone) and their lady journalist friend wears a smart black or dark blue suit (perhaps the hue of dark consciousness as it is in *The Shining*). The orange outfit worn by the writer while plotting with his other well-to-do, anti-government cronies confirms that they are part of the same elite order—even if they are at odds with it. Perhaps this indicates that when a particularly high financial threshold is reached, selected upwardly-mobile individuals are required to serve the upper Masonic orders if they wish to maintain a certain level of success and high standard of living, whatever their realm of expertise may be.

Towards the end of the film, manservant Julian wearing his pink shirt aids his boss Alexander and his cronies to drug and then torture Alex in order to damage the government's involvement in mind control. After Alex almost kills himself in escaping, the head doctor in charge of Alex's wing who allows the Minister of the Interior to enter his ward, wears a blue suit with pink pin stripes himself underneath his white lab coat.

When Alex is bedridden after his suicide attempt (that he is literally bandaged from head to toe is humorous in itself), he is first visited by his parents. His mother has donned on a bright red latex ensemble while his father wears a grey suit with subtle XOX textures. Alex initially is not too happy to see them but rallies when a cheerful, blue-wigged lady psychiatrist comes to check in on him and gives him a test. The test is to determine if their previous operations on Alex's mind bore fruit ("I kept having this dream ... like all these doctors were playing around with me Gulliver," Alex slyly asks Dr. Taylor). The blue wigged Dr. Taylor wears an orange dress with black XOX lettering under her white lab coat; if we go by Kubrick's now established color code, the orange of her dress infers that high degree Masonic Luciferianism is enmeshed within the structure of MK-Ultra-type programs. This collusion is hinted at again with the Ludovico Head Matron Dr. Branom first sporting an orange tie and then later a black and white XXX tie. Dr. Branom's name happens to make the anagram for MOB RAN, which might suggest where mind control programs get some of their needed funds. When the Minister of the Interior makes his special visit to see Alex and gets him to agree to show public support for the government, the Minister has minions wheel in Beethoven music, flowers, and two gigantic speakers, whose tweets and sub woofers together just happen to add up to 18 (6+6+6) sound apertures. The Minister's lackey who brings in the portable phonograph wears a black suit and devil red shirt and keeps strangely still during the rest of the frenzied paparazzi scene.

## The Look of *Clockwork Orange*

Other illuciferian motifs and mind control apparatus masquerading as futuristic furnishings can be found within Alex's family dwelling. Their hallway walls are painted in glittery gold, while the other rooms have highly

## 15. A Clockwork Orange: *More Disturbing Than Ever*          131

reflective surfaces and brightly colored, bumpy, plastic textures which hide XXX patterns in the couch and chair and checkered curtains in his parents' living room and kitchen. The white table legs form an X as well. Other illuciferian sigils are hidden in room furnishings and props. Even the daze-y/sunflower on the parents' dining table is a co-opted illuciferian symbol for the sect's claim on the sun. The kitchen and bathroom wallpapers both have disorienting orange, yellow, and mirrored square or rhomb patterns. Alex's bedroom is glaringly white thanks to his gigantic, blinding light bulbs, which are noted tools used in hypnosis.[7] These huge light bulb motifs can be also found in the writer's living room and the visually overwhelming shopping mall.

The most obvious mind conditioning motif inside the mall is the music kiosk Alex patronizes, for above him, two more browsers and the music shop keeper, is an immense black and white hypnotically spiraling speaker. The size of it is imposing and vaguely threatening, at least in a demented fun-house sort of way. Its presence intimates not only how music is used to manipulate people in advertising but also in MK-Ultra/Monarch type programs. Photos that look like singing (or missing) children line the back wall of the record shop behind the Beatles' *Magical Mystery Tour* album, mixed in among other music covers and rock band posters. Among these, Kubrick could not resist adding the soundtrack album of *2001: A Space Odyssey* among his examples of the hypnotic, influential power of music. Not even poor old Ludwig Van Beethoven escapes this sort of scrutiny. On Alex's white bedroom poster of Beethoven, there are decorations of flipped satanic S's and hidden 6's in the poster flourishes. More specifically Masonic images appear on both Alex's Beethoven tape that he switches from his decidedly satanic colored "Goggly Gogol" tape; they both have single eyes as distributor logos. Even the name "Goggly Gogol" has rather eye-evoking word associations, as well as Old Testament world domination allusions. Along with "Johnny Zhivago," names like Goggly Gogol keep to *Clockwork Orange*'s Russian–English vernacular. To add to that, Gogol's Russian-sounding distributor "Dolvaoi" provides the anagram option OVALOID, yet another apparent eye reference. In an earlier scene, when Alex is shown walking home through his local residential urban blight, a stand-out pyramidal concrete island passes by him in front of a row of inverted crosses, even inverted double crosses, upon a lighted tenant block building behind Alex.

### Light Effects in *Clockwork Orange*

Light effects are so well executed in *Clockwork Orange* that even though they do much to call attention to themselves, viewers either do not really take heed of them or just accept them as part of the film's dystopian ambiance as lights placed in a futuristic setting. But light itself does appear to have a certain primary importance in *Clockwork Orange*, as the lights in the film's various sets, rooms, and environs can be almost painfully bright. It is as though the movie's lighting crew is practically screaming at you to notice them.

Such is the case with the Milk Bar sculpture bulbs and the two gate lamps outside Mr. and Mrs. Alexander's home. These gate lamps are glaring white yet cast a red aura about themselves, with the left one spitting fluttering light upon the writer's gate. It is natural to write this shot off as simply one of the bulbs needing to be replaced and think no more about it. But as this is a Kubrick film, the light sputtering on the gate draws attention to the gate's design for a reason; as it makes an XOX frame. Then the fact it is the *left* (hand path) light revealing this feature makes sense in a most fitting, esoteric way. This may be the film's first indication of illuciferian presence (or influence) within *Clockwork Orange*'s symbolism.

The mall Alex visits is itself designed quite like a hall of mirrors in terms of the barrage of light reflections and refractions bouncing off its metallic gold walls. The brightest lights in this shopping area have a curious halo effect as Alex walks underneath them. These lights extend a pale rainbow noose that goes back into their bulbs as Alex walks about the shop kiosks. Yet the bulbs themselves emit a baleful red glow similar to the writer's "Home" gate lamps. Some of the mall's indoor reflections and lights look suspiciously like distressed or demonic faces or unfriendly eyes surveying its shoppers. Strategically placed eye imagery peppered throughout the shop displays direct the audience's eyes towards things to notice. When purple clad and snake-skinned Alex approaches the last music kiosk, to the left of the *2001* soundtrack, a black record cover's shiny packaging reflects in the guise of a serpent's eye.

Newspapers in the film refer to Alex's family as the Burgesses, something the author of *Clockwork Orange* hopefully got some amusement out of. The family's apartment lights in the entryway shine on particular pictures of brown-skinned ladies, which look to be the dominant paintings throughout their family unit. Do they hold any other significance besides being more examples of women as objects on display? Perhaps their coloring gives clues to what brown conveys in *Clockwork Orange*'s color code. As they are all in natural outdoor settings, it would make sense that brown in *Clockwork Orange* is the Earth color, particularly since the color brown also symbolizes the Earth in Masonry.[8] Additionally, the placing of these paintings in the Burgesses' gold entryway and hallway connects to *2001*'s connection of the color gold to both sanctified Earth and the ascended female principle.

Two light effects infer illuminati influence within the Ludovico program. The first is a very pyramidal spotlight that is choreographed during Alex's public performance as a reformed citizen. This triangular column of light is shot straight on, a few times, with its source light emanating extra illumination, similar to the Freemason's Eye of Providence pyramid herald. The second is when the Minister of the Interior sits down after introducing Alex. As the Minister leans towards his colleague, the Prison Governor, to indicate his "complete faith" in Dr. Bronski's Ludovico system, a small rainbow emits from the pyramid spotlight and alights right under the Minister's left eye, staying there for most of the shot. Its symbolism may refer to the illuciferian caveat to keep the masses "spiritually under the rainbow." When Alex cries out for the doctors not to use Beethoven's 9th Symphony in his aversion therapy, as Dr. Branom responds, the camera spies her duality-themed, black and white XXX tie. Though the Nazi footage Alex is forced to watch makes an allusion to an ostensible source of such brainwashing methods,[9] Dr. Branom's tie and the eight-rayed projector light are yet other dark hints in *Clockwork Orange* of the disturbing overlaps between mind control programs and Luciferianism.

Glaring light, often as artificial light, alerts us to the presence of great evil. Mr. Alexander's house is lit by tall column lights that glow so hot it is at times hard to tell whether they are topped with light bulbs or torches. The Cat Lady's gym table lights and floor lights are especially bright, nearly blinding, as if broadcasting the evil committed on women in the Cat Lady's "health center" as extrapolated further by the shocking paintings on her walls. Considering the number of atrocities Alex commits on a regular basis, the fact that Alex's room is blazing white when all the lights are on now makes a sort of sense. Alex's Ludovico hospital room's bleached light, where the icy Dr. Branom is in charge, is bleaker than the ward where he recuperates from his injuries; that space has warmer tones and less septic grays. Last but certainly not least, the brightest light coming into his mother's room literally shines on her row of beta kitten wigs and reveals evil incarnate on her closet panel.

## Rooms, Colors and Environments in *Clockwork Orange*

Orange, yellow, and reflective surfaces stand out the most in Alex's parents' apartment. The kitchen area walls have orange and yellow squares on a reflective background. The bathroom wallpaper has instead orange and yellow diamonds on a mirrored background. Alex's pointy coverlet has gradations of orange ending in yellow, with one side of his room being a mirror. Their entryway and hallways are shellacked gold, with reddish carpeting covering the floors (the other Earth/Woman color). The living room wall behind the couch is mostly blue and black done in a slightly disorienting figure eight style. The parents' living room's white plastic couch and chair have black and blue seat cushions as well with a repeating X pattern. Even their living room carpet is blue with strange, cloudy shapes. The wall to the kitchen is dark magenta as are the walls in Mum's bedroom and Alex's floor. We might assume

Mum's bedroom is solely hers because there is nothing in the room to indicate that Dad occupies it. Mum's bedcover is perhaps the largest green hued item in the entire apartment. Her curtains are a combo of green, pale green, and blue. When Deltoid visits Alex, he notably wears a pale green shirt himself under his gray suit. As in *The Shining*, pale green is likewise an indication of perverse evil, and in *Clockwork Orange*'s case, wan green is a particular evil of a most predatory nature.

Arrangements of X's show up in other places to testify the existence of under-the-radar devilry going on. Alex's own strangely pointy bed cover creates strings of XXX's depending on how the camera frames it, further connecting the colors orange and yellow with Masonic evil. Orange and yellow reappear where sinister events are possibly conducted or where they have strongest influence. Yet there is very little orange or yellow in Mum's room and that is where some of the film's most veiled horrors happen. Considering what went on in there, it is appropriate that Mum's bed covers simultaneously contain both dark and pale X's that run along the length of the bed, doubling as the feminine rhomb. For those naysayers who assert that such textile patterns are a fluke, considering the multiple times X/XX/XOX already appears within *Clockwork Orange*, it is highly improbable that the bed pattern is just a "happenstance" design. Again, the sickly pea soup green of Mum's coverlet strengthens the association of the bed with infernally perverse actions.

Alex's mother's bedroom is dominated by green and dark magenta. Magenta is repeated as seats in the kitchen, and their new tenant Joe, embodying the golden son the Burgesses never had, wears a form-fitting, fuzzy dark magenta sweater that matches the walls outside the kitchen. Green and dark magenta also dominate the Cat Lady's beta kitten gallery, where Alex's mother also resides on a wall, displayed in a painting. The Cat Lady herself is dressed in a dark magenta wig and green leotard. Perhaps dark magenta and dirty green are the color of sex slave victims, which would indicate that strapping Joe is one as well, as were the two magenta and green wigged shop girls Alex passes by in the market center. Purple and red seem to be another sex-related color combo, as Alexander's live-in attendant Julian and the brunette Alex picks up at the mall both wear purple and red attire. Most tellingly, red, purple, and white feature prominently in the Beta Kitten paintings and generally depict skin tones, especially breasts. Perhaps purple, red, and white represent nurturing, both wholesome and obscenely profaned.

Covert images of serpents, not just Alex's boa Basil, run through the film. When Alex courts the young ladies in the indoor shopping center, his purple ensemble is resplendent in snakeskin lapels and cuffs. During his biblical fantasizing, Alex wears alligator hide and other reptilian regalia. More ominously, when Alex walks out to his parents' living room in his underwear, he stands right upon a snake's head on the blue and white carpet and the rest of the rug looks to be roiling with other serpents and hostile faces. In his mother's room, above her bed, is a landscape painting that from a distance also looks like a snake's head. Whether this is to humorously suggest either Alex is *the* "Serpent" or is a by-product of the evil the serpent portrays, or a bit of both, is open to debate.

## The Ultimate Diamond Heist

Another very important discovery in *Clockwork Orange* is that Kubrick reveals the diamond shape's most ancient female symbolism at least three times. Once it is used as patterning on the Cat Lady's gym room wallpaper. There, the diamond is part of a repeating fleur-de-lis textile, with the diamond itself being depicted as an intentionally anatomically rendered motif. This fleur-de-lis pattern is accompanied by multiple, smaller, ankh-shaped Trees of Life. A closer look at the base of these glyphs may be devil heads claiming power over these symbols. The audience is given a few chances to inspect the wallpaper up close when the Cat Lady and Alex are near the gym door. The second example is where Alex is locked in a very feminine room whose white wicker chairs are detailed in downward-pointing (female) chevron stacks with X-frame backing and whose wallpaper is also made of diamonds with vaginally inspired detail. The chairs' down-facing chevron stacks assert power over the feminine in nefarious shadow script, and its X-shape backing is its satanic reinforcement. Here in the same room, Kubrick subtly showcases how the feminine powers is one of the main symbols the illuciferian set appropriates and sublimates at the same time, as they double the diamond to represent their eight-pointed morning star, originally stolen from the ancient (4000 BCE) Sumerian goddess Inanna's eight-pointed star (later named Venus by the Greeks) and therefore historically *not* Lucifer's.

Alex's pet boa Basil is very interesting in itself, since its skin conveniently displays the nested rhomb shapes Luciferians equate to their Fallen One. Notice where it is directing its head on the nude Black woman painting when placed on its branch. Here, Kubrick indicates the exact symbol the illuciferians stole for their "light bringer," the ages-old African diamond symbol of Womankind/Earth, the source of Life. The fact that the boa displays its diamonds while the lady on the wall is obviously missing hers bluntly brings home the symbolism of the "Serpent's" theft.

It is possible that the nested rhombs on the boa's scale pattern are in fact natural (mazacuata and emperor boas have underside rhombs), but just as likely someone may have added a few cosmetic touches to its flanks—making the visual connection between Woman's stolen yoni-diamond and the Serpent's nested "morning star" rhombs all the more clear. This single use of serpent imagery in *Clockwork Orange* symbolizes one of the world's oldest spiritual crimes. That the boa, Basil, provides the anagram LABIS further strengthens this argument. Quite a feminist statement for an otherwise testosterone-drenched, "ultraviolent" film to make.

During Alex's audio torture, the government opposition instigators wait it out while their red-shirted leader rolls red balls across a green pool table. The only other balls placed prominently are a black ball and a white one, presumably representing the duality of existence. Why is it he only uses red balls? Take a look above Mr. Alexander's head to see why: an attractive mural or Victorian style poster gives the vague impression of impersonating a large pound note or the general concept of money. Underneath it, but just above the writer's head, is a wooden floral border that from a distance looks just like a running XOX pattern. Another example is in Alex's room as he opens his bed drawer to access his illegally obtained earnings. The only two cameras in there (antique ones that a young Kubrick would be more tempted to steal than Alex) happen to be near paper money as if to say "take a closer look." On the drawer's upper right is the reassuring visage of a young Queen Elizabeth on a monetary note (with no numeric amount indicated), and near the drawer's lower left is another note that is hard to make out—but does not look pleasant. It appears to be an ugly visage sticking its tongue out with a skull to its right. When viewed from upside down, the note's detailing does not improve much. A mother huddles with her children on the right while from the left a glowering bearded man with hollowed out eyes scowls outward and below him at left is a large, malicious looking serpent, eyeing the family. In between them is what from a distance seems to be an evil eye but when looked at close up turns out to be a smaller female figure (a girl child) with her arms wrapped protectively over her head. If one is to surmise Stanley Kubrick's thoughts on our modern money system, the above described must be a definitive example.

## Cycles in *Clockwork Orange*

Circularity is another theme in *Clockwork Orange*. In the disorienting kaleidoscopic shopping center, the scene of Alex walking around the shops starts and ends with the same popsicle-licking girl with strange yellow hair color.

When Alex engages to struggle with the Cat Lady, they circle around each other almost as in a dance parody. Later in the jail yard, Alex and a group of inmates out for their exercise are going around in a tight circle while an engraved pyramid looms over them from a grim, concrete prison wall. A closer look at this wall will dredge up X's and inverted crosses around the pyramid ghost carving and disturbing faces on the other walls. How Alex leaves

## 15. A Clockwork Orange: *More Disturbing Than Ever*     137

home and then returns to it is circuitous as are the events of him revisiting the writer's home.

What does this circularity theme entail? One take on this is the idea Kubrick is illustrating cinematically how all levels and channels of society are thoroughly corralled, contained, and maintained by the powers that be. The entirety of modern Western civilization operates like a highly complex hamster habitrail, where people are kept in their own special sets of hamster wheels. Meanwhile, those in power are continuously spinning schemes, be they educational, judicial, medical, institutional, or political, on how to keep the growing population under control.

While arguably this outlook is nothing new, it is striking how thoroughly and repeatedly Kubrick appears to be emphasizing that, yes indeed, illuciferians are running the show. Such a realization may make more people wake up to how dire our situation is, living under this truly corrosive system. Kubrick is sounding the alarm, not on the various human flaws of civilization itself but on the increasingly evident reality that the uppermost echelons of Western authority have over the centuries (perhaps starting in the mid–1600s)[10] thoroughly rotted, due to a gradually expanding Luciferian influence throughout various power centers of modern society. Such institutionalized evil does not benefit the majority of humanity. This top-heavy power crisis proves the adage that absolute power does, over time, corrupt absolutely.

The circularity of abuse in a variety of forms is covered in *Clockwork Orange*. Many who have already seen the movie have observed the educational/correctional abuse in the guise of Mr. Deltoid, the abuses that go with life in incarceration, and abuses of justice committed by police, humorously portrayed by ex-droogs Georgie and Dim who later become official thugs paid by the state. Last but not least are the institutionalized abuses committed within *Clockwork Orange*'s spotlight on terrible brainwashing programs. But domestic abuse is also highlighted in a more veiled manner. When Alex first looks in on Mr. Deltoid from his mother's bedroom door, horrific images can be seen on the right side of the room from its interior. First there is the glaring light on the left side of a dark panel. It is a brightly lit devil face, evilly surveying the rest of its marbleized wood. Its attention is on three dark, disturbingly demonic animal heads with large rotting mouths that decorate the side of Alex's mother's mud-colored wooden closet. When viewed in high contrast and brightness, they turn out to be caricatures of a crazed Alex's mum wearing a cat-eared wig and what appears to be a closed third eye sealed shut by an X. Together with the imagery of the creepy Mr. Deltoid drinking from Mum's false teeth glass, the mouth imagery used during the death of the Cat Lady, and Alex's Mum at one point wearing the exact red boots that the gym's most fearsome beta kitten painting wears (not to mention the matching makeup), the evidence is fairly clear that Alex's mother sexually abused him sometime when he was fairly young, especially with the aforementioned scary lady painting holding up a captive "little Alex" at the gym. It is no wonder, then, that Alex has a literal safety lock as his bedroom doorknob. Now we know the lock wasn't just to prevent detection of his room's stolen swag. Here Kubrick is illustrating another circular theme: that Alex's mother, in turn, was previously abused and broken in her earlier slave conditioning transformation into a beta kitten. Thus *Clockwork Orange* demonstrates the cycle of abuse by how past abuse feeds future abuse.

## Wearing One's Aims on One's Sleeve

Sleeves are very important in *Clockwork Orange* in providing clues to how power works. The droogs' outfits brandish disembodied eye sockets on their sleeves, advertising not only their fearsomeness as a gang but as a big visual hint to pay attention to *other* characters' sleeves in *Clockwork Orange*. The Prison Governor's pink sleeves have already been mentioned. During Alex's public presentation as a fully-reformed young man to showcase the success of Dr. Brodsky's Ludovico conditioning, the minister of the interior puts his hand on Alex's shoulder, revealing black and white checkered sleeves. This checkerboard pattern has overlapping associations both with the Masonic concept of universal duality and as a hypnotic mind control device in MK-Ultra/Monarch-style programming.[11] Therefore this government official's hand on Alex's shoulder symbolically underlines what has been done to Alex and by whom.

The second time the Minister is with Alex is in the medical ward. Here it appears the Minister has gone as far up the illuciferian ladder of power as possible. He arrives wearing a sleek black suit with a gold silk pyramid-shaped pocket handkerchief and a black silk shirt with gold patterning. Together, black and gold embodies the true occultist nature of the illuciferian elite. When the PM feeds Alex and later again puts his hand on Alex's shoulder, his sleeves are revealed to contain satanic S's, XOX's, or triangles, depending on the angle of the pattern. The moment the Minister puts his arm around Alex is also when Alex starts to dissociate, another indication that illuciferian interests and MK-Ultra/Monarch techniques are nefariously linked.

An earlier connection is the film projector light shining as an eight-point star behind Alex as he is being prepped to endure a real "horror show." Considering all the real-world horrors *Clockwork Orange* exposes, it makes sense why Kubrick treated the appalling subject matter with a wicked, sardonic sense of humor and recognized that the use of a totally unsympathetic protagonist was necessary to reveal the brutal inner workings of power and black site experimentation. If Alex was made a more compassionate or sympathetic character, audiences of the time would have found the awful situations in *Clockwork Orange* even harder to stomach, if not completely unwatchable.

## The Most Misunderstood Scenes in *Clockwork Orange*

Though the girls Alex pick up at the shopping center do not wear wigs, their rainbow-striped popsicles and the white clad lady's vibrantly dyed hair suggest Monarch conditioning.[12] The brunette even wears a soul sigil choker around her neck to make her enslavement clearer to those with occult knowledge. Her cane-shaped ice doubles as a satanic initial whose coloring keeps consciousness "under the rainbow." When Alex takes them to his room, most people think they are about to watch a humorous take on a consensual three-way. The other clue that the girls are conditioned sex slaves is how they put on their clothes almost automatically after they have sex. The reason this is not as consensual a scene as is generally assumed is that Alex keeps taking off their clothes again in the effort to continue having sex when each of the girls is obviously trying to leave. With the film sped up, the two girls' strangely robotic actions are emphasized. It usually goes unnoticed in this sequence that neither of the girls actually gets to rest nor stay on the bed but keep making motions to leave.

The other most misunderstood scene in *Clockwork Orange* is at the end, when Alex is doing a glad-handing photo-op with his new friend, the Minister of the Interior. The common opinion is that Alex has essentially gone back to his evil old ways with his "fantasy" at the very end of the film. But he has not. He is, in fact, dissociating. The old Alex's fantasies were violent and cruel, but Alex's last vision is actually of consensual sex, where the woman is on top and obviously enjoying herself while a gathering of early 19th-century folk applaud Alex for finally being a real human being and not a complete psychopath. Dissociation is a result of some form of extreme trauma or abuse a person has endured.[13] In one of Alex's bible-inspired fantasies, he is being tended by hand maidens he presumably had his wicked way with after he killed their previous owners. The blonde lady on his right only limply stares out past the camera, hardly moving, like she is not really there. She is exhibiting characteristics of being in a dissociative state. It is the same state we see young Danny in when he puts up with his father's pawing in *The Shining*. For *Eyes Wide Shut*, it looks like the same condition we see Mandy the call girl in when Dr. Bill Harford attempts to revive her in Mr. Ziegler's bathroom.

Alex reacts the same towards the film's finish. He goes stiff under the minister's hand on his shoulder and Alex's eyes slowly crawl up into his head as he becomes slack jawed. His vision shares similarities with other descriptions of dissociative states. Alex and his dream lover, together with their crowd of admiring on-lookers, are in a cloudy, misty place that victims of trauma often describe going to when they are dissociating.[14]

The final clue that Alex is exemplifying trauma brought about by Monarch-style conditioning is the faceless lady wearing a butterfly mask on the far left of the closing scene. Objects shot on the left side of the screen can suggest the left hand path of Luciferianism, as is appropriate considering the insidious processes involved in MK-Ultra/Monarch brainwashing programs. Her butterfly mask being primarily black and gold is another Kubrick color clue of satanic occult influence within these (formerly) government-ordained mind slave conditioning techniques.

Some debate the existence of Monarch over the proven MK-Ultra projects, but it is doubtful Kubrick would have used such butterfly/rainbow symbolism if Monarch was not a real program. Especially since the same imagery is repeated in *The Shining* and *Eyes Wide Shut*.

## How *Clockwork Orange* and *The Shining* Connect to *2001*

Looking back on what we know now about *Clockwork Orange* and *The Shining*, we can compare how the two films relate and link back to *2001: A Space Odyssey*. On the surface, all three of these movies look completely different and they are in genres that are poles apart from each other. But observing the details, we find that both *Clockwork Orange* and *The Shining* relate back to *2001* through their use of themes and motifs originated from *A Space Odyssey*.

The monolith appears more often throughout *The Shining*, but it does have a few meaningful cameos in *Clockwork Orange*. The first notable monolith shapes in *Clockwork Orange* are the blinding hexagonal podiums the Milk Bar beta kitten sculptures stand on. In the sectioned area of the bar where the droogs sit, the six statues and their six-sided stands do symbolize 666, twice. The second time the monolith appears as a white rectangle of space behind a tall torch light placed inside the writer Alexander's bookcase. It provides a clue to what the monolith symbolizes in *A Space Odyssey*. That meaning is carried through most of Kubrick's films that came after *2001*, starting with *Clockwork Orange*. The other times the monolith outline makes an appearance in *Clockwork Orange* is as a giant poster, mural, or tapestry behind the writer's coterie when they torture Alex with sound. In the room where Alex is held captive, a large dresser displays two monolith sized mirrors. The left rectangular mirror either starkly reflects light as an evil influence or more likely portrays light as emitting the *presence* of evil,

## 15. A Clockwork Orange: *More Disturbing Than Ever* 141

like an alarm. The iconic *2001* monolith's last incarnations arguably are the slab-sized fluorescent lights in Alex's ward at the end of the film. They are shrouded in black to dim his room but a monolithic light above the approaching Minister of the Interior blazes intensely on the ceiling as a warning. Here, the monolith is primarily used as a signifier towards important *Clockwork Orange* concepts, such as highlighting how wholesome things are profaned in evil purposes.

*Clockwork Orange* gives the impression of having its own color code system that *The Shining*'s color code partially continues and also combines with *A Space Odyssey*'s original color code. *Clockwork Orange* introduces orange and yellow as invoking Masonic evil and Death respectively, whereas in *A Space Odyssey* the colors held the more lofty associations of yellow exhibiting Embodied Life and orange signifying Life Functions or Life Signals. In *The Shining*, orange still pertains to Masonic evil and yellow as Death, yet the Duality championed in *2001* exhibits the benign flip side of these colors, depending on their color hue. For example, yellow may equal Death or commonplace evil in *The Shining* but gold still embodies Sanctified Life and the Divine Feminine in both films. Green in *2001* is Creative Intuition and Growth but in *Clockwork Orange* its pallid shades alludes to themes of defilement. As pale green is displayed on Mum's curtains and worn by Deltoid hints at the hue portraying perversion or evil mindedness in both *Clockwork Orange* and *The Shining*. It would certainly make a dualistic, holistic sort of sense if the colors in *Clockwork Orange* symbolize the near polar opposite of what universal themes the same colors represent in *A Space Odyssey*. If "good" orange in *Clockwork Orange* is how life operates or more specifically how Alex's modern society normally operates, then "evil" orange underlines the invisible hand of Masonic manipulation.

Yellow in *Clockwork Orange* as death occupies the same space as orange in the Burgesses' kitchen and bathroom and Alex's bed coverlet. Yellow is also the dominant color in Frank Alexander's dining room's large, monolith-sized floral painting. It is also the blanket color Alex finds himself on when he wakes up in the very feminine sound torture room. Just before he commits suicide by jumping out of the window, there is a shot of Alex from the back as he looks towards the window area. The pink and light blue room looks to be totally covered in wall to wall X's before Alex jumps.

Blue stands for Consciousness in *A Space Odyssey*, and in *Clockwork Orange* blue looks as if to represent normal, day-to-day consciousness of the average working stiff. Alex's father is dressed in a blue but also wears a pale blue shirt. The 'daze-y' flower on the table has leaves positioned to point this out. Light blue in *A Space Odyssey* is Higher Consciousness, but in *Clockwork Orange* it could be corrupted higher consciousness, as dark blue equals degraded ordinary consciousness. Both Alex's mother and the brunette he meets in the shopping center wear dark blue. Light blue is the dominant color of the feminine room's furnishings where the author's lofty, in-the-know allies subject Alex to sound torture. The couch and chair in the parents' living room are covered in repeating black and wan blue X's. The wall behind their couch is a disquieting design of black, dark blue, blue, and light blue infinity swirls that also may double for flipped satanic S's. When Alex later "graduates" from the government backed Ludovico program, his blue suit may advertise normalcy, but its actual colors of glowering dark blue and weak pale blue give away his true moral fiber.

Grey, as a mixture of black and white, most likely as a neutral color stands for everyday morality or normalcy, which becomes forebodingly less so the darker it gets. Deltoid wears a grey jacket declaring his official governmental position that literally covers his own perversion.

The Burgesses' reflective bubble wall symbolically links to the metallic mirror sections of the apartment's orange and yellow kitchen and bathroom wallpaper. As orange indicates Masonic influence and yellow means death, the reflective bits represent the self as one looks into a mirror and sees oneself. All together, the wallpapers are most probably a warning of how Masonic entanglements can destroy the self, even the soul. Their shiny bubble wall is constructed in an ovoid chain pattern that is popular in Luciferian occultism as wallpaper. Possibly this is because its repetitive S-curve pattern can hide flipped satanic S's in its outlines to frame and claim ovoid "soul" sigils and circular "fulfillment" glyphs of power.

## How *Clockwork Orange* Connects to *The Shining*

*The Shining* in many respects picks up where *Clockwork Orange* left off, covering similar themes of misogyny, child abuse, and illuciferian exposure. It also revisits the topic of how extreme abuse in any form can lead to trauma and dissociation. In Alex's case, in *Clockwork Orange*, his trauma and dissociating was brought about by institutionalized abuse, though we learn he was sexually abused by his mother as well (and she, in turn, was destroyed spiritually by institutionalized beta kitten programming). With Danny Torrance in *The Shining*, his trauma is mainly brought about by the physical and incestuous abuse committed by his father. Misogyny is expressed mainly through Jack Torrance's treatment of his hapless wife, Wendy Torrance, which comes out mainly as dismissive and condescending verbal abuse until late in the second half of the film, where it escalates to all-out attempted murder. Themes of institutionalized abuse in *The Shining* are more suggested and covert, as their related symbols are hidden within the Overlook hotel and are indirectly associated with Danny's situation as sinister echoes to what he is experiencing and its root cause. The Monarch trope has a more direct link to the Grady twins, whose own past traumatic ordeal reverberates back to Danny's present suffering.

*The Shining* doubles down, laying bare the existence of the illuciferian elite by exposing their secret symbols. *Clockwork Orange* contains plenty of their symbols as well but its focus is on outing the corrupt, high-degree Masonic influence in various sectors of society in Western civilization, especially the political, legal, medical, and artistic establishments. *The Shining* centers on the covert diabolical aspects of the illuminati set in America's ruling class.

As the reality of MK-Ultra programs came to light and were allegedly closed down after a U.S. government investigation in 1977, credit for their exposure can in part be given to films like *Clockwork Orange* and *The Manchurian Candidate* which brought such institutional abuses to the public's attention.

## *Clockwork Orange*'s Ending

Alex's dissociative vision at the end of the movie contains many keys to *Clockwork Orange*'s color symbolism. His clapping, Edwardian crowd is dressed in the most utilized colors of the film. Appropriately the people, specifically the ladies, on the left side (with the Monarch masked woman) wear the "bad" or warning colors, and those to the right wear the good-but-compromised/threatened colors of *Clockwork Orange*. All the men are in grey. The monarch masked lady happens to wear colors that match the décor of the room Alex was trapped in. Her white and yellow-tipped parasol reflects the same colors of the bed Alex found himself in that same room. In the group with her, a lady wears a black, orange, and white (or pale gray) dress. Both her hat and parasol are black and she is the only woman wearing black and orange in the crowd. She is also the only person not applauding Alex's spiritual breakthrough. She just puts her right hand on her left hand holding the black parasol, the most triangular looking one in the gathering. Her orange, black, white zigzags can suggest beta-kitten animal print patterning or hidden shadow script. There appear to be a few black X's tucked into the black parasol lady's dress pattern.

On the right are three women that can be seen most clearly. First there is a lady in white, a woman in brown, and the third is in a pink and purple ensemble topped with a red scarf or collar. If white represents innocence and purity, then the Monarch maiden's yellow and white parasol may represent the Death of Innocence, similar to what Alex's light yellow shirt signifies about himself. The brown-clad woman represents the Earth and possibly womankind. The tan-skinned lady wearing the red, purple, and pink gown portrays the colors of sex, love, and nurturing, respectively. In *2001*, purple stands for Self-Illumination and holds the same connotations in *The Shining* and within *Eyes Wide Shut*, so in *Clockwork Orange* purple possibly means love as a doorway to ascension. The purple-pink clothed lady's complexion connects her to her brown garbed sister. In the background on the right is a young woman wearing a magenta-colored hat. Magenta in *A Space Odyssey* conveyed the Seat of Higher Consciousness and in *Clockwork Orange* it might mean the same, but we mostly see it in a murkier, dirtier shade that would more represent compromised or *abused* love. As this is one of Alex's mother's main colors along with dingy green signifying perversion, this color interpretation makes the most sense. It is also the colors the Cat Lady (as a wig) and Alex-replacement Joe (furry sweater) wear as appropriate for used-and-abused sex kittens and beta boys.

Examples of *Clockwork Orange*'s color coding reside in the following scenes. Alex's purple outfit in the shops declares he is looking for love, but his snakeskin collar and cuffs betray his true intentions. His light yellow shirt underneath hides Alex's dead innocence. Mrs. Mary Alexander wears a full red sexy pantsuit (emerging from a pure white, egg-shaped lounge seat) and the writer's male caretaker wears rather revealing red shorts with his white-purple (innocent love) tank top. The unusual abstract sculpture in Frank Alexander's living room is red, pink, and purple with weak blue shading, and its contours possibly suggest the writer's bisexual nature. Sadly, its weak blue may suggest perversion defiling or abusing love and sexuality (originally pure and healthy, be it straight, bi, or gay). Far in the back of the living room is a disturbing statue of a woman with various gaping holes in her body. She is lit by giant, almost unbearably bright, light bulbs to call attention to her. She is accompanied by rather ominously shaped foliage, one in the apparent shape of a dog and the other uncertain. When their lights are off, the foliage and the statue are at their most menacing, viewed from a distance. Final proof of *Clockwork Orange*'s color code lies in its end credits, which roll magenta, blue, green, etc., to the end, marking the key colors Stanley Kubrick encourages alert viewers to investigate.

# 16

# A Woman's Take on *Full Metal Jacket*

Iconic Full Metal Jacket helmet (model by Gary Blakeley/Shutterstock).

Stanley Kubrick's 1987 war drama *Full Metal Jacket* featured a group of marine privates training and embroiling themselves within the 1970s Viet Cong Tet Offensive. It could have been in danger of being swallowed up by all the other major war pictures (*Red Dawn, Platoon, Good Morning Vietnam, Hamburger Hill*) that came out in the '80s. So many war films being released in the spate of a few years no doubt stole a bit of each other's box office fire. Based on war veteran Gustav Hasford's book *Short-Timers* on grunts' experiences in Vietnam, one can easily think that a film as metaphysical as *2001* would carry little over into a seemingly nihilistic war picture like *Full Metal Jacket*. However, some surprising spiritual elements from the 1968 science fiction classic and Kubrick's following films do make it into *Full Metal Jacket*, and they are usually employed as grim warning signifiers to what is going on in a given scene.

Though the story's main character is Private James T. "Joker" Davis, the movie starts with a group of young men getting their heads shaved; they will end up in the same corps barracks together, and the first part of *Full Metal Jacket* focuses on their training as a unit. Actor R. Lee Ermey does a superlative job as their marine drill instructor Sgt. Hartman, whose main objective is to harden, toughen, and get his "maggots" fit for battle, with grueling military discipline. Sadly, one poor soul gets singled out to be the scapegoat, as an example to the rest of the troop of what *not* to be, thereby giving the others more incentive to perform as expected for their demanding drill instructor.

Constant insults, verbal abuse, physical abuse, and newly designated nicknames do their fair share of psychologically stripping the troops of any remnant tender feelings to protect or any notion of marked individualism that would impede essential military group cohesion. The grunt who gets the worst of Sgt. Hartman's ire is man-child Leonard Lawrence, now named Private Pyle (after the insipidly annoying TV character Gomer Pyle), the most overweight recruit in the corps. Though some of his fellows may feel bad for him forever being singled out (like Joker and Cowboy), they also sincerely do not want to end up like him by becoming Hartman's next victim of constant ridicule. This common training tactic of selecting a scapegoat can inspire fervent troop solidarity to obey and excel.

The camera captures Private Pyle in shots that portray him as almost baby-like. The first is when, by either cinematic illustration or through punitive infliction, Pyle is seen dragging behind his marching troop with his pants down and his thumb in his mouth. A later training session views Pyle in silhouette sucking his thumb as he watches the men continue their physically draining workouts. The last example is just before the infamous "Towel Party" hazing scene where Private Pyle is sleeping in his top bunk, looking very much like an overgrown infant before he is mercilessly attacked by his bunk mates. Before that, when Joker becomes Pyle's training mentor, the almost puppy-like gratitude Pyle exhibits towards Joker helping him out is quite heartbreaking. Actor Vincent D'Onofrio expresses Private Leonard Pyle's innocence with aching sincerity. Pyle's character is a victim of the impersonal draft board process, for as a person with the mind of a child, someone like Leonard had absolutely no business being selected for military duty. But the Marines just want bodies. Thanks to Hartman's unceasing vicious harassment and Pyle's resulting alienation from the rest of the troop, Private Leonard Pyle's originally sweet nature curdles and dies in psychosis.

## Light FX and Secret Symbolism in *Full Metal Jacket*

Light used as cinematic signifiers is used to full effect in *Full Metal Jacket*, echoing their spiritual component portrayed in *2001: A Space Odys-

## 16. A Woman's Take on Full Metal Jacket

*sey*. When Private Joker is on night fire watch duty, his flashlight emits two wide rainbow arcs while the torch bulb itself glows warning red, a pointed throwback to alarm light FX used in both *Clockwork Orange* and *The Shining*. The two rainbows are symbolic of Duality. How the rainbows are positioned place a pink-purple diamond light as polar opposite from where the satanic lit flashlight is at Joker's lower left. The diamond light appears either right by Joker's head or most upper right from his point of view. The magenta diamond recalls *2001*'s illumination symbol now with its more ethereal, pastel rainbow, whereas the opposing red flashlight's rainbow is its more earthly, unenlightened opposite (in *Eyes Wide Shut*, occult rainbow symbolism emphasizes who is illuminated and who is not). As Joker is about to come across Private Pyle experiencing a severe mental breakdown, the unusual light effects for an otherwise ordinary torch act as a warning, especially when its beam first falls upon highlighting the words "ill" and "instruct" on the Drill Instructor's door sign and "Head" for the bathroom Pyle is in. The light effects revealing the door signs are interesting in themselves as they are not normal round pools of lamp light but instead throw sharp, triangular shadows that single out the particular text being highlighted. Looking back on this scene in hindsight, there is no logical reason for Joker to bother shining his light upon these doors as by now he should be well acquainted with every inch of his own barracks. That in itself provides proof that the flashlight beams in this sequence are supposed to hold more meaning than merely being functional light effects.

Another scene with impressive lighting is inside newly transferred Joker's Vietnam barracks with the rest of his newsroom grunts. As they lie in their bunks boasting about who has seen "action" out on the field where the fighting is at its fiercest, four intensely bright diamond shaped lamp lights stretch their luminosity far out beyond themselves, each one making a giant "T" cross whose arms reach to the barracks side walls and whose beams of light spear right down to the floor. Three of these diamond lights are near a wall plastered with photos of scantily clad and naked women, which the lights' intensity bring out from the background, making them hard to ignore. One of the lamplight arms alights on a racist Asian face caricature next to Latino grunt Chili's bunk (who most likely got his nickname the way Black marine "Snowball" did), its cartoon eyebrows itself suggest disguised shadow script for a profaned Tau cross, a sort of demented Third Eye. The almost cruciform lamp glow literally shines a light on the marine grunts' low-grade machismo of comparing wartime experience to "gettin' some *real* action."

When Joker gets reassigned to the front lines with his buddy Rafterman in tow, whom he is reluctant to take along due to his youth and inexperience, a helicopter takes them close to the scene of the battle. As the helicopter's shadow is seen flying over treetops, it develops a halo of pink-purple light just before the next shot cuts to a close-up of the helicopter in the sky. The sky itself is a dazzlingly strange pink-purple hue, and pink-purple light effects flicker about the helicopter before changing to a close up of Joker and Rafterman inside the craft talking with the helicopter's door gunner man. The extra light effects in the sky emphasize the sky's unusual color, the same color of the newsroom window glass. This pink-purple may be a color flag for the esoteric Plane of Existence theme for the planet Earth.

The same color was used to depict the same Physical Realm trope in *2001: A Space Odyssey*. In contrast, outside above the helicopter door is a wire satanic script S with a line through it, similar to part of a steel fence design Joker sneaks past when he later hunts a sniper. Inside the helicopter to the left of Joker are gear shelves made of shadow script: diamond headed ankhs with bars across their faces provide voiceless commentary on the door gunner's substituting his machinegun for a penis. With strains of *Dr. Strangelove*, Kubrick returns to the now not-so comedic refrain of the military regularly utilizing sexual euphemisms for their war games, such as "This is my rifle, this is my gun, one is for fighting, the other's for fun," intense gunfire being "hardcore action," and retreating as "pulling out" of a conflict.

*Eightball* actor Dorian Harewood mentions that Stanley Kubrick wanted to make an unromanticized war film: "This was his answer to *Rambo*.... He wanted to show what war is really like." This belies any casual notion that Kubrick would make an entirely ambiguous, relativistic movie on war, as Michael Herr suggests.[1] *Full Metal Jacket* in effect takes a page from *The Shining* in that much of its presumably Vietnamese building décor is in fact either not Vietnamese at all or is mainly shadow script piggybacking on Vietnamese design. The Vietnamese posters and signage are authentic-looking, but Kubrick implants some of his *Clockwork Orange* and *The Shining* illuciferian alarm symbols amid the ravaged Vietnamese architecture, as well as among the Marines' military supplies. One example is when Crazy Earl in Cowboy's troop shows off his kill inside a temple moon gate, a dead Viet Cong soldier that he set in a chair to look as if the dead man was just taking a nap. While Crazy Earl makes a mock eulogy for his deceased enemy, a large woven rice thresher behind him most fittingly displays the zigzag shadow script pattern for insanity, originally exposed in *The Shining*. When trooping behind a tank in an attempt to take Hué city, Cowboy's Sergeant Touchdown gets killed and falls right under the tank's rear supplies, which contains a cardboard box with a left-facing black crescent moon; a satanic moon. The tanks continually show these supplies in addition to fuel jugs with carved shadow script that parody god's-eye weavings (as seen again during Joker's showdown with a sniper), and bumper wire rolls made of repeating infernal S's. Sometimes the tanks brandish wide X's on their sides. All of the above provides evidence Kubrick is making a very definite statement about modern warfare as an intentionally infernal phenomenon. Whatever Kubrick may have said to Herr originally about his new war picture, he fully intended to put his esoteric stamp throughout the actual filming of *Full Metal Jacket*.

In another sequence, a shell-damaged building has at least two gray signs with three large red diamonds outlined in black. The two outside diamonds overlap the center, meeting the other's corner points which forms a big black X. This motif of a large X cutting a diamond's center is an occult sigil for 'War,' a symbol apparently not lost on Kubrick and select members of *Full Metal Jacket*'s prop crew who built it. This X also turns the middle rhomb into four smaller diamonds, which make six to seven diamonds total, if the large, central diamond is included as separate from its smaller divisions. If these are to be counted as seven diamonds, they echo the seven diamond Advanced Beings from *2001*'s Star Gate and a seven-diamond, wan green cloth wall hanging featured in *The Shining*. That puce wall hanging made of both diamonds and XXX's was a warning of illuciferian power perverting thought and imprisoning humanity's ability to spiritually ascend. In *Full Metal Jacket*, the imposing black X superimposed over the diamonds is most likely Kubrick warning about the same diabolical threat. Cowboy himself dies right underneath an upright version of this augmented "War" shadow script with three diamonds and a big X in the center diamond, intimating death of the Third Eye as well as War. Its message in this sad sequence is clear: Ascend or Die.

Later, as Joker's *Stars and Stripes* news crew film Cowboy's troop invading the Vietnamese city of Hué while their camera dolly rolls along, a distant red XXX gate can be seen clearly. Red XXX ironwork makes repeat appearances in *Full Metal Jacket* as either building scaffolding or stairwells. Some gutted windows on fire show XX window frames. A tower block with "Văn Hûę" in pale blue has below it eight black squares, each with a white X inside. Below each X box is four window boxes in a weak blue column. Animal Mother ends up blasting out most of the white X squares and pale blue windows near the "Văn Hûę" sign. On the same wall just above those mentioned we see several rows of stacked chevrons ("chevre" is "goat" in French), this time turned upward to declare illuciferian power. It has sixteen to eighteen chevrons across, and eight chevrons down in columns, each number with important Luciferian symbolism. A second building in the same area has a pinkish "Mỹ Tpăn" sign (together meaning "Perfect" or "Complete" but separately either "America/Beautiful" or "America Finished"), which underneath has it a design of two overlapping diamonds inside a latticed panel. In total the mosaic makes up 18 pieces; a possible 6+6+6 reference. Considering how Animal Mother demolishes the above with strafing gunfire leaves one to ponder the weight of each translation. The two rhombs' points equal eight and may suggest the illuciferian presence influencing or overseeing how the Lusthogs contribute to their hellish environs.

## *Full Metal Jacket*: Misogyny as Original Sin

The inherent misogyny in *Full Metal Jacket,* that in other war films is simply taken for granted as gritty realism, is arguably one of Stanley Kubrick's main important recurring themes. Here, misogynistic dialogue is not used simply for authentic barracks patter but is regularly used to point out misogyny's ingrained presence within the military (and western culture) in general. It comes up so frequently in *Full Metal Jacket* that Kubrick does seem to be making a strong statement about the damage done by normalizing such an ugly mindset. The constant trash talk about women is kept up continuously throughout the film, from Sgt. Hartman's salty troop chants and gun-as-girl soliloquies, Cowboy and Joker's regular friendly ribbing about who sleeps with whose sister (or mother), the new boss Lt. Lockhart explicitly telling Rafterman to get revealing shots of Ann Margaret during her scheduled visit, the "Get Some!" trigger-happy door gunner merrily mowing down peasant women and children, the ever-present barracks skin mag photos on display, to the very end with how the remaining men react to the maimed little girl sniper who had just earlier picked off their mates so effectively. *Full Metal Jacket* has only three stand-out women characters, two of whom are working girls and the third a very young child soldier. The gross underpricing of prostitutes underlines how they are valued as human beings and the appalling scene of one—most likely underage—girl ("Hey there, little schoolgirl!" cat calls Cowboy) who is expected to service the entire squad is exacerbated by the men's base behavior towards her. Not inquiring about the hooker's age may very well be Kubrick illustrating the original U.S. military's "Don't Ask, Don't Tell" policy. As racist Animal Mother grabs her from fellow marine Eightball ("Don't come between a dog and his meat!" Eightball warns) and drags her towards the derelict theater entrance boasting to the rest that he'll "skip the foreplay," one of *Full Metal Jacket*'s biggest Luciferian XXX signs is portrayed on the theater doors they go through as Kubrick's warning for where mankind is shown at its worst.

Since this same scene fades into darkness with the other "Lusthogs" replying to Animal Mother with, "Fuck you!"—one can make the case that *Full Metal Jacket* underscores how such a phrase constantly used denigrates what is supposed to be a physical expression of love into an oft-used degrading epithet—whose dreary, commonplace usage truly does have real corrosive effects on relations between the genders.

## Intentional Continuity Errors in *Full Metal Jacket*

*Full Metal Jacket* has its share of intentional continuity errors. In the *Stars and Stripes* newsroom stationed at one of the U.S. military bases near

## 16. A Woman's Take on Full Metal Jacket        151

Saigon, Joker and his younger friend Rafterman listen to the newsroom Editor Lt. Lockhart review their submissions for the next issue and gives advice on what to write and how to write it. Behind their boss' head is a big red banner with yellow lettering that reads, "First To Know And Last To Go," with the amusing subtitle "We defend to the death your right to be misinformed." In the first scene of the newsroom the banner doesn't have anything near it, but in the second scene, after their base is attacked, a large yellow Snoopy stands left of the banner. Photos and comic strip art festoon the length of the wall opposite. While the news reporters talk, the camera goes around the room showing Charlie Brown in uniform brandishing a sword towards another yellow Snoopy punting a bomb on a pale blue background, reminiscent of Mickey Mouse kicking a football on one of Danny's blue sweaters in *The Shining*. As most people familiar with the Peanuts comic strip know that Snoopy is always depicted as a white dog, his yellow visage gives support to *Full Metal Jacket* having a color code like most of Kubrick's previous films. In both *Clockwork Orange* and *The Shining*, yellow was the color of Death, and wan, weak hues were corrupted forms of what their purer, vibrant shades represented in *2001: A Space Odyssey*. Snoopy's light blue background may either represent higher consciousness à la *2001* or its polar opposite, weak consciousness. In the second newsroom scene this same picture of punting Snoopy has a mini magenta lampshade with a black skirt above Snoopy's head that originally wasn't there. That lampshade's coloring perhaps depicts how the ability to self-illuminate is blocked by inadequate consciousness. Operating mainly in survival mode on a military base in wartime is sure to snuff out anyone's ability to self-illuminate.

Comic book characters feature prominently in *Full Metal Jacket*. Mickey Mouse and Snoopy make frequent appearances either on screen or are mentioned in speech, especially Mickey Mouse. Not only does their presence suggest a certain American immaturity or naiveté on the grounds of a much older South Asian culture, but Kubrick may in particular be using such comforting imagery as a way to telegraph significant messages. Close ups on Joker as he verbally ripostes with his senior officer in the newsroom reveal three Mickey figurines on the windowsill behind him. One Mickey wears a red shirt with blue shorts and sits on a pale blue stand. His eyes are directed at another Mickey to his left, one that wears a yellow shirt with red shorts, and next to him lies, rather disconcertingly, just a decapitated Mickey head without a body. The window glass behind them is curiously purple colored and happens to be double monolith-sized panes. These purple glass panels recall the rectangular windows in *2001*'s moonbus revealing a violet moonscape. The red and blue Mickey can embody Masonic colors for the duality of earth (red, female principle) and heaven (blue, male principle). His pale blue stand conveys either undeveloped or higher consciousness that "Masonic Mickey" surveys /controls while keeping an eye on the Mickey with the yellow (Life or Death) and red (Seat of Consciousness or Material Realm) coloring. The disembodied Mickey head can exemplify the warning: "Ascend or Die." Later, Masonic Mickey is seen *pointing to* the purplish window glass, inviting viewers to take note of it. This reinforces that the Masonic colors red and blue together make purple, which is why purple is both seen as the union of heaven and earth and is also the crown chakra color for ascension as covered in *A Space Odyssey*. The Mickeys first seen behind Joker in the second newsroom scene later disappear from view altogether during another Joker close up, a definite Kubrick signal for his audience to pay attention and try to interpret what is being presented.

A third example of intentional continuity errors happens during the filming of Cowboy's Lusthog city raid of Hué. Several of the men in his troop are interviewed, and Animal Mother, the toughest grunt there, is filmed in front of a tank. The first two times the camera is on Animal Mother, a wide X is shown on the side of the tank behind him. On the third shot, there is no "X" on the tank when Animal Mother replies, "…as Americans, of course we want to win." As Cowboy answers questions, a grotesque, screaming head emerges out of wreckage behind him. Shadow script lurks behind Eightball as he talks while Snowball's interview is overseen by a face made of stone ruins.

The hunting-of-the-sniper sequence reveals Joker carefully entering a burning building, where he passes two ornate steel guardrail partitions, one nearest him and the distant other covered with a dark green and dark red Viet Cong flag. The upper center of the flag is a big inverted pentagram. So if this is a true Viet Cong flag, it is upside down. Through the fire, the flag looks black and red, giving it a more satanic look than South Asian. The steel guardrails are based on actual Vietnamese temple screens whose iconography has been purposefully profaned. Their centers have inverted swastikas (originally benign four-direction symbols) that also double for interlocking satanic "lightning bolt" S's and flipped S's. As Joker slowly creeps by the gate, the inverted pentagram in the background moves along too, highlighting the shadow script "L"-for-Lucifer shapes that make up much of the gate frames. Many of the illuciferian motifs masquerading as Vietnamese decorative flourishes contain inverted and flipped "L" shapes, similar to matching Vietnamese motifs but are perverted and exaggerated. The flames raging behind a decorative screen framing the startled girl sniper illuminate still more shadow script. This time the decoration takes on the appearance of X's framing diamonds that in turn bind or imprison a central diamond representing womankind and/or the Earth. Like the scenes featuring the city working girl and the motorbike prostitute, here we have another occurrence where some of the most prominent illuciferian sigils appear where women are either in imminent danger or are being devalued.

Joker and company singing the "Mickey Mouse Club" theme at the end of the movie is yet another hint to pay attention to all the other Mickey Mouse references Stanley Kubrick purposefully put into *Full Metal Jacket*. Same goes for Sergeant Hartman's "What is this Mickey Mouse bullshit?!" outburst. Unlike Private Leonard "Pyle" whose inner child was essentially destroyed during the new marine recruits' merciless training, the surviving soldiers singing a children's TV theme song as the film closes appear to revert back to childhood, at least momentarily, as they march into a brave new world scorched by fire and poisoned gas, some of it courtesy of Monsanto, makers of the fetal-destroying Agent Orange. Somewhere in Vietnam there is a museum dedicated to the effects of war where several horrifically deformed fetuses and babies are on display, victims of the abominable Agent Orange.

## The Color Code of *Full Metal Jacket*

*Full Metal Jacket* effectively contains both the positive color code system of *2001: A Space Odyssey* and its colors' polar opposite meanings demonstrated within *Clockwork Orange* and *The Shining*. The island barracks Leonard, Joker, Cowboy, and Snowball share has a mainly pale green interior with a red floor. As the previously mentioned Kubrick films have established pale green as representing destructive perversion or evil mindedness, together with the red floor symbolizing both Danger and the Seat of Consciousness, the military ideal of the barracks being a healthy environment conducive for marine trainee development does not bode well where the color symbolism in *Full Metal Jacket* is concerned.

Pasted to the *Stars and Stripes* newsroom walls is a large yellow fan with a dark red or dark magenta handle. The photos next to it may help determine whether its yellow stands for life or if it stands for death. The newsroom interior itself is painted yellow, and considering the message its red banner emblazons, perhaps yellow in *Full Metal Jacket* also stands for yellow journalism, with yellow Snoopy in part representing the *Stars and Stripes* "newshounds." Joker's boss Lt. Lockhart makes no bones about it: their paper's job is to win "hearts and minds" and provide proof of the Vietnam War's relevance and effectiveness.

Dark pink smoke is the first sight to greet Joker and Rafterman when they jump off the helicopter they shared with the gung-ho door gunner to go find where the "enemy action" was the "hottest." If bright pink-purple colors in *A Space Odyssey* allude to self-illumination, then the billowing dark pink gas acts as a literal smoke screen that blocks self-illumination, or represents unconsciousness, in *Full Metal Jacket*.

The almost jovial, matter-of-fact way team leader Sgt. Touchdown being interviewed by Joker calmly discusses how the white-powdered Vietnamese in the lime ditch were killed is quite chilling. How it happened was essentially a dirty trick done by the U.S. troops to weed out potential "leaders and troublemakers" by knocking on all village doors to inform the male inhabitants to report back for "re-education." The unfortunate souls that actually bothered to show up were shot for their troubles and ended up in the ditch. White in *2001* portrayed Life's Essence and in *Clockwork Orange* and *The Shining* it conveyed Innocence as well as Life's Essence (the Self), which in this sad instance makes for a poignant scene in *Full Metal Jacket*.

The burnt sky glowing yellow at the end of *Full Metal Jacket* while Joker and the remaining Lusthogs sing the Mickey Mouse Club theme song is a sobering use of Kubrick's Color Code. As the squad sings, they go marching off into a yellow firestorm of Death.

The final song for the rolling credits is the Rolling Stones' "Paint It Black." The first line is a possible *Full Metal Jacket* color cue referring back to the satanic symbolism on the red and black painted props (like the derelict movie theater doors with XXX window frames) and all the other color-coded "wake-up humanity" warning motifs entrenched within *Full Metal Jacket*.

## How *Full Metal Jacket* Connects to *Clockwork Orange* and *The Shining*

*Full Metal Jacket* surreptitiously hides horrors in a similar manner as *Clockwork Orange* and *The Shining*. In the sequence when in Vietnam, Joker finds his best friend from the Marines training island, he sees Cowboy shaving inside a Vietnamese temple that his platoon had previously shot up, contained, and now occupies. As the combative Animal Mother goads Joker and Rafterman takes photos of Crazy Earl posing with a dead Vietnamese soldier, the rest of the platoon relaxes, leaning against the pockmarked temple walls. However, the walls are not all that they seem. The wall behind Animal Mother and the one behind Rafterman (when he crouches with a camera) are filled with frightening faces, some demonic and skull-like, while others hold clues to Kubrick's esoteric symbolism within the film. Where Eightball sits, his rifle rests on one of the larger demonic faces, its grimacing mouth with black teeth hover threateningly over Eightball and his nearby comrades. The wall behind camera-clicking Rafterman has a particularly evil head right above his own, and next to it on the left is a trio of scary grotesques. The first one of these looks like a despondent or melting face made out of exposed brick, and behind it lurks a menacing darker visage that is then followed by an even scarier leering face that links back to the horrible skull right above Rafterman's head. Still farther to the left on the same wall, is a more cartoony face (perhaps feminine) with large eyes shedding what appear to be diamond shaped tears. The other previously described ghoulish faces stand for a man shedding his humanity, masks behind masks. Behind Animal Mother, the entry door wall showcases great jeering demons, some fading half-in and half-out from its surface. The wall where the killed Vietnamese soldier sits has giant demonic faces slowly emerging from scorched plaster. Such disturbing imagery provides a canvas duplicating the platoon's own loss of humanity. Kubrick's using this "writing on the wall" technique to communicate messages not only harkens back to the brick illuminati pyramid and contorted faces inside *Clockwork Orange*'s prison walls, but also correlates to how walls and furnishings contain terrifying clues in both *Clockwork Orange*'s state, city, and home living spaces and within *The Shining*'s Overlook hotel. The above scene exemplifies Kubrick's method of putting symbolic imagery near people's heads as well.

Like *Clockwork Orange* and *The Shining*, *Full Metal Jacket* has more than its fair share of illuciferian warning signs. From the satanic crescent moon boxes riding tanks, the several X to XXX signs strewn across battlefields and destroyed buildings, Marine DonLon's Alabama confederate flag with X's instead of stars on his helmet, Eightball's helmet doubling as a veiled Luciferian reference to the eight-pointed morning star, the zigzag insanity shadow script making a comeback from *The Shining*, the Lusthogs' inner demons hiding in the above-mentioned shelled temple walls, and Joker's encounter with ultimate evil at the end of the film, proves *Full Metal Jacket* is well stocked with occult imagery that is highly unusual for a war picture. Certain metaphysical motifs repeat, and *Full Metal Jacket* introduces a new shadow script glyph that is seen both on portable gallon tanks and the hellish lattice screen behind the discovered sniper. It looks similar to a four-pronged power pinwheel enclosing a central diamond. It can either be a Luciferian rhomb or an entrapped female/earth symbol its four power rods are binding. The flaming screen has multiple patterns, one where a Luciferian X ensnares a diamond, also upward-pointing chevron stacks indicating satanic power and a woven 'senses snare' shadow script. Even the girl sniper's scarf contains shadow script: it is a pale green cloth (perversion) covered in black checkerboard mesh, the curse sigil for "to keep in darkness." In the scenario the sniper finds herself in, one can certainly see that she is *a child* choking in a darkness created by the evil-mindedness of manufactured war.

## How *Full Metal Jacket* Connects to *2001: A Space Odyssey*

Out of all of Kubrick's pictures after *2001*, *Full Metal Jacket* may be the least likely to be deemed having any remote connection to *A Space Odyssey* after *Barry Lyndon*. It is by many accounts his most realistic, current, and least surreal film. Yet there are elements of surrealism that exist in *Full Metal Jacket*. The sight of new marine recruits praying to their guns in bed, the jarring image of overgrown Private Pyle tagging last behind marching exercises with his pants down and thumb in his mouth, the light effects on Joker's unrealistic torchlight and a helicopter's pastel aura are soft-spoken instances of surrealism. One other beyond-real scene is the sight of a camera crew filming a battle as it happens, including interviewing the soldiers as chaos reigns about them. Though filming live war footage is a reality that has preserved important historic events, Kubrick actually filming filmmakers' film such combat creates a strange kind of cognitive dissonance, a sort of eerie reverberating, cinematic feedback loop.

One of *2001: A Space Odyssey*'s serious tropes is duality that spans throughout its runtime. Joker's peace symbol pin and "Born to Kill" helmet is an attempt at a more lighthearted take on duality in the most grim of circumstances. When he is grilled about his peace pin by a senior officer, Joker responds by declaring, "I was trying to suggest something about the duality of man ... the Jungian thing, Sir!"

*Full Metal Jacket*'s main symbols of duality are, first and foremost, the new marines themselves as their personalities change through the crucible of war, some to an almost bipolar extreme, such as Rafterman. First Rafterman threw up at the sight of women and children being strafed with gunfire and later went to grinning maniacally at the flush of his first kill, a child soldier. The second is visually symbolic, the round temple Moon Gate Joker and Rafterman walk through to meet Cowboy, versus the deceptively ornate, pale green and satanic red round window where Joker encounters the girl sniper. The first-round gate, being part of a temple, is holy. In the sniper's holdout, the round latticed window surrounded by flames and next to an inverted pentagram, is actually a large consolidation of shadow script sigils (similar to the Overlook's lobby floors). Each lattice section from left to right, top to bottom counts to eight power rod partitions for the Luciferian "morning star." In the center is a swastika shape that balloons out to a large X that doubles as a big binding spell. The whole window makes up a giant X-in-O sign, an illuciferian Fulfillment declaration of power as well as another "Luciferian Sun" sigil. The infernal window also has two small lines at each of its cardinal points, which just happen to mark the points of entry for a satanic circle's Gate of Inception.

To reinforce the situation's evil, Joker and later Cowboy are seen near columns with torn remnants of black and white posters of clenched fists with XXX on their sleeves (a symbolic shout-out to *Clockwork Orange*). The girl herself is first seen behind another steelwork gate whose elements are flipped Luciferian 'L's that form larger flipped satanic S's. Just before the twelve-year-old girl is shot, the camera sees Joker's partially melted column from a new angle, where

## 16. A Woman's Take on Full Metal Jacket

Joker is pinned between a flag's inverted pentagram on his right, and on his left reveals a most terrifying demonic visage wearing what looks to be a small, black, crucified baby head (Death of Innocence) speared on an inverted cross, which is also ingeniously a profaned *2001* Third Eye † glyph. Above the demonic head are the words "Doan Ket," which has the dual Vietnamese meaning of "Unite" or "The End/Ending" depending on the diacritics used.

Most Kubrick films after *A Space Odyssey* have a scene with mirrors in the background, usually in bathrooms. In *Full Metal Jacket*, there are no mirrors at all in the island barracks' bathroom, which amplify the feeling of being cut off from oneself. The only mirror in the entirety of *Full Metal Jacket* is Cowboy's small, round mirror that invokes the same shape of the temple doors he and his troop have entered and taken claim of. The significance of this reflects the mirror's ability to aid self-illumination. That Cowboy's mirror is located on the right side of the screen is another indication of it being a positive symbol. But as an example of contrasting duality, the round temple door itself in turn mimics Cowboy's mirror and thereby through its walls, holds up the inner reflections of the other Lusthog marines in a quite disturbing Dorian Gray–style group portrait.

A third scene showing specifically Masonic duality comes just after a Vietnamese boy steals Rafterman's camera. The working girl near Rafterman wears a red tank top and a black mini skirt. Opposite on Joker's left side (but to the audience's right) is a placard of a praying Jesus wearing blue on a black background. The girl and Jesus together exemplify Masonic red (female, earth) and blue (male, heaven) principles and share the color black, the Source color where everything first originated. To emphasize this, above the Jesus sign is a shop sign with a red pentagram (female, earth, good) and an inverted pea green pentagram (profaned earth/star symbol, bad). The other positive feminine reinforcement is the Hot Xoan ("diamond") sign with two red diamond shapes with diamond stones inside each. The diamond <> is an ancient African symbol that is virtually synonymous with the Earth and the divine feminine. Diamonds appear again as the cross-like lights in the newsroom grunts' barracks and also hidden within a temple wall as clues to their meaning. As in *2001*, the diamond/rhomb shape and the "T" for Third Eye surface in *Full Metal Jacket* as symbols for accessing the human ability for ascension. In relevant instances of showcasing duality, the inverted "†" also makes grim appearances within *Full Metal Jacket*. The inverted "†" in *Full Metal Jacket* stands for the same extreme negative (as in evil) polarity as *A Space Odyssey*'s inverted "i" sigil did in the form of HAL.

*Full Metal Jacket* carries on *A Space Odyssey*'s color purple as a symbol for self-illumination. Kubrick's Vietnam movie puts forward most of the color code he previously set up in either or all three films *A Space Odyssey*, *Clockwork Orange*, and *The Shining*. It also champions the diamond shape, either as symbol for earth/womanhood and/or the seven rhombs representing the physical symbol of self-illumination. In *Full Metal Jacket*, the seven ascension diamonds are usually seen sublimated by an infernal X. Seen as three large diamond shapes they also symbolize our eyes (like the diamond tears on a temple wall), with the Third Eye being ominously X'd out while doubling as the shadow script for War. Either way of viewing this symbol means the same thing: the ability to ascend being destroyed by human evil.

*Full Metal Jacket* also exhibits several Kubrickian intentional continuity errors as hidden messages; similar techniques done before in *2001*, *Clockwork Orange*, and *The Shining*. In addition, Stanley Kubrick's last war movie utilizes lighting and props as message signifiers, cinematic techniques that were engaged within most of his preceding films. The issue of trauma so well covered in *Clockwork Orange* and *The Shining* is explored again, this time within a military environment. We watch as each new recruit's identity is shaved off in more ways than one, with some adjusting better to corps discipline than others. We see the dark side released even in our favorite protagonists due to the dehumanizing consequences of battle. No one comes out of war unscathed, and by the end of the film Joker has achieved his Thousand Yard Stare. The sequential stripping away from Private Lawrence (now Leonard Pyle) of his sense of self, self-worth and inner child is one of the most heart-rending scenes in *Full Metal Jacket*.

## Anagrams and Word Play in *Full Metal Jacket*

It is possible that hidden anagrams exist in the Vietnamese city signage and some names of *Full Metal Jacket*'s cast of characters.

There is a surprising amount of wordplay within *Full Metal Jacket*. As the first working girl walks towards Rafterman and Joker, the song "These Boots are Made for Walking" plays in the background. The shop sign for Hot Xoan ("Diamonds") is symbolically right above the orange sign where the working girls have congregated. The "Hynos" toothpaste ad with the pea green fonts is an anagram for the old English word "Hyson" for green tea. The orange sign "Con-Nai" above the bordello Rafterman and Joker sit next to (and most likely patronize) means "deer" as appropriate to the deer images on the signage. Deer in Vietnam symbolize innocence, as generally most women don't choose to do sex work but through life's circumstances are either forced into or are sadly born into it. A stark yellow and black sign "Las Vegas" really reads as "AS VEGAS" since the "L" is more of a black border that's pointing to where the two marines are sitting. The most likely anagram for "AS VEGAS" is "SAVAGES," so that Stanley Kubrick is effectively calling out Joker and Rafterman's behavior in this scene where they talk down the hooker's already low price for "everything." Thus, *Full Metal Jacket*'s so-called "nice guy" protagonists get a silent tongue-lashing from the director's subtle use of signage.

As stated earlier, "Mỹ Tpān" is a sign seen on top of a building in the city the Lusthog squad invade. "Mỹ Tpān" means "Perfect" together but separately the words most likely translate as "Complete/Finish America" or "America Finished," which may be Kubrick commentary on the grunts playful but caustic movie-making quips while being filmed taking the city of Huế: "'T.H.E. Rock' will star as a rock," "I'll be Ann Margaret," "Animal Mother can be a rabid buffalo," "I'll be General Custer," "Well, who will play the Indians?" which ends with Animal Mother himself saying, "We'll let the Gooks play the Indians," as a flippant aside to America's (and Europe's) long history of colonial genocide.

Deer Symbolism in *Full Metal Jacket*: As deer represent innocence, deer do seem to be a recurring theme in *Full Metal Jacket*. There is the scene where Private Leonard Pyle literally shoots Sergeant *Hart*man right through the heart, a more symbolic act than previously realized. Newsroom chief Lt. Lockhart's name may not only infer what marines must do to survive the hell of war, but also serves as a reminder to what Joker's *Stars and Stripes* real news purpose is: to capture "hearts and minds." Deer are featured on the orange Con-Nai ("deer") sign above the brothel entrance Joker and Rafterman just happen to be hanging out nearby. The innocence of the Vietnamese women forced into prostitution is killed just as Pvt. Pyle's innocence was killed in Sgt. Hartman's relentlessly brutal training. Due to their current conditions, both have been chewed up and spat out by those that capriciously use them.

"Con O Ben" ("Black Eagle") on the beer sign across the street from Joker and Rafterman creates the English anagram "No Bonce" which is slang for "No Head," an interesting anagram for a beer ad. "La Ve Hâo Hang" on the same beer sign is Vietnamese for "First Class Beer." "Con-Nai" the deer sign creates the anagram "A Nonic" in English that just happens to stand for a type of "No Nick" pint glass. Appropriately for the women involved, the deer in the Con-Nai ad appear to be in "non-nonic" shaped glasses themselves, in other words, "nick-able" glasses. Beer imagery features throughout *Full Metal Jacket* as well, and quite a few times bottles and cans are placed in the foreground or somewhere prominent to be noticed, including nonic and non-nonic glasses. There are times in the film where both women on display from magazines and cans or glasses of beer are displayed prominently within the same scene, usually within a barracks. The strong evidence that both beer and deer imagery are linked may well be Kubrick's stern warning of the dire consequences of mankind "consuming" innocence like a mere commodity. It continues *A Space Odyssey*'s "vessel-as-body" trope as well.

Lastly, there is Animal Mother's name. His character and personality are the direct opposite of what the shamanic term "Animal Mother" originally means, and yet his role in the film truly juxtaposes what an Animal Mother purportedly does in shamanism. Traditionally in Siberian and ancient South Asian tribal cultures a shaman must take an Animal Mother, usually a female deer, as a visionary guide through the spirit realms.[2] In the book *Short-Timers*, "Animal Mother" is a belligerent, rapacious, violent, adrenalin junkie who was a sergeant demoted to a grunt for flipping off a superior officer. He serves as the Lusthogs' Animal Mother, being their devolved spirit guide through the hellscape of war. As an entirely ruthless yet loyal soldier, Animal Mother to a certain extent is someone the others look up to.

But beware the role model whose helmet reads: "I Am Become Death."

## 17

# The Uncanny *Eyes Wide Shut* Connection

**Venetian mask with Luciferian motifs (photograph by Klassenlehrer/Pixabay).**

Out of all of Kubrick's films that came afterwards, it is *Eyes Wide Shut* that surprisingly makes the most direct references to *2001*. We're not just talking one-offs like the *Space Odyssey* soundtrack cameo in *Clockwork Orange* or the "Best Bowman" building ad in *Eyes Wide Shut* either. *2001*'s fingerprints appear all over *Eyes Wide Shut* throughout its entire runtime. It appears as he was making his last movie, Stanley Kubrick wanted to leave clues linking back to his sci-fi classic whose deeply esoteric surface was as yet barely scratched by film critics. Perhaps, more than any other of his past films, Kubrick felt the need for people to revisit *A Space Odyssey* and discover its deeper spiritual layers, not just its technological and futuristic themes. As someone aware of his own advancing mortality and concern for the state of the world as it was, this cinematic self-referencing of Kubrick's most important work seems a sort of clarion call, especially in light of *Eyes Wide Shut*'s more sinister subject matter. Kubrick was very keen to finish *Eyes Wide Shut*, a work he considered his greatest contribution to film, so much so he was willing to cut his losses and hand over to Steven Spielberg the reigns of their ambitious blockbuster project *A.I.*, which started as a joint enterprise between them.[1]

It is understandable if people first balk at Kubrick considering his deceptively low-key drama *Eyes Wide Shut* as approaching anything near the grandeur of a film like *A Space Odyssey*, so it is worth taking a closer look at *EWS* to see why Kubrick thought this was his best film to date. In the story, as main protagonists Bill and Alice Harford get ready to leave their spacious NY apartment to attend a swank, pre–Christmas Eve party held by one of Bill's wealthiest patients, Victor Ziegler, the camera passes through the Harford's rooms and a hallway bedecked with paintings, one in particular being a large painting of a cat (painted by Katherina Kubrick) and other paintings which either contain cat imagery or hidden demonic faces. The couple's own bed headboard has a flipped, old English "S" (*f*) border which flanks "illumination crowns" disguised as flowers, another common Left Hand Path motif found in *EWS*.

It is a bit incongruous when at the party dance Alice asks Bill, "Why do you think they (the Zieglers) keep inviting us to these parties?" Yet when the Harfords first come through the Zieglers' grand entrance, it is Alice who first kisses Mrs. Ziegler on the left cheek, which indicates more familiarity than mere acquaintance. This suggests Alice knew the Zieglers before Bill and may have even originally introduced Bill to the Zieglers. Another curious thing Alice does when Bill wants to meet an old school friend (Nick Nightingale) turned pianist, Alice excuses herself by saying, "I desperately need to go to the bathroom." Yet when she leaves, the first thing she does is guzzle down a drink and does not go to the powder room at all, which gives the impression she was either simply not interested in meeting Nick or for some reason wanted to avoid him.

After that, both Alice and Bill get waylaid by rather ardent admirers. Alice finds herself dancing with a charming, Hungarian silver fox while Bill gets hit on by two flirtatious models. As both move around the Zieglers' palatial mansion, save for a few oddly lit Christmas trees, there is actually very little in the way of traditional Christmas décor. The wreaths and lighting look unusual or just odd to people unaware of their symbolism. Pentagram flowers top curling branches of overly large light wall displays. The bright light-bulbed curling branches themselves are typical baroque Luciferian spirals, stolen from ancient Near East and Greco-Roman styles.

Another appropriated Near East symbol is Inanna's eight-pointed star (Venus) which Luciferians have arrogantly claimed as their light bringer's "morning star." Stanley Kubrick rightfully restores this star back to the divine feminine as Alice's head is constantly crowned with the large lighted star again and again as she's twirled around the room in a quite impressive camera one-shot. Tom only gets framed with this light-bulbed star once or twice, so Alice being repeatedly haloed in Inanna's eight rayed star reinforces what it originally stands for and to whom it historically belongs. In contrast, the oversized "lady lamps" at Somerton House are super-sized "light bringers," symbolizing the Luciferian concept of achieving Illumination through Darkness.

On the same theme, the Harford's apartment, and especially Ziegler's and the Somerton Estate display strangely pronounced and at times brightly painted furnishings whose marked largeness literally sticks out for notice. The Harfords' apartment is stuffed with paintings, many whose size and number dominate the rooms to the point of overwhelm. It has been noted before that the Harfords' Manhattan abode is too stately and spacious even for a successful doctor, which Bill virtually explains when he informs Alice, "This is what you get, when you make house calls [for the wealthy]." Another of Bill's rich patients, the dying Lou Nathanson (Marion's father) resides in an extravagant apartment built of expensive marbles, guarded by tall and imposing ornate iron torch stands, displaying sculpture, collections and paintings of decorative funerary urns. Victor Ziegler's princely bathroom has a fireplace, which is highly unusual even for luxury mansions of its era. The bathroom fireplace that drugged (or dissociating) Mandy sits next to, features oversized Agathodemons masquerading as monstrous fish, a Kubrickian tactic to get people thinking, "What do *fish* have to do with a fireplace ... and why is there a fireplace in the *bathroom*?" The bathroom wainscoting and window seat are done in a bold green with gold inset rectangular trim, shadow script for "power over ignorance." This is contrasted by Mandy wearing a large "pearl beyond price" ring, seated in a vibrant red sofa chair while wrapped in a blue blanket that matches the blue fireplace "fish." Above Victor Ziegler's head as he attempts to explain Mandy's condition is a large, very red portrait of a pregnant woman, the masonic color most associated with the feminine/earth principle. An intentional clash of color symbolism appears to be going on here, with Mandy sitting in a satanic-colored seat swathed in the benevolent blue masons traditionally associate with heaven and the male principle, juxtaposed against the fierce, blue agathodemons and the red-for-feminine powers painting. Throughout *Eyes Wide Shut*, the double-meanings for red and blue continually swap or oppose each other, with the originally "heavenly male" color often associating with the feminine or the earth (bright, blue-lit windows indicating the world outside), and the age-old, fertile feminine/

earth red being co-opted or contrasted with the more masculine, satanic red of the Sonata Jazz Club, Somerton House's carpeting, and Victor Ziegler's unusually-colored pool table. It is hard to see kindly Sydney Pollack portraying a callous monster, but he does a good job of it, as Victor's paternal, condescending tone to a woman whom he just used in a bathroom (real class, there) underplays the situation as a normal occurrence, just as Bill's "gentleman's agreement" with Victor to keep it quiet is meant to be taken in stride. The call girl was to be promptly dismissed as soon as she came to until Bill Harford intervened, but his acquiescence to stay mum about the incident still makes Bill an accomplice to a much-abused "male honor" code.

How women negotiate, maneuver, and are in turn manipulated by today's still male-dominated society is showcased through the actions of *Eyes Wide Shut*'s female cast. Alice Harford exercises her intuition by continually honing in on the most salient point of what is being discussed. She is also good at calling out men on their self-delusions. Alice holds her own against her overly aggressive would-be suitor at Ziegler's party, nailing the true moral of the seasoned sophisticate Sandor Szavost's posturing on Ovid's *Art of Love*: "Didn't he [Ovid] end up all alone, crying his eyes out, in some place with a *very* bad climate?" she counters. When Alice's dance partner becomes too insistent, she wrests her arm away from Szavost while still letting him down easy, as he previously suggested he could provide Alice future employment in her preferred field of art gallery work. When Bill later visits his other rich patient, Lou Nathanson who just died, he eventually finds out the mourning daughter, Marion, has a crush on him. The gold chair she sits in forms a soul sigil textured in darkness crosshatching. When her fiancé Carl shows up, he turns out to be a poor-man's doppelganger of Bill Harford, Marion's consolation prize in place of the doctor she cannot have. Mandy, the call girl, is making money however she can, given her not-so-fortunate circumstances compared to securely-married Alice and the bereaved rich daughter, Marion. Considering the psychology textbooks in Mandy's shabby apartment, she or her roommate are putting themselves through college. Unfortunately, Mandy's economic situation renders her more vulnerable to exploitation. "Sorry, maid's day off," Mandy sheepishly jokes to Bill Harford when they enter her rundown, messy apartment.

It is curious that most of the main women characters in *Eyes Wide Shut* have red hair, especially the Harford's young daughter, Helena. The color red refers to earth, life, and the feminine powers in Masonic iconography. It is also a reference to Aleister Crowley's Thelemic appropriation of the Scarlet Woman (the Whore of Babylon, an age-old, hoary desecration of the Mother Goddess),[2] in another attempt of Kubrick to lift up and resacralize that which has been denigrated within the Divine Feminine, namely natural female sexuality. In addition, almost every female main character in *Eyes Wide Shut* wears some semblance of red, purple, or blue colors of the Goddess (Mary) or "Whore of Babylon" in the New Testament's Revelations.

Though at first glance, *Eyes Wide Shut* can be viewed as having a harsh misogynistic edge, it is interesting to note that *Eyes Wide Shut*'s cast and crew end credits boast an impressive number of women working on the film in significant movie positions. It certainly rosters more female crew members than the average box-office movie hired at the time. As similarly covered in *Clockwork Orange*, *The Shining*, and *Full Metal Jacket*, Kubrick's last film seems more of a final treatise against the deeply entrenched misogyny of those who truly run Western civilization and its ramifications throughout the modern world's cultural and social strata.

## *2001* Symbolism in *Eyes Wide Shut*

Like *A Space Odyssey*, *Eyes Wide Shut* consistently repeats the monolith shape. It appears as apartment vents, floor tiles, ground mats, sidewalk sections, window panes, display cases, rotating doors, wall paneling, signage, columns, and paintings: particularly the huge monolith-shaped one in the Harfords' dining room, invoking Grid Field duality (Christiane Kubrick's *Seedbox Theater*). The monolith image simply shows up much too frequently (often in pairs) to be merely coincidental and while open to different approaches in capturing a scene, Kubrick was famous for being meticulous about a shot's set-up. While considering this, the prevalence of paintings, Alice's gallery work, and Bill's medical profession can be an allusion or doppelganger to the Kubricks themselves, as Christiane is a painter and Stanley could have been a doctor had he followed in his father's footsteps. The fact that the Kubrick family's own furniture furnish much of the Harfords' apartment is another clue as to whom the Harfords may double for.

The diamond is a frequent symbol all through *Eyes Wide Shut* too. In *2001*, it appears sparingly as an entity of great import and double-meaning: both as Perfected Being (flying octahedron) and the Divine Feminine/Earthly Realm (yoni figure). In *Eyes Wide Shut*, this shape continues emphasizing the Divine Feminine since among the movie's core topics is the many sociological ramifications of being a woman (married, single, working class, or otherwise) in modern society. The diamond is seen in Alice's party dress, as vent screens, blankets, slanted Christmas cards, rug patterns, marble floors, and in various architectural motifs. Sometimes it is accompanied by hidden ankhs, Inanna's stolen eight-pointed star, or other Goddess imagery such as fleur-de-lis wallpaper and Helena's Birth Goddess–like (or her mother in cape with cowl) kitchen fridge doodle. Along with the monolith, the diamond is *Eyes Wide Shut*'s most ubiquitous hidden symbol. Throughout the movie, its dualistic opposite is the double Luciferian rhomb, either nested inside one another or side-by-side. These versions are derivative Luciferian palimpsests claiming Venus as their now-masculine morning star while staking their claim of dominion over the Earth for themselves.

Another example of the sacred feminine is Kubrick invoking the Goddess Trinity concept again as he did in *2001*. One of the biggest clues lies in *Eyes Wide Shut*'s end credits: it is shown that actually three actresses play the same woman character: Mandy, who is also Domino (alter/call girl name indicating her classic Venetian mask and her potential posthumous AIDS revenge on the evil elites), and when masked at the black mass she is billed as the Mysterious Woman. This harks back to the Goddess Trinity appearing as the three women scientists in *A Space Odyssey* and in a sadder and more unrecognized way, the three main ladies featured in *Full Metal Jacket*. Kubrick's familiarity with Frazier's *The Golden Bough* and Campbell's *Hero with a Thousand Faces* would inform him of such ancient mythic archetypes.[3] At one point in her apartment, Mandy takes off her female-chevron fur coat, revealing gold lining inside and a smaller purple jacket with light blue 'Y's on it. The symbolism underlines Mandy as the precious woman she is, the light blue 'Y's-as-Vavs as conduits of Higher Consciousness. Her Y-necked purple dress underneath completes the three sacred six's, presenting Mandy as Divine Union made flesh.

In contrast, those who might claim that *Eyes Wide Shut* has no satanic symbolism because Red Cloak sports no horns and carries no pitchfork need only look at Bill Harford's mask if they wish to see devils. Bill has quite an evil one right on his forehead, complete with flipped S horns and leering face created from an inverted palmette-styled third eye. Above that is an even larger eye that can double for the Evil Eye and the "Illuminati" Eye. Ever since *Lolita*, Kubrick has presented these as one in the same. Devils decorate the walls of Somerton, hiding in plain sight. There are two quite frightening ones to be found within the marbled surroundings of Marion's deceased father. Demonic visages haunt and hunt Harford through the streets of New York wherever he goes and visits.

The *2001* portal () sign unmistakably shows up in Bill's office lobby as two yellow tables. It also is seen as neon signs, hospital hallway lights, and reflections. Another *2001* reference which contrasts with the ankh symbols is the inverted **i**, the anti-life symbol which exposed HAL for what he really represents. The inverted **i** is found as wall paneling within an opulent marble hallway and on hospital walls in *Eyes Wide Shut*. To spiritually combat this, **i**'s also reappear as Third Eye sigils on floors and wall paintings, often on the same set where ()'s or –**i**'s are. The **i** sigil is yet one more regularly occurring *2001* motif throughout *Eyes Wide Shut*; it is almost as frequent as the monolith and diamond glyphs.

## Lighting and Anagrams in *Eyes Wide Shut*

As they were mostly overlooked in *A Space Odyssey* (and his other films), Stanley Kubrick employs lighting as a signifier again in *Eyes Wide Shut* but this time in more obvious ways (for Kubrick) than the much subtler lighting techniques used in *2001* and *Clockwork Orange*. Anagrams can appear as names or street signage. The most fitting anagram for the deceased Lou Nathanson is NO SOUL NATHAN, considering the hidden horrors on his deathbed headboard and throughout his stately residence which confirm Lou's Left Hand Path loyalty.

Other examples are when Tom Cruise's Bill Harford walks around New York and becomes aware he's being followed. On the buildings behind him shine shafts of light in the literal shape of hands pointing at examples of Kubrick wordplay in city signage; the shop name "Krysete" turns out to be an anagram of "SEEK, TRY." After Bill is accosted by drunk frat boys, he walks under a satanic-haloed streetlight whose white shaft beams pointedly towards a strangely designed Christmas tree image mounted on a building. It is made out of "branches" of increasing size from top to bottom whose segments turns out to be upside-down "horned suns" or profaned boteh (Middle East/India fertility/wealth symbol) motifs. Another instance is when Bill enters a hospital to inquire about Mandy at the front desk. Between Bill and the lady helping him is a computer whose screen displays a hand-like graphic that juts its finger at some demonic lights on the hospital lobby Christmas tree. Light effects are in turn put to more ominous use in highlighting unsavory faces and frightening figures throughout *Eyes Wide Shut*. As Bill strolls past a "Kitty" lingerie shop, some shimmering light effects at left happen later upon the buildings near him, that at times form shadowy visages that seem to trail Bill.

One place where Stanley Kubrick's love of anagrams shows up is in Dr. Harford's patient exam room, where he checks a boy's throat. In the background is an eye chart where its first two rows display an unusual choice of too easy-to-read letters: OAHVXT, which may form the anagram TV HOAX. Add the words GTA underneath and it can become GVT TAX HA. Kubrick wordplay resurfaces again on a Muralo Paints building sign and the Sonata Jazz club. The Muralo Paints sign shows up more than once in *Eyes Wide Shut*'s streetscapes; a definite Kubrick tactic indicating he wants viewers to notice a potential message. It turns out to yield several interesting anagrams, the first being MANIPULATORS and the second OUR LIMP SATAN (a medieval "Fallen One" reference) and third: U.S. MORTAL PAIN. Even more intriguing (and more likely), subtract the p*aint* sign's "P" and you get MASON RITUAL and NASA TURMOIL.

If possible, the Sonata Jazz club's anagram is even more damning.

"Sonata" turns out to be an anagram in Esperanza ("spanglish") for SATAN (Satano). So Satan's Jazz turns out to be a very appropriate name for Nick Nightingale's garishly red-lit underground club, especially when its walls and light fixtures are decorated with Luciferian shadow script motifs, and includes the threatening sign "ALL EXITS FINAL" behind Bill as he descends the club's ember-glow stairwell. Other infernal events unfold as Bill Harford goes about his business on the city streets. At one point, Bill even walks by an iron grating fence where light briefly highlights the word "LOOK" (Warning: what you look for in this particular scene is not pleasant). What you do find is more evidence for Kubrick's urgent underlying reasons to make *Eyes Wide Shut*. Basically, if you take all the previously discussed occult clues found in Kubrick's earlier films from *Paths of Glory* to *Full Metal Jacket* and condense them all into one movie, in effect you get the major illuciferian alarm system that is *Eyes Wide Shut*. All those multitudinous Luciferian motifs and shadow script sigils that were overlooked in his past films, Stanley Kubrick made sure to put in everything including the Hell's kitchen sink for what he possibly surmised might be his last film.

As Bill watches an imposing bald man following him on the street, several lighting techniques are employed to provide clues of how dire a situation Mr. Harford is actually in. Above the bulky man as he crosses the street is holiday lighting in the form of "XX," the Luciferian occult glyph which co-opts the Earth diamond sign (between the XX's) as another Lucifer's morning star sign. Before then the stalker passes a series of art and jewelry galleries which carry "House" names of diabolic connotations such as "Nic(k)os" or "Tobias." One "Artinis" art gallery directly invokes the name of an Armenian sun god. Now, whose supposed entity do we know that has pretensions of being a god of light?

Kubrick's production crew keeps piling up the clues in signage, props, and entire movie sets. In fact, one can make a good case that Stanley Kubrick's re-made areas of downtown New York are whole city blocks showcasing endless examples of Luciferian sigils. We've gone from one hellish Overlook hotel to shadow scripting an *entire city*. Now what is the message in that?

As the Crowley-esque man stalking Bill walks by an Italian restaurant with monolith-shaped windows, light casts a tree shadow on him which fractures the man's hulking figure into a spidery, asymmetrical black net, yet another dark occult motif for being bound and enmeshed. At one point, the webbing assumes a giant, unpleasant face on his tan trench coat. Bill also gets this tree shadow thus signifying he is entangled by sinister powers beyond his current understanding. Alice, his wife, however turns out to be already entangled within the occult elite's machinations. She is already knowledgeable of higher spiritual realities, as the red candles and burnt incense holder right near her large silver mirror attests (Mandy also has a stick of incense near her bed mirror). The fact that this very same ornate mirror is the one Kubrick chose for his primary *Eyes Wide Shut* poster campaign is actually an extremely important tipoff. Currently, the *Eyes Wide Shut* poster is usually shown on a black background, but that was not Kubrick's initial poster design. In his original poster, the background was originally purple and the lettering show Kidman's and Cruise's names in a lighter purple and *Eyes Wide Shut* in light blue (or pale green), which very neatly ties into Kubrick's long-held cinematic Color Code of Illumination and Higher Awareness (or evil mindedness), respectively. This poster of Alice's right eye looking straight into the mirror therefore indicates her use of it as a "Soul Portal," one of the most direct tools for Self-Ascendance. Here, Stanley Kubrick is showing us on this very poster what *2001: A Space Odyssey*'s deepest inferences were all about. The *Eyes Wide Shut* poster's carefully chosen colors fully support this spiritually symbolic association, while at the same time warning us of those in power who are abusing this ascension technique. As such, Alice looks afraid staring into (or out of) her big silver-framed looking-glass, which eerily echoes the scene in Mandy's room where under her misshapen dark mirror is a book titled *Shadows in the Mirror*.

## Color Symbolism in *Eyes Wide Shut*

The continual contrasting of the meanings behind red and blue being used in *Eyes Wide Shut* has been mentioned before. Alice Harford is at times lit in blue light, and when she calls Bill (at Mandy's/Domino's place) she even wears a shimmering blue robe of aware consciousness. The Mysterious Woman (Mandy) who saves Bill Harford at the Luciferian fete is lit in a heavenly blue glow as she intercedes on Bill's behalf while the rest of the attendees standing in their satanic red circle look up in amazement. Perhaps the most obviously satanic red used outside of Somerton's Black Mass and the Sonata Cafe is Millich's Rainbow Fashions luridly red manikin display room. The Manhattan street lamps also give off an unusual red halo similar to *Clockwork Orange*'s shopping lights and *The Shining*'s more ominous hotel lights. The neon wigs lined-up where Millich finds his daughter with two half-dressed Japanese businessmen belie the sex-kitten conditioning of Millich's daughter. Wigs, especially neon or pastel colored ones, can indicate the reinforcement of alternate programmed personas.

The horrors of MK-Ultra/Monarch programming that were the underlying focus of *Clockwork Orange* and deftly revisited in *The Shining*, resurface again inside power elite Ziegler's bathroom (a dissociating, drugged out call girl), the exclusive costume shop ("beta kitten"/sex slave wigs, lingerie, and the costumer Millich's underage daughter being sexually groomed) and also suggested in Alice's spooked reactions to her own mirror reflection and (perhaps) dream recollections. As in *Clockwork Orange* and *The Shining*, mirrors in *Eyes Wide Shut* evoke haunted expressions and altered personas. Mandy/Domino has three mirrors in her room, one framed black with masks, a white-framed mirror and an ugly, dark ash-gray misshapen one with a ritual candle on the wall opposite. The white and dark mirrors might also suggest the occult theme of duality which is also used in mind conditioning programs. Mirrors, bright lights, hypnotic patterns, wigs, costumes, and masks are part of the inhuman handler modus operandi used in MK-Ultra/Monarch brainwashing to break victims' spirits and split their personalities for control.[4] In essence, this is the practice of soul-shattering, a great evil.

The beta kitten symbolism continues in the Harford's house, which have paintings containing cat imagery (such as a gold one that is right above Alice as she sits on the TV couch) and a tiger lamp. Tigers show up in the form of stuffed animals both on Mandy's bed and at the toy shop at the end of the film. Teddy bears appear in both Helena's room and Mandy's room and only once a bunny plush is seen trapped inside her dark soul mirror. Teddy bears symbolize childhood and a person's essential self. Once that is captured or held captive, a person loses their sense of self and is rendered more vulnerable to exploitation. Perhaps that is why a smaller pale blue teddy bear makes up part of a malevolent, one-eyed viper in the center of Mandy's room. Its color-coded high-or-weak consciousness is held captive by a much larger evil. Above the viper hangs a grinning, eight-rayed Luciferian sun mask.

*The Shining* touches upon Monarch conditioning by fastening it as an insidious linchpin to the sadly more prevalent, everyday reality of family abuse which is one of the true underlying horrors of *The Shining*. *Clockwork Orange* too, has a deeply hidden vein of child abuse which sheds more light on why psychopath Alex is what he is. Beta kitten wigs line the window of his mother's bedroom and later she is seen wearing the same red boots which appear in the painting of a lady molesting "little Alex." Previously, Kubrick's *Clockwork Orange* provides a shocking, much more in-depth expose' of the processes of MK-Ultra's/Monarch's brutal conditioning and the social systems that use them, whose above-mentioned paraphernalia appears consistently throughout the exploits of Alex and his droogs (who dress like handlers themselves). As in *Clockwork Orange*, *Eyes Wide Shut* suggests that some of those in power use these awful techniques not only to keep targeted underlings under heel but also as a form of vile entertainment.[5] The Korova Milk Bar in *Clockwork Orange* casually has female manikins bound or made as furniture in distressfully compromising positions wearing fluorescent-colored (beta slave) wigs and nothing else. In *Eyes Wide Shut*, people are seen being used as furniture during the Black Mass orgy, harkening back to desperate Claire Quilty's plea to persuade the vengeful Humbert that he could use his friends "as pieces of furniture" in the film *Lolita*.

When Alice and Bill waltz around Ziegler's not-so Christmas party, the predominant colors women are wearing there are black, red, gold, some pastels, and very little white. One lady drifts by with a black-with-gold XOX patterned dress as Bill and Alice dance together. Later when they separate, a young woman's black dress with black straps in a crisscrossing "darkness" pattern passes near Bill's two beta-kitten models, perhaps hinting at their mental imprisonment. Black and gold, the most revered Left Hand Path color combo, is what makes the Rainbow Fashions "Merry Christmas" signs look decidedly *un*–Christmas-y. The Somerton Estate exhibits absolutely no Christmas décor at all.

Other colors are also prominently featured in the movie. Yellow returns as the color of Life and Death. "Life" yellow appears in the form of the portal-shaped tables in Bill Harford's office lobby but yellow-as-Death presents itself more often throughout the film. Marion's father's marble-encrusted apartment contains hallways painted in decidedly "Death" yellow, as their wilting brown bouquets and funerary urn motifs in a dying man's abode would indicate. Nathanson himself lies in a yellow baroque-style bed covered with inky dark blue sheets. As lighter blue indicated higher consciousness in *2001* and *Clockwork Orange*, dark blue could indicate literally dark consciousness, as befits an illuciferian. Dark blue mixed with gray coats the doors of Mandy's apartment complex entryway, whose interior is painted both pale green and gray. Pale green suggests the presence of corrupt or evil activity and gray indicates either neutrality or average, middle-ground existence. During the sad scene when Bill later visits the now-deceased Mandy, the hospital morgue her body rests in is done in yellow and pale green tiles, apt for a drugged victim of possible gang-rape.

Once people finally recognize the illuciferian symbols and sigils Kubrick has laid bare for decades, watching *Eyes Wide Shut* can be almost funny in a grim, gallows humor sort of way by how absolutely stuffed with shadow occult symbolism the film actually is. You can barely turn around in any given *EWS* shot without tripping over XX's, XOX's, Lucifer-spirals, devil faces, varied flipped satanic S's, inverted pentagrams, hexagrams, and there are more "light-bringer" lamps strewn about than you can shake a rhomb stick at. Even clothing, such as what Mandy's roommate wears, carries copious Luciferian motifs that link back to those found at Somerton and within the Harford's own home. It is as if Kubrick and his *EWS* crew compactly crammed all these symbols to doubly (even triply) ensure that with *this* film, someone would be sure to discover at least a few of their planted illuciferian alerts and hopefully pick up and follow Stanley Kubrick's final cinematic trail of false worldview-wrecking clues. For truly our eyes have been wide shut on this unpleasant reality for a very long time indeed.

Yet positive symbols abound in Kubrick's final film as well. The Ankh itself resurfaces in *Eyes Wide Shut* and is found in bed headboards, door frames, marble floors, and in Ziegler's pool room. Some ankhs and goddess symbols are seen trapped in the exclusive mansion's masonic blue gate, its entry door and its mosaic floors. Again, *2001*'s most hidden Hebrew pictogram depicting perfection/vessel-of-Life/Yoni reappears as well on Domino's purple jacket and dress, inside Bill's office as a painting, and last but not least—as the lady participants' Y-shaped black thongs in the Black Mass circle, placed in a way that is very easy to miss. Among addressing its several socially relevant tropes, *Eyes Wide Shut* is Kubrick's flagship finale vehicle for unmasking the hidden Luciferian illuminati motifs that are flagrantly used in the real world without the public's knowledge. Some examples are the tall rhomb sticks that flank the Sonata Jazz Café and the diner next to it. Another likely real-life art example of Lucifer-as-cherub is Jeff Koons' "Ushering in Banality" sculpture, where two winged, fair-haired putti accompany a large pig that a child clothed in red and black is almost made to be kissing the rear of. The blonde "cherub" at the pig's left is dressed in a sun yellow robe, left hand laid over his right, while accompanying the procession with slit eyes and a most condescending smirk. For the power elite, pigs are a mocking symbol[6] of the masses which makes for a most fitting exhibit theme for Jeff Koons.[7] There are paparazzi photos of Koons rather cozy with the likes of Philippina de Rothschild (when alive) and Marina Abramovic.

One of Kubrick's core intentional parallels in *Eyes Wide Shut* is that misogyny is very purposefully cultivated in power elite illuciferian ritual as it is culturally ingrained in the modern world. When costumed Bill Harford first enters the great mansion's ballroom, one of the more chilling masks he first sees is the hostess': it is a woman's crying, beat up face in a jester's hat with bells, a quite horrible harlequin. This is how the illuciferian elite depict abused women: as clownish figures to be ridiculed. The traditional "teardrop"-crying domino masks exemplify this perverse thinking. Unbeknownst to Bill, his own mask sports that leering devil over his third eye that stresses what he's attending is not a mere costumed swingers party for bored rich people—it is a serious Black Mass occult ritual celebrating December 22–23, when Capricorn (the Goat constellation) and the sun first overlap in the sky. Further proof of the Luciferian connection is the attendants' ritual of only kissing the left side of the face, indicating loyalty to the Left Hand Path. The fact Alice first kisses Mrs. Ziegler's left cheek at the film's beginning would further indicate Alice was already enmeshed in the Luciferian elite long before Bill was. When Mandy the Mysterious Woman singles out Bill at the ritual, she slowly kisses his *right* check to contrast the others kissing their left (which is why this kiss scene is drawn out). Further on during Bill Harford's later defrocking, one particular two-or-three faced female mask in the crowd bears a remarkable resemblance to performance artist Marina Abramovic. This mask's eyes are ringed in gold, reminiscent of how the black-and-gold clad opera singer's forehead in *Clockwork Orange* was ringed in gold, a possible Luciferian high priestess marker or other occult designator of high status. The closest central mask in that same shot looks uncannily like Baron Jacob de Rothschild. It may be that some of *EWS*'s more realistic face masks are purposely designed to "out" certain people.

A later allusion to illuciferian misogyny (with satanic XOX's on his rug) is Ziegler's shadow obliterating an Ankh light effect linked to Bill's news clipping of Mandy's death. Earlier when Ziegler is standing near his pool table, a demonic face hovers above him in the guise of a lighted painting. The elite occultists' exploitation of women (and beta boys) as disposable sex slaves share disturbing correlations with "formerly" CIA-ordained traumatic brainwashing techniques Kubrick unsparingly exposes in *A Clockwork Orange*. One of the more obvious signs of the Illuminati/Luciferian overlap in *Eyes Wide Shut* is the double-headed eagle throne that Red Cloak sits in, which is a herald for the highest degrees in Scottish Freemasonry and the regal crest for several aristocratic families of Europe (including the Rothschilds). The world globe that sits atop the eagles' heads makes a strong statement to that effect. *Eyes Wide Shut*'s unsettling undercurrent of Masonic-flavored satanism is tied to its frequent *2001* references that rise up as Bill Harford comes to realize his family is snared in an insidious web they cannot escape. Even the toy shop at the end of the film is replete with Luciferian motifs, including an XOX made of two windmills flanking a central sun rotating above Bill's head. When Bill despairingly asks his wife Alice, "What do we do?" towards the movie's end, the real answer may be Stanley Kubrick emphatically pointing back to his more uplifting revelations within *A Space Odyssey* as a way to transcend and overcome the existing evil he warns of in *Eyes Wide Shut*. Just like Floyd's Squirt in *A Space Odyssey*, the Harford's daughter Helena holds crucial esoteric keys.

## Pointing a Finger at Venetian History

For a movie based on an Austrian novella, *Eyes Wide Shut* makes a lot of Italian references. Szavost mentions "the Italian poet" Ovid to Alice. Throughout the film, Italian signs, Italian names, Italian restaurants, and Italian ads set in Venice pop up. The costumed attendees at Somerton wear classic Venetian masks, many marked with centuries-old Luciferian styles. It may be that late-Renaissance Venice or Turin is the birthplace of elite Luciferianism which then gradually spread throughout the aristocratic and rich merchant families throughout Europe as evidenced through local styles that exhibit moderately uniform Baroque occult symbolism, piggybacking their diabolic palimpsests upon mainly Greco-Roman and Near Eastern imagery. It was at this time Venice's extremely affluent ruling classes were notoriously over-the-top decadent, as the flip-side (or mirror) of the Church's Vatican history. By the end of the 17th century, Luciferianism had already become wealthy Europe's well-established dark side of the Enlightened Age.

*Eyes Wide Shut* has a sparkling surface that layer by layer, reveals what lurks underneath. It slowly draws you in what first looks to be a light sex farce with not much actual sex happening, then repeated viewings sinks you in deeper and deeper into the icy cold realization of what is actually happening to the main characters and what the film is really about. It is then *Eyes Wide Shut* can really shatter your cozy worldview.

Yet *Eyes Wide Shut* ends on a hopeful note. Whereas *Clockwork Orange* is ostensibly Kubrick hoisting his mid-digit high to those engaged in inhuman brainwashing programs by laying bare their props, tools, and techniques for all the world to see, *Eyes Wide Shut* does the same by blowing the lid off the surreal-yet-disturbingly-real truth behind those who are at the financial and political apex of Western civilization. *Eyes Wide Shut* is a fascinating film dealing with unpleasant realities and dispenses wisdom on how to rise above such realities. That transcending wisdom emphatically points back to *A Space Odyssey*'s hidden, mind-blowing esoteric instructions. Considering the importance of what is revealed in *Eyes Wide Shut* and perhaps cognizant of his own waning energy during its production, it is small wonder that Stanley Kubrick chose to bite the bullet and leave A.I. in the more-than-capable hands of Steven Spielberg in order to finish his own comparatively "quiet" masterpiece, *Eyes Wide Shut*.

Part III

# The Films Before 2001

As we move on to explore that which came before *A Space Odyssey*, it may come as a surprise that a certain amount of Kubrick's visual esotericism initially thought to first originate in the deeply metaphysical *2001* actually appeared in some of the director's earlier mainstream films. Continuing to go further back in time from *Dr. Strangelove* ('64) to *Paths of Glory* ('57), a common thread can be found representatively linking back to the masterful science fiction's own symbolic lexicon. In addition, such films as *Spartacus* ('60) and *Lolita* ('62) unexpectedly connect back to how films from *Clockwork Orange* to *Eyes Wide Shut* serve as both omens and harbingers for humanity.

Three of Kubrick's early mainstream movies which had international release, *Paths of Glory*, *Spartacus*, and *Dr. Strangelove*, all deal with war themes, from the historic to the topically and uncomfortably present. *Paths of Glory* is a tragic series of events exacerbated by military politics set in World War I, *Spartacus* is an ancient Rome sword and sandal epic loosely based on the Servile War slave revolts, and *Dr. Strangelove*'s absurdist satire tackles nuclear Armageddon head-on with unrelenting 1960s irreverence … and each film hides a selection of sigils in plain sight which unexpectedly connect them not only to *2001*, but to Kubrick's later films as well.

Sandwiched between the releases of *Spartacus* and *Dr. Strangelove*, Vladimir Nabokov's *Lolita* is given a cynically funny Kubrickian onceover that is simultaneously yet deceptively lighthearted and compassionate, but not for whom you may think. In Kubrick's *Lolita*, the deviants may cast themselves as sympathetic heroes in their own telling, but symbolically the ingenious director gives Nabokov's characters no quarter in his film and spares no under-the-radar opportunity in showing them for what they truly are.

Starting with *Dr. Strangelove*, the first of Kubrick's four big-release films before *2001: A Space Odyssey*, each movie makes their own contribution in spearheading Stanley Kubrick's covert combat with western civilization's worst adversary: the enemy within.

# 18

## *Dr. Strangelove*: Horror Beneath the Humor

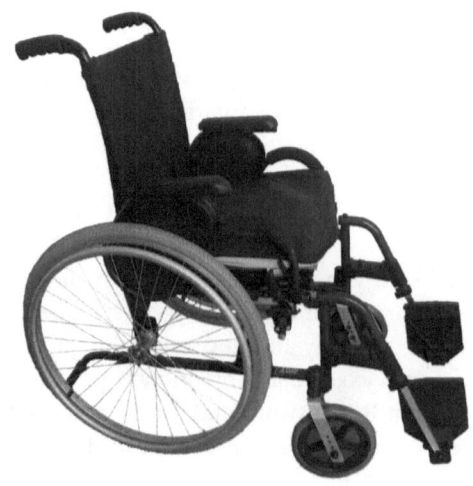

*Dr. Strangelove* wheelchair (photograph by Richard Revel/Pixabay).

*Dr. Strangelove* stands as Kubrick's funniest laugh-out-loud film compared to *Lolita*'s sunny yet sadly dark satire (considering the subject matter involved), and *Clockwork Orange*'s wickedly mean-spirited sense of humor. *Dr. Strangelove* sticks to mainly political and military spheres with a smattering of personal interplay, yet all through the picture runs a humorous underlying current of Freudian juxtaposition on the insanity of war. There would at first glance seem to be scant evidence of any esotericism within *Dr. Strangelove*. It would be easy to assume that *Dr. Strangelove* may be Stanley Kubrick's least esoteric film, with movies like *Clockwork Orange* and even *Full Metal Jacket* containing much more metaphysical content than would be expected from such unnervingly dark films. But even though *Dr. Strange-*

## 18. Dr. Strangelove: *Horror Beneath the Humor*

*love* is an all-out comedy, Kubrick apparently had every intention of inserting esoteric messages, positive or negative, into *Dr. Strangelove*, addressing the absurdities "nuclear strategies" generate into life and death scenarios. As it turns out, Kubrick's clandestine use of arcane symbolism within the famous comedy takes place within a surprising number of scenes.

The gist of *Dr. Strangelove*'s storyline opens with a cunning but mentally unstable General Jack Ripper unleashing a military ruse to force nuclear war with the Russians, thereby hamstringing the U.S. Pentagon's top brass who debate with President Merkin Muffley (Peter Sellers) on how to resolve the situation. The president's own name and General Ripper's (Sterling Hayden) are just a few examples of the tongue-in-cheek Freudian current running through *Dr. Strangelove*. Major Kong (Slim Pickins) and his airmen represent one of several nuclear-carrying B-52 bombers ordered to bomb Russia by the mad general. Meanwhile President Muffley, General Turgidson (George C. Scott), General Faceman with his toady Stains, and Russian ambassador De Sadeski (Peter Bull) agitatedly scramble to find a solution, which after much deliberating results in a confessional phone call to the Russian Premier himself, Dimitri Kissoff.

Other Freudian touches is the constant presence of smoking and chewing gum, particularly Wrigley's gum; a staple in military K-rations since World War II. Inside the Pentagon's War Room, General Turgidson is seen repeatedly chewing Wrigley's Spearmint gum, even offering a stick to Stains at one point. Wrigley's gum is also found in the survival kits Major Kong hands out to his B-52 flight crew. At one point, Group Captain Mandrake (Peter Sellers again) anxiously plays with a silver gum wrapper as the dawning realization General Ripper is insane begins to fully sink in. There are many shots of Ripper chomping on his ever-present cigar and several Pentagon officials seen smoking away in the War Room along with the cigarette-puffing Dr. Stangelove. Both gum and (unofficially) smokes were encouraged in the military because they helped to lower soldiers' "tension." Yet psychiatric boards of the time also considered such habits to be no less than forms of oral masturbation.[1] It is apparent Stanley Kubrick was gleefully aware of this when making the movie. Another thing perhaps not lost on *Dr. Strangelove*'s savvy director is the fact part of Wrigley's gum recipe contains polyvinyl acetate, a synthetic Wrigley's obtained from the *explosives* manufacturer Hercule Powder Company.[2] Guess that is the real reason why we are told not to swallow gum. So this sheds some more light where the War Room boys are concerned, for as they say … you are what you eat.

Building on the Freudian theme is the film's use of water glasses. Here, *Dr. Strangelove* continues the glass-as-body theme of *Lolita*, where a glass' contents symbolized both innocence and the essential Self, and where *Strangelove* ingeniously applies General Ripper's "Purity of Essence" theory to accommodate Kubrick's already established glass-as-body motif. One example in *Lolita* is when Claire Quilty and Humbert face each other in Humbert's own house. Two empty coke bottles, each with two straws, are placed in front of both Humbert and Quilty, representing how both pedophiles have drained Lolita's innocence-as-essential self (as repeated in *Full Metal Jacket*). In one of *Lolita*'s film trailers, a coke bottle graphic is shown with a white flower losing a petal. Quilty's coke-bottled eyeglasses as "Dr. Zempf" provide another visual link to the coke bottles' other metaphor for vision (glasses relating to eyeglasses). All the glassware on the War Room table appear unusually crystal clear, clean, and shiny, including beautifully cut-glass ashtrays. Quite a few War Room table shots are framed so its glassware is strategically positioned to be seen. On the huge War Room table in *Dr. Strangelove*, a number of Pentagon officials have been provided clear glasses containing pencils sticking out. The fact the glasses just contain pencils and no pens or other utensils is easy to miss. The same is true for General Jack Ripper's desk. The film's Freudian interplay carries on as it turns out the etymology of the word "pencil" itself traces back to a Latin diminutive for penis. Figures.

In *Dr. Strangelove*, the "Purity of Essence" theme appears to link to clear glass containers, perhaps intimating what many of the men in *Strangelove* are substituting in place of what they desperately need most: clarity of vision. When Group Captain Mandrake first enters General Ripper's room, reflections in a glass eagle stopper and set of glasses at right actually look like an eye, staring straight at the audience. Whether this is an Evil Eye warning or

In *Dr. Strangelove* (1965), an Eye reflection made of an eagle-topped glass inkwell and drinking glasses at right. Ripper's (Sterling Hayden, left) head perfectly covers the "crazy face" which he reveals later. Peter Sellers is also pictured.

## 18. Dr. Strangelove: *Horror Beneath the Humor*     179

hint that glasses can substitute for eyes in *Dr. Strangelove* is something to consider. It does seem strange that most of the glasses on the War Room's round table look filled with only water, when there is a long buffet table with various drink and alcohol options. While General Turgidson in the War Room makes his war-mongering arguments, the water goblet next to him alternates with its top being off and then on. When it is on, the body of the glass reflects a very clear "i" reflection. Stanley Kubrick will continue to use his glass-vessel-as-body symbolism in *2001: A Space Odyssey*, *Full Metal Jacket*, and even *Eyes Wide Shut*.

    Mirrors feature as well in *Dr. Strangelove*; both General Turgidson's bedroom and General Ripper's office have their share. When we first see Secretary Miss Scott, she is in front of multiple square mirrors that give General Turgidson's quarters a house of mirrors feel. General Turgidson's first appearance is in a square-patterned shirt that compliments Miss Scott's diamond-covered bikini: juxtaposing very traditional masculine and feminine shapes. The lighting behind the War Room's buffet area consists of square-shaped projection lights and the lighting forming the great halo ring above the immense conference table are rectangular. Such repeating elements may imply a correlation between mirrors and lights and one's essential nature within *Dr. Strangelove*.

    One of the binders Turgidson looks over during the War Room meeting is the *War Alert Actions* book, whose covers have a U.S. military top-secret logo on top of a diagonal white band covered in black stars. Patriotism aside, a plain band motif oriented to the upper left also happens to be a Left Hand Path allegiance emblem (historically displayed as a herald or shield) and somehow Kubrick ostensibly knew this when making *Dr. Strangelove*. This is made more apparent when the binder's band is seen straight-on: most of the "stars" become inverted pentagrams. Its herald of a knight's fist even clutches satanic "lightning bolt" S's. To top it off, there exists a photo-op picture of Kubrick peeking over the War Room table exhibiting this Left Hand Band binder in the foreground with the funny but still disconcerting "Megadeaths" binder.

    It was a habit of Kubrick to cameo in promotional photos of his films, where his presence could specifically hint at the deeper concepts his movies were targeting. For *2001*, there are photos where Kubrick is pointedly looking up at his Square-the-Circle portals in *Discovery*'s centrifuge area, where he poses right in front of *Discovery*'s center pod bay (Third Eye) hatch with a rather knowing look, and his more famous photo-ops with Arthur C. Clarke when he and the *Sentinel* author take turns standing inside one of his Portal-door elevator sets. Taking all this into account, though it was normal for Kubrick to survey a scene in preparation for camera setups, the fact he let himself be photographed with one eye open while peering over the War

Room's above-mentioned binders may be one of the slyer ways the director intimated the more serious issues *Dr. Strangelove* covertly addresses.

*Dr. Strangelove*'s more veiled Masonic/Left Hand Path associations emerge through lighting as the high-ranking General Faceman and his sidekick Stains are separated from the other Pentagon brass by a markedly triangular shadow (an effect put to more unnerving use in *Clockwork Orange* and *The Shining*). Faceman exerts his superior command power over General Turgidson by flatly stating how his "boys can easily sweep your men aside with no trouble." When Turgidson struggles to wrest away Ambassador de Sadeski's spy camera, he appeals to President Muffley, "but I saw him with my own eyes!" When this is said, the lighting on George C. Scott's face frames only his right eye and distinctly blots out the left side of his face in shadow.

In a previous War Room scene, General Turgidson protectively grips his top-secret war binders close to his chest while walking up towards President Muffley. As he argues with the president about the rashness of letting the Russian ambassador into the War Room, a man standing behind Dr. Strangelove's wheelchair covers his left eye with his left hand as his right hand grips Dr. Strangelove's chair. The motion is decidedly not natural; the official simply covers his left side while watching the interchange between Turgidson and Muffley. This man does not put his left hand down until General Turgidson says "lousy commie punk." Since the eye-covering movement is done in a rather deliberate—even affected manner, it presents itself as a possible message. In effect, it is a recurring Kubrickian theme, as the renowned director has put visually metaphoric hints of the Masonic Eye of Providence and the Luciferian Evil Eye as overlapping or even being symbolically one in the same in the majority of his movies. It is understandable that many people would not want to believe that either "eye" symbol has much historic significance or relevance, yet once recognized, their *continual* appearances in Stanley Kubrick films, from *Paths of Glory* to *Eyes Wide Shut*, makes them increasingly harder to ignore.

Ambassador Alexei de Sadeski's miniature spy camera in question is shown up close to be a fake matchbox with two matches on one side of the lens and three matches on the other. Three Russian peasant women are on its cover, each with her right hand raised to lift up the right side of their headscarves; in effect, lifting the veils from their eyes. They all appear to be blind by wearing shades—or perhaps the eyes are made large. The Russian acronym "CCCP" labels the matchbox spy camera's base. It could be that this is an early Kubrick eye portal hint or some other allusion; otherwise why bother showing such an extreme close-up of the spy camera's design details? Further evidence of eye portal allusions take place in Major Kong's bomber as the flight crew are seen to look straight up into sun-like or eye-like light fixtures.

## 18. Dr. Strangelove: *Horror Beneath the Humor*

As will be noted later, James Earl Jones' Bombardier is even graced at times with celestial diamond lights.

Later, Ambassador de Sadeski is forewarned by one of the Russian Premier's lackeys about Russia's top-secret Doomsday Device, which he informs the American president and General Turgidson will, once detonated, produce a "Doomsday Shroud" that will encircle the Earth for 93 years, causing the death of all human and animal life on the planet. It was built as a military deterrent to ensure that no one would dare bomb Russia. As it is the Russian ambassador who delivers this news to the War Room brass, it is quite interesting and most appropriate that the last name de Sadeski also creates the anagram DEAD SKIES.

Other hidden images show up in *Dr. Strangelove* as well. When the battle rages to take over Burpelson's Air Force Command Base, Group Captain Mandrake finds himself trapped with a madman as he is locked inside crazy General Ripper's office. An overlooked comic touch in General Ripper's interior design is that all his doors are *padded* from the inside. While Mandrake sits in growing consternation, a gun rack display on the wall behind him takes aim towards some elongated grotesques craftily concealed within the faux wood paneling at Mandrake's left. Here light is employed again as a revealer when a lamp shines on a picture of a plane in flight above a round island (or volcano) that on second glance looks like a large, baleful eye. The dark painting next to it at times displays shifty serpent eyes. Nearby the threatening eye photos are wood grain specters on the walls. Depending on the shot, sometimes the wall panels look like stretched demonic faces and at other times they take on the appearance of long-faced "war hawks." Occasionally the office lighting hits the wall so their hostile eyes pop out from the paneling background, inviting detection.

While General Ripper fends off attack with a machine gun, the now darkened "Peace Is Our Profession" emblem on the wall takes on the appearance of a grinning, malevolent one-eye creature looking off to the right with a white triangle in its design pointing the same way. This lidded one eye is actually another Evil Eye motif that Kubrick also inserts into *Paths of Glory* and *Barry Lyndon*. It must be a particularly nefarious motif because earlier in the film we see Ripper's cigar forming smoky devils right in front of it, which seem to bring evil shapes to the fore. In addition to the mounted gun rack, this mocking evil eye picture directs the gaze towards the hidden wall panel entities near the office doors. Mandrake himself points to these same frightening figures as his head turns towards them when recalling his torture by the Japanese.

During the time General Ripper explains his fluoridated water theory to a quietly panicking Captain Mandrake, the unsettling wall war hawks glare

In *Dr. Strangelove* the cigar of General Jack Ripper (Sterling Hayden) points to a squinting Evil Eye behind him formed in dim light.

out behind the two men. The creepy visages at times appear to share the same eye, with one "hawk" seeming scared as the other appears mad in a perfect wood-grain caricature of Mandrake and Ripper. General Ripper's own shadow also alights upon other evil images, such as a terrifyingly insane-looking bald eagle-man on the right side of the office's Burpelson's base aerial map.

When not looking like an evil eye in murky light, the "Peace Is Our Profession" herald actually has a Bomb Wing Strategic Air Defense's raised knight fist holding three short lightning bolts (that easily pass for satanic S "lightning bolt" initials). This is another occult co-opted sign which originated from ancient Roman shield designs, along with the elongated spears or arrow symbols which symbolize War and Death. There is a time when one of these lightning bolts is brightly lit to stand out from the rest of the wall hangings in General Ripper's office.

When his office is shot up by enemy fire, Ripper intrepidly fights back with a rapid-fire machine gun. During the gunfight, the "Peace Is Our Profession"/Evil Eye sign is shot off from the wall and General Ripper's big home-base map more obviously displays an XOX configuration.

After the base surrenders, General Ripper is dejected by the outcome. As he walks toward to sit in front of the large base aerial map, a wall devil head near the ceiling reveals itself at left. When General Ripper sits down, his shadow falls right on top of then next to the fearsome, evilly grinning visage that makes up the wall map's right side behind him. Gradually, Ripper gets up to go to the bathroom with Group Captain Mandrake following and en-

## 18. Dr. Strangelove: *Horror Beneath the Humor*         183

**Captain Mandrake (Peter Sellers, left) and General Ripper (Sterling Hayden) are mirrored by long-faced "war hawks" in the grain of the wall paneling behind them (at right), seen more clearly on screen, in *Dr. Strangelove*.**

couraging Ripper to give him the B-52 bombers' communication code clearance. While Mandrake follows, the machine gun he carries literally points to M-shaped wall devils and war hawk faces the general and his shadow passes. These M- or W-headed demons may refer to actual shadow script M and W sigils that later appear in films like *The Shining* (above elevators and in Ullman's office curtains) and *Eyes Wide Shut*. Perhaps all the war hawk imagery is connected to the reason why *Dr. Strangelove* is Kubrick's first film listing "Hawk Films Ltd" as its production company. It is then General Jack Ripper shoots himself in the locked bathroom to avoid his imagined torturous interrogation he expected to receive upon surrender. This leaves Mandrake having to figure out the security clearance code himself by pouring over the deranged general's scribbled notes.

Afterwards, Captain Mandrake is later confronted by a Colonel Bat Guano barging in, after shooting out the door handle. As Colonel Guano pushes open the door, revealing its wood-grain paneled exterior. Here, the outside of Ripper's door contains scared-looking wood-grain war hawks to accompany the office walls' wood-grain demons. Strangely, the Burpelson Air Defense picture is mysteriously remounted on the wall, where Guano's own rifle even points to it. Afterwards, Guano then escorts a furious Mandrake at gunpoint down a hallway where another hidden menace lurks behind the two men in the distant background. The cross-framed window at the end of this hallway at first does not seem like much, until one notices the unwholesome grin behind it. Whether it makes up a jeering face or not, Mandrake and Colonel Guano point to it at least three times during their argument in the hallway. A similar sinister hallway set-up is to be found in Kubrick's *Eyes Wide Shut*.

Returning back to the War Room, differences of opinion over the origins of the title character Dr. Strangelove have ranged from sporting Operation Paperclip member Wernher von Braun's hairstyle to RAND's martial strategist Herman Kahn, bomb designer Edward Teller and the Manhattan Project's John von Neumann. All four may have indeed contributed to shaping Peter Seller's titular nemesis, including an eccentric New York photographer nicknamed "Weegee" (for Ouija) whom Peter Seller's himself credits as inspiration for Strangelove's voice.[3] Another hint to whom Sellers' Strangelove emulates is the man sitting to his left at the War Room round table. This man's face bears a strong resemblance to Wernher von Braun.

One scene in particular effectively captures Dr. Strangelove's sinister nature. During General Turgidson's call to prayer after most of the B-52 war planes have been successfully recalled or shot down, When Turgidson says the words, "Lord.... You have deemed fit to deliver us ... from the forces of evil..." the camera has cut to Dr. Strangelove sitting in near total darkness, with only his cigarette smoke and eye shades glittering spits of light.

A visual carry over from *Dr. Strangelove* to *2001: A Space Odyssey* is the result of placing a camera behind helmet glass. In *Dr. Strangelove*, this camera effect is used to enhance the claustrophobic feeling of being enclosed within the cramped quarters of Major Kong's war plane. In *A Space Odyssey*, the visual trick is enacted during the moon monolith sequence as Dr. Heywood and his Clavius base coworkers walk down its ramps to inspect the Tycho crater excavation site. In both movies the light effects look like they reflect off helmet glass, giving the audience the feeling they are wearing a helmet as well. But the first time this lighting effect is executed in a Kubrick film is *Killer's Kiss*, when the noir-esque movie's dance-hall heroine is seen inside a bus and the camera looks as if it is peering through smudged window glass.

## Comparing *Dr. Strangelove* to Kubrick's Other War Pictures

Whereas Kubrick's *Spartacus* was based on the noble premise of escaped Roman slaves going to war in a valiant bid for freedom, his earlier *Paths of Glory* (the film whose star Kirk Douglas later hired Kubrick to direct *Spartacus*) cast the reality of war as the inglorious exercise it usually is. Yet even in *Spartacus,* Kubrick saw fit to show the piles of dead bodies of warriors and their families as the aftermath of a doomed military campaign. In contrast to *Spartacus'* inspiring rallying cry for liberty, *Paths of Glory* has no illusions about the futility of war from the outset. World War I at the "German Anthill"

## 18. Dr. Strangelove: *Horror Beneath the Humor*

is shown as a grim, grey, waste of humanity, where French soldiers' lives are cheaply sacrificed to gain just a few inches of German ground. It is this rather bleak outlook on war and its accusatory stance of high-ranking French generals treating their ground soldiers as expendable pawns which resulted in *Paths of Glory* being banned from screening in France until 1975. Compared to *Paths of Glory* and *Spartacus*, *Dr. Strangelove* approaches the added horrors of thermonuclear war as a mad farce where the tactics of U.S. military strategy in such a dire situation is particularly lampooned. The only rational heads bobbing above *Dr. Strangelove*'s sea of insanity are President Merkin Muffley and British Group Captain Mandrake, who despite their best efforts fail to avoid nuclear Armageddon.

*Barry Lyndon* may not be considered a war picture per se, though a good part of it takes place during the Seven Years War where Britain, Prussia, and Hanover battled France, Russia, Austria, and Sweden over contested territories. Whereas *Dr. Strangelove* completely rejects the outrageous arguments for nuclear war and mercilessly attacks them, the titular hero in *Barry Lyndon* initially uses war as a way to advance his position in society. Barry, an Irishman, joins the British army in the hopes that one day it will earn him the rank of a gentleman. In *Barry Lyndon*, war is reduced to the purview of one man as simply events happening within his own personal story, whereas in *Dr. Strangelove*, the terrifying specter of nuclear war involves the fate of the entire Earth. Though *Dr. Strangelove* actually focuses on a limited number of characters in mainly three locations, the scope of *Strangelove* is effectively the world stage.

One important similarity both *Dr. Strangelove* and *Barry Lyndon* do have in common is they both carry their own load of repetitive esoteric sigils; *Dr. Strangelove* with its hidden "war hawks" and *Barry Lyndon* with its background masonic owls just being one example. Another theme they share is the diabolic double-bind symbolism of chosen military insignia, such as the intentionally changed Prussian army flag in *Barry Lyndon* and the Evil Eye hiding in Ripper's mounted air force base banner.

*Full Metal Jacket* is often described as Kubrick's most realistic portrayal of war set in '70s Vietnam from the view of the marine grunts who battled and died there. In *Dr. Strangelove*, its satire primarily focuses on the extremely skewed points of view of top military brass, leaving only a few air force base soldiers and Major Kong's flight crew to witness the movie's crazy happenings from the position of the common man. As Kubrick's last war film, *Full Metal Jacket* is credited as showing war just as it is and simply show how men trained to be soldiers actually act and behave, leaving the audience to decide for themselves how to feel about what is happening in a given scene. Being an out-and-out dark comedy, *Dr. Strangelove* itself does not hold back in making the entire nuclear military gambit look like a complete crazy train run by three-ring circus clowns.

What these films do share are endings that all serve as a warning future epitaph to humanity. Comparatively, *Paths of Glory* manages to end on a somewhat uplifting note while *Barry Lyndon* ends quite sadly for its title character losing his leg, yet closes rather ambiguously for everyone else in the movie. In *Full Metal Jacket*, the surviving members of the Lusthog Squad are seen marching off into poisonous yellow gas for their closing sunset. It goes without saying that unlike all the above-mentioned Kubrick war films, *Dr. Strangelove* is paradoxically the lightest in tone while tackling the darkest of truly life-threatening subject matter.

## Funny Touches

What makes *Dr. Strangelove* such an excellent satire is its attention to comedic detail. Signs are used to comic effect during the Burpelson's base raid scene with shots of billboards declaring "Peace Is Our Profession" as grenades and bombs explode as soldiers desperately dodge bullets around a "Keep Off The Grass" sign. The most amazing thing about this sequence was that it was partially shot by Kubrick and Director of Photography Gilbert Taylor dressed in fatigues crawling into an actual military training exercise while capturing the footage. How they managed to shoot film without being shot-up (or arrested) themselves is a major miracle. That is some serious guerrilla filmmaking that took real guts. Before the fighting begins in earnest, a base entry point has a bombardment shelter boldly stating "After the Wreck Comes the Reckoning."

To add to the lunacy, the perfect deadpan denseness of Keenan Wynn's Colonel Guano somehow makes the inspired touch of grenades attached to his nipple area all the more funny. The visual of swinging grenades on an officer named "Bat Guano" cries out mental instability. Perhaps the colonel's hang-up with "preversions" are meant to spell out the anagrams SERVE PRISON or PENIS ROVERS. Yet at his balking to destroy private property, Colonel Bat Guano's own most likely anagram is ACTUAL NOBLE GOON. As he and Group Captain Mandrake argue at a phone booth, a nearby '60s ad-style poster on Civil Defense depicts an entire family in a bomb shelter with Junior declaring, "Gee Dad, Thanks for Thinking of US."

Continuing with the Freudian anagram theme, Mandrake's own name may make out the anagram DAMN RAKE, and taking into account General Turgidson is the only Pentagon official with a visible girlfriend, his anagram is possibly STUD GROIN … or DUST GROIN. Speaking of Miss Scott, the only woman in the film, her name may be a playful reference to George C. Scott playing General Turgidson who at one point promises her, "One day

## 18. Dr. Strangelove: *Horror Beneath the Humor*  187

I hope to make you Mrs. George Turgidson." The air force base Burpelson's name happens to make the quite apropos anagram BONER PLUS, but not in the way perhaps General Jack Ripper would hope it would mean. In this case, considering the catastrophe brought about at Burpelson Air Force Base, BONER PLUS more rightly translates as "Major Cockup" or "Big Mistake."

Though not too surprising given that this is a comedy, even the nuclear warheads are funny in this picture. Besides the "Hi There!" and "Dear John" messages scrawled on the bombs' backsides, there are signs that read "Nuclear Warhead: Handle with Care" and "This Side Down."

Considering that Stanley Kubrick and producer James B. Harris were originally making a statement on the insane rationale for the nuclear arms race, perhaps it should not be so shocking that the director would insert other illuminating themes into *Dr. Strangelove* as well. The diamond symbol for Woman makes a humorous comeback in the form of Miss Scott's bikini as she fields a phone conversation for her lover/boss General Turgidson, who wears a more masculine, square-patterned shirt in similar hues. Diamonds also show up as dangling picture frames and as scribbles on General Ripper's "Purity of Essence" sketchpad.

In a more unexpectedly spiritual context for a comedy, diamond light effects possibly symbolizing self-illumination (which pre-date their appearance in *2001*) repeatedly alight to the right of the Bombardier (James Earl Jones) as he endeavors to give coordinates to Maj. Kong's B-52 plane's guidance system. This diamond light effect also shows up in *Full Metal Jacket* as flashlight beams and barrack lights. On Kong's plane there are many close ups of the crew's eyes looking straight up into light or light fixtures. Many of the plane's lights themselves are paired like eyes and at times are seen right above or right next to crewmen's heads. Sometimes diamond effects float near these "eye" lights, as if to bring attention to them. At one point Major Kong even commands, "Fire the explosive bolts!"—"explosive bolts" being a phrase prominently placed upon the doors of the eye-shaped EVA pods in *A Space Odyssey*, a film noted for its prevalent eye imagery. The Diamond shape also continues on to appear in other Kubrick films as either positive symbols for the sacred earth/feminine or as a sign of ascendance. As a negative symbol, the hijacked double diamond (side by side) or nested rhomb (one inside the other) are both used as Luciferian power glyphs.

The previously mentioned scenes in the bomber and others in General Ripper's office not only use subtle lighting to great affect but also contain examples of Stanley Kubrick's "Association by Proximity" cinematic trope. In General Ripper's case, his head is at times framed next to or even over the frighteningly insane face on the "XOX" base aerial map. His shadow falls upon or passes over it as well. Both Ripper and Mandrake are also shot either with their heads right by or they are looking directly at the evil specters hiding in the wall panels. As mentioned above, Major Kong's B-52 crew often have eye-like lights somewhere around their heads while lighting effects literally highlight the connection between them.

This approach is similar to the bed headboard demon & lampshade snake near Jack Torrence's sleeping head in *The Shining*. One of the generals in *Paths of Glory* has their head rather dubiously close to an unmistakable Eye of Providence. While riding a taxi in *Eyes Wide Shut*, Bill Harford's head happens to be adjacent to a pyramid-topped building in the background. Under a projection light's pyramid cone, most of the left side of General Turgidson's face is in shadow as he proclaims, "I saw him with my own eyes!" during his scuffle with the Russian ambassador. In *Barry Lyndon*, owls, devils, and XOX's at times appear within the vicinity of influential friends and relatives, if not Barry Lyndon himself. Such listed examples should well establish Kubrick incorporated his "Proximity as Association" framing technique in the majority of his movies, as did his recurring use of lighting as a subtle signifier.

One of the final instances of under-the-radar shadow sigils in *Dr. Strangelove* is Major Kong's B-52 nuclear warhead area. The low entryway to its overhanging bombs is marked by a large X. An XX is above the Bombardier's weapons release controls. As Major Kong straddles a prone and ready missile, its tip bears the black-&-white checkerboard pattern of Masonic duality, followed by the American star that in certain *Strangelove* production stills appears as an inverted pentagram. As the bomb finally drops with Major Kong astride elatedly whooping up a storm, the back of the warhead is shot so its fuselage is an unmistakable X/O, a Left Hand Path variant for Luciferian Fulfillment. All jokes aside, the nuclear warhead in *Dr. Strangelove* aptly symbolizes the diabolic death of all known realms of earthly life.

Stanley Kubrick's *Dr. Strangelove*, much like *Lolita*, is a black comedy in which under the humor lurks unexpected horrors, even for a dark satire about nuclear Armageddon. It would have been fascinating to be a fly on the wall and overhear what Kubrick described to the prop and set designers responsible for meticulously creating such intentionally hidden visuals. In the same vein of his films that came before (*Lolita, Spartacus,* and *Paths of Glory*), *Dr. Strangelove* continues Kubrick's undercover exposé against the corrupt powers which he apparently believed dominate—or at least severely compromise—the western world's ruling classes.

# 19

# What Underlies the Film *Lolita*

There are those who would be astonished to hear *Eyes Wide Shut* was not the only film in which Stanley Kubrick endeavored to expose the corrupt ruling class and perhaps yet be more shocked to hear that even *The Shining* cannot be credited with the same benchmark, though the techniques it utilizes to do so are a stunning achievement of cinematic mastery. Its precedent, the illuminati-colored *Clockwork Orange* has its share of hidden Luciferian revelations as well, but its focus is more on recognizable Masonic iconography while uncovering existing government-sanctioned brainwashing techniques. Here we shall find Kubrick's habit of inserting illuciferian alarm motifs into his films go back as far as *Lolita* (1964), and perhaps even further.

In the film version of *Lolita* as well as the book it's based on, it at first looks as if more attention is paid to the antics of the atrocious adult characters than to the humanity of the title character herself, so the movie could well be called *A Tale of Two Perverts: Hilarity Ensues* or *Nabokov Unveiled*. From the beginning it appears James Mason's Humbert Humbert is supposed to have more of the audience's sympathy, but part of both the film's and novel's deeper humor is based on the fact that on closer inspection, Humbert Humbert is shown to be a manipulative, weak, selfish sleazeball who in his own way is just as sickeningly pretentious as his posturing shadow, the more threatening yet ridiculous TV writer Claire Quilty, who spends half the movie stalking Lolita and Humbert. Nabokov's novel can be faulted for treating Lolita like an object while at the same time placing her on an obsessive's pedestal. In his intention through Humbert's words to make his pedophile protagonist sympathetic, Nabokov's decorative prose for this conceit can be just as poisonously deceptive as the film's darkly florid walls hiding evil in Quilty's mansion. In the film *Lolita*, Kubrick does here as he did later in *Clockwork Orange*: to showcase how depravity and acclaimed "high art" aspirations can exist side by side within society's designated glitterati.

The most intense graphic warnings for illuciferian presence in *Lolita* are most suitably found in the film's opening scenes in the perverted Clare Quilty's mansion. Peter Sellers' over-the-top performance as Clare Quilty can distract people from taking in the details of his forebodingly opulent surroundings, but the estate's interior décor is most significant in the illuciferian imagery it contains. Its disorderly state has several black statues scattered about, some holding up items in a "light bringer" posture. The whole interior of the manor suggest the aftermath of a swinging party, with glasses and bottles on the floor, open crates of expensive liquor, and leftover plates of food strewn here and there. Some furnishings covered in white cloth hint at Quilty being away a lot. Chairs in white cloth may symbolize something else (such as shrouds), as they move around.

When Humbert first enters, he stumbles over some bottles and wine glasses on the floor, a filmic device to draw the audience's attention to an 18th-century painting of a girl near the door. In addition, a female nude sculpture crowned with a white shoe is turned toward the painting as reinforcement. The young lady in the painting reminds us of Lolita, and the shoe-as-indicator not only alludes to the opening scene of Lolita getting a pedicure, but also a later scene when Lolita kicks her same-styled high heels off on a hotel bed. All are visual cues to associate this particular portrait with Lolita, and its later appearance on top of the stairs where Quilty dies behind it from Humbert's gunfire not only seals this assessment, but seems to beg the audience to look into the question of why this painting is the last thing to be seen in the movie.

Diligently researched by author Juli Keams, the portrait turns out to be of a young Frances Puleston (Mrs. Bryan Cooke) painted by artist George Romney.[1] Romney himself was besotted with a young muse of the name Amy Lyon. Her history is a sad one of being passed from one rich "gentleman" to another starting at a very young age. Mr. Bryan Cooke's second wife was Charlotte Bulstrode, which name-wise connects her to Shelly Winter's Charlotte Haze as the unfortunate Anne Lyon connects to Lolita's Sue Lyon. As the film *Lolita* progresses it is revealed that Charlotte herself was married very young. Both mother and daughter are tragically fated as formerly used playthings of debauched, over-privileged males. An eerie, bearded portrait near Quilty's fireplace bears a strong resemblance to Charlotte's now deceased husband Harold, who for some reason attempted suicide before he succumbed to some yet unknown malady. Originally when this bit of backstory is brought up it is humorously framed that overbearing Charlotte must have driven him to it. But if it is true that when alive, Mr. Haze was enough of a compatriot for Quilty to own a painting of him at his estate, suggests the rather dicey nature of having such "high class" people as friends. Throughout *Lolita*, clues that Mr. Haze may have expired from despair or from the result of other vices are posited. For some reason Lolita herself does not appear to mourn her father's passing the way her mother Charlotte does, even though it was only seven years ago when he died. All things considered, a particularly appropriate anagram for the Haze's town of Ramsdale is SAD REALM, wordplay that would be neither lost on Nabokov nor Kubrick.

Back at Quilty's mansion, which was originally called Pavor Manor (for dread/child night terrors) in the screenplay, ingenious wallpaper is covered with leering Beardsley-esque faces, each glaring with one eye that link into elaborate mocking goat heads, which in turn are surrounded by grimacing devils and serpent-like skulls. As we have seen in other Kubrick films such as *Barry Lyndon*, such insidious wallpaper (though less obvious) designs are startlingly commonplace among estates with long histories (as those in Highclere castle, both *Downtown Abbey*'s and *EWS*'s location site, demonstrate). Lighting the wallpaper are two-candle lights, both held up by a dark figure in an unmistakable "light bringer" pose. Quilty's silk robe bear an XOX pattern (for Luciferian sun or success). Even the piano bench he sits on has XXX's on its cushion. As Quilty manically distracts the vengeful Humbert with a game of "Roman ping, Roman pong," an anagram for "MAN-GROPING-MAN PORNO," which sounds like something right up Quilty's alley (Does the visual of two perverts playing ping pong hint at some sort of coded euphemism? The scene is not in the novel.), a tall and menacing, decoratively carved mirror looms over Claire Quilty. In far shots it looks very much like a large, shadowy devil head crowning its mirror's frame. This devil head has at least three eyes, its central Third Eye doubles for an Evil Eye. There are times when Quilty's head is right underneath the mirror's devil head, which is clearly intentional, and at one point Quilty even sports the devil's horns. The devil head frame also clues us in to its standing mirror's possible use as a black soul mirror; a sad reminder that while illumination expands people of good conscience, this realm of free will does not reserve the fruits of ascension to just the well-intentioned. Enlightened evil can be wise. Such awakened evil is clever, calculating, and plans for the long run … as our present modern world can attest. Where the Left Hand Path power elite are concerned, unfortunately crazy does not always equal stupidity.

Kubrick has done a number of shots throughout his films where a character's head is closely aligned to some visual theme of the director (*Paths of Glory, Dr. Strangelove, 2001, The Shining, Full Metal Jacket,* and *Eyes Wide Shut*). To top it off, overhanging the infernal mirror while gilding the entire lobby ceiling is a palmette-styled XOX pattern. When Quilty is shot crawling up the stairs backwards, the goat and devil heads in the cleverly conceived wallpaper are easier to spot on the upper floor. As Quilty backs himself behind the 18th-century painting of a young lady (that originally Humbert almost trips over at the mansion's entrance), one eye of a frightening tiger head on the ground is illuminated. There are other illuciferian motifs peppered throughout *Lolita*, particularly the unusually large XX upstairs arm banisters inside Charlotte Haze's home, but craven Clare Quilty's gloomy mansion holds the lion's share of such alarming imagery. The serpentine Evil Eye and predatory tiger eye seem to complement or even equate each other, as wallpapers, window curtains, shower curtains, and other textiles repeat both malevolent motifs throughout *Lolita*.

At one point Claire Quilty grabs some boxing gloves that just happen to be in a Boelens crate and begins to playfully throw some punches at Humbert. The fact this scene is not in the book is significant. For one, Quilty's boxing posture mimics a real photo of Nabokov boxing, as Irena Księżopolska was first to point out.² Second, the "Boelens" crate does not actually refer to any fancy drink but to a New Guinean boa constrictor known for its glittering rainbow pattern. When the sun hits its scales, the results are dazzling. Yet in all its brilliance, like Quilty, it is still a dangerous beast. There are instances throughout *Lolita* where Kubrick is unmistakingly comparing Claire Quilty to his creator Nabokov, and themselves to deadly things, and like the boxing gloves, this is one of those moments. Considering Kubrick's open respect to Vladimir Nabokov as a writer, slyly comparing him to a reptile is hardly complimentary. So among other things, this proves in Kubrick's film adaptation of *Lolita*, Quilty is Nabokov's doppelganger as well as Humbert's. In addition, between actor Peter Sellers and younger Nabokov there are some physical similarities that were purposefully played up in the movie. Though Stanley Kubrick genuinely appreciated Nabokov's expert skill with language, throughout the movie it becomes apparent that as a human being, Kubrick does not let the author off the hook.

Actor James Mason, while playing the pedophile protagonist Humbert, recalls Vladimir Nabokov once saying to him that the girl playing Lolita should have been much younger. Considering that actress Sue Lyon had just turned thirteen when she took the role of Lolita, this left Mason with the chilling thought of just how young the infamous author wanted the girl to actually be. Some years after the film was made, Vladimir Nabokov suggested that prepubescent actress Catherine Demongeot (star of 1960's *Zazie dans la Metro*) would have been the ideal Lolita (yikes).³ Even in a violently raw, gritty '70s film as incendiary as *Clockwork Orange*, Kubrick was careful with such subject matter. In Anthony Burgess' book, Alex actually drugs and rapes two underage girls (à la the "Polanski Technique™") but in Kubrick's *Clockwork Orange*, the girls were made to be young ladies of more consensual age. Even the young actress in *Eyes Wide Shut* who plays the costumer Millich's scantily-clad, prostituted daughter, mentions how "Stanley was very protective" of her and made sure she was comfortable doing her scenes.

In the film *Lolita*, Claire Quilty's fairly odd dialogue regularly differs from the book. As Quilty desperately crawls upstairs backwards after being shot in the leg (amusingly contrasts Nabokov's Quilty "majestically" walking upstairs), he tries to placate and appeal to Humbert by at first offering his house (as in the novel), and then later offering his friends whom "you can use like pieces of furniture (not in novel)." When Claire Quilty first becomes visible, he is found under a chair's white sheet cover himself. Using others like furniture apparently can be an unsavory pastime of the occult power elite. In *Eyes Wide Shut*, there is even a scene of a mansion orgy attendee being used as a sex table. One real life example was the Watermill Center's charity theme "Devil's Heaven" in 2013 that had various painted, nude performance artists assume chairs, tables, and other inanimate objects.[4] It was this same event where, arriving with a rather dazed-looking Lady Gaga in tow, Marina Abramovic partook in annoyingly scraping a spoon lengthwise down a nude lady's torso whose job for some reason was to lie still in a tub of chocolate syrup.[5] Other guests and performance artists showed up either as devils, or dressed in costumes with Luciferian diamond masks, XO's, eight-pointed stars, etc., or as decidedly clownish angels. The "human sculpture" usually depicted humanity in a dejected manner.

As Humbert and Quilty move about his oppressive mansion, the lobby and living room are filled with occult-looking furnishings of their own. The living room with a fireplace has Luciferian double-diamond wallpaper and contains plush chairs with evil faces staring out of the embroidery. Several unpleasant faces glare from walls in the background. The marble fireplace behind the sparring deviants has unfriendly eyes in the shape of "universe" shadow script and the center mantelpiece displays a satanic unity sigil or another Evil Eye radiating quiet menace.

When Charlotte Haze (Shelly Winters) shows Humbert around her house in the hopes he will rent out a room she tries to impress him with her collection of decidedly lowbrow art (Mexican velvet paintings and tchotchke folk art). In her bedroom, Humbert is faced with the ashes of her former husband, held in a rather sinister-looking urn juxtaposed by a saintly icon wall panel of Mary, Mother of God with baby Jesus, which the evil black urn is placed in front of. There is a mysterious light between the icon and the urn which at times casts an eerie glow on the urn while illuminating the icon. After Charlotte confronts Humbert with his obsessive journals about Lolita (that deride Charlotte as insufferable), she later locks herself in her room and strangely cradles the urn as she mourns the loss of her husband, thereby drawing more attention to the urn's Mephisphelian goateed devil head on its side and Luciferian child topping its lid. Having angels, cherubs or some actual depiction of the deceased on an urn is one thing, but the combo of babies, women, and demonic faces on a *funerary urn* as *decoration* is more than a bit disturbing. As was seen earlier in Quilty's mansion, using funerary urns as décor appear to be all the rage on the estates of the super-rich that often appear in their gardens as statuary, as gate or fence fixtures, on fireplace mantelpieces, or placed in front of mirrors. Such decorative funeral urns are curiously often found framing mansion entryways and are understandably mistaken for simple vases when used as planters. Inside stately homes they are sometimes placed upon marble stands that may be carved in Left Hand Path motifs. Funerary urns are a most eerie use of "upscale" ornamentation that repeatedly appear in Kubrick films like *Paths of Glory*, *Clockwork Orange*, *Berry Lyndon*, *The Shining*, and *Eyes Wide Shut*.

A very consistent Evil Eye/Tiger Eye is a visual motif which runs throughout the entire movie. Whether the tiger eyes represent Charlotte or Lolita in sex kitten mode in regards to Humbert, or whether it also includes the predatory nature of Humbert himself is up for debate. In *Lolita*, the tiger eye can be either synonymous with the occult Evil Eye or stand on its own as a specific signifier for predatory motives. Tiger/big cat themes are everywhere in Charlotte Haze's house. Tigers hide and lurk in shower curtains, as stylized wallpaper in different rooms; particularly the rather large patterned wallpaper in her kitchen. Remember we first see the tiger eye symbol in Quilty's roaring tiger skin with its frightening eye particularly highlighted, signifying Quilty's own predatory nature.

The other adults in *Lolita* such as Charlotte Haze's closest friends, the aptly named Jean and John Farlow, are depicted as a slightly unsavory pair, of whom hint to Humbert that they are swingers who probably swung with Charlotte and her husband Harold when he was alive. The creepiest couple seen at the high school dance though are Claire Quilty and his slinky girlfriend, Vivian Darkbloom, whose name being an anagram of Vladimir Nabokov further proves Quilty is Nabokov's double both in the film and the novel. At the dance, Vivian wears a coiled snake bracelet, another reptilian dig at both Nabokov and Quilty. As Claire Quilty is the local theater producer and TV writer, he and his icky paramour are allegedly the hippest pair in the crowd the neighborhood bourgeoisie crave social favor from, including Charlotte. To be part of Quilty's clique is to be among the so-called sophisticated set who are invited to his hedonistic parties.

Does Kubrick paint this permissive atmosphere as intrinsically bad in itself, or is it just shining a light on real adult sexual habits, which are harmful only when they adversely affect children? It turns out Quilty has socialized with Charlotte and her husband before in the past which is why Lolita knows who he is and why she is infatuated with him herself, being the big erudite celebrity in town. What Lolita may or may not have been aware of what Quilty and the Hazes got up to together in the past is anybody's guess. What Lolita herself may have been exposed to during those times is also anybody's guess, but Kubrick's set designers leave disquieting thematic visual clues throughout Charlotte Haze's house.

## 19. What Underlies the Film Lolita

Arguments can be made how Nabokov through Humbert vivisects crass American suburban hypocrisy versus their actual adult sexual mores as a way to make Humbert less of a monster. *Lolita* producer James B. Harris stated how "Humbert was made to be the only innocent" in the film.[6] One can also put forward the query of who is preying on whom? Both Charlotte and Lolita vie for Humbert's affections by varying degrees as the Farlows clue Humbert into their swinging lifestyle. Be that as it may, it is still quite a preposterous ethical stretch to propose the predatory habits of a pedophile are somehow more virtuous or less repugnant when compared to simple adult flirting or seedy-yet-consensual adult relations. As a dark satire that casts a pedophilic kidnapping as a romantic love story, *Lolita* is a tragic farce both in book and film.

Delores "Lolita" Haze herself is cast as a normal, growing teen who is naturally interested in boys and enjoys flirting with Humbert. Humbert in turn inappropriately encourages this while jealously keeping her from socializing with boys her own age. There are too many times Humbert is physically abusive in his jealousy when he more than once wrenches Lolita brutally by the arm. This smothering possessiveness proves Humbert's downfall after Charlotte Haze's death, as his virtual imprisonment of Lolita afterwards encourages her to run away from him, as she has been carefully groomed off-screen by the shadowy Claire Quilty, who most likely presents himself to Lolita as her playwright in shining armor.

The Haze house's upstairs paintings and Mexican knick knacks provide the strongest proof that little Delores was sexually abused by her father. As Charlotte shows off the trinkets from an old family trip to Mexico, one tall Mexican folk painting shows the backside of a large, sombrero wearing male standing within a door frame. "Oh, I keep telling Lo to put this back in *her* room," Charlotte says as she moves the bulky painting aside. Inside Lolita's room hangs a similar adult-sized sombrero and poncho whose guitar neck points to a pin-up of Claire Quilty as if to say, "Playing my tune?" Finally, on the wall opposite between Delores' parents' room and her father's old study is a big painting of a girl crying, head in hands. Between all the mounted bull fight mementos is the undertow of a wretched family past. Knowing this, it is no wonder gazing upon the portrait of the late Howard Haze can give a person the heebee jeebees. Arguably, Mr. Haze's visage is a strange mixture of both Humbert's and Quilty's facial features. As Harold's Luciferian urn complete with Mephistophelian heads and an evil pentagram specter that appears cheek-to-jowl to Harold's living-room ebony bust can attest, where immorality's concerned, Mr. Haze must have given Claire Quilty quite a run for his money. This seems to suggest that, unlike Nabokov's Humbert and Charlotte crying out to her dead husband, "How did we raise such a little *beast?*" Kubrick does not blame Delores for any sexual precociousness she might exhibit, as the house's backstory hints she was groomed to be that way at a much too-young age (she was only seven when Mr. Haze died) through no fault of her own.

The theme of respectability vs. depravity pops up again whenever the words "civilized" and "normal" are uttered by (and largely by) such ethically-challenged pieces of work like Humbert and Quilty. So according to this logic, if Charlotte calls her late Harold "the soul of integrity," that should red flag him as having been a fairly reprehensible human being. Humbert sees himself as an urbane, sophisticated writer whose delusions of gentility vanish whenever he wrenches teenage Lolita by the arm in a pique of jealousy and takes advantage of her. When he repeats this abusive behavior to Lolita at the telephone booth, there is appropriately an auto garage ad with a large hand and the words "BRAKES ($)14."

There also seems to be a fair amount of gaslighting going on in *Lolita*. Quilty gaslights Humbert with his often confusing, hypnotic patter. Humbert attempts to gaslight Charlotte after she discovers his debased journal. "Your name and Lolita's were put in by pure chance, because they were handy," Humbert whines. "That's the way novelists work." When Humbert interrogates Lolita where she's been and who she's been with, Lolita gaslights Humbert's jealousy with "You're sick. You're not well. You should see someone," which indicates Lolita was exposed to this brainwashing tactic enough times before to learn how to use it herself.

Throughout the entire film, predatory eyes are a constant visual motif, particularly tiger and serpent eyes. Evil eyes haunt the wallpaper and furnishings in Claire Quilty's estate. His manor walls' single human eyes becoming one with satanic goat eyes may well symbolize those elite that profane the Eye of Providence and those who follow the Left Hand Path are one in the same. Quilty's other Luciferian trappings such as light bringer lamps, nested-rhomb wallpaper, XOX ceiling border trim, and demonic upholstered furnishings would strengthen this assumption.

Feline imagery dominate the interiors of Charlotte Haze's house. She has a tiger image on her bedroom rug and snarling tigers prowl her bathroom walls and curtains. Charlotte herself more often than not dresses in leopard print. When she makes overtures towards Humbert at home and at the high school summer dance, big cat visuals follow right behind her. As she talks to Humbert at the dance, a tiger materializes in vent slats behind her head. At home, before Lolita rejoins them, tiger eyes and faces appear on the wallpaper. Later, a black cat appears in the background shrubbery between the frame of Charlotte's and Humbert's faces. A more sympathetic view of Charlotte is the two-fold nature of her feline trappings, which do not just signify predatory vampishness on her part but possibly hints of socialized sex kitten grooming in her past. We learn Charlotte was married young, perhaps too young, to the late Howard Haze.

Of course Humbert well deserves his own predatory eye imagery, which like Quilty's, are more serpent-like Evil Eyes. When Humbert courts Lolita with poetry in his rented bedroom, his window curtains are full of snake-in-the-grass eyes which visually link to Humbert's strangely ostentatious ascot sporting a matching snake eye. Evil reptilian eyes watch Humbert's intentions wherever he goes, they glare at him inside his Enchanted Hunters hotel room on the walls and in paintings, At one point a great serpent's eye is found on Lolita herself as she sleeps in the hotel room, the slow dissolve to the next scene giving an audience more time to see it. These evil eyes lurk in wallpaper, tablecloths and upholstery, leering equally at Humbert, Quilty, and their potential prey throughout the entirety of the film.

The car trip section of Nabokov's novel was in part inspired by a real, not-at-all romantic kidnapping that was covered in the newspapers of the times.[7] The poor 11-year-old Sally Horner that was finally rescued from her pedophile kidnapper Frank La Salle was scarred and never really recovered afterwards. To find that this sad event and earlier books with similar pedophilic storylines fueled Nabokov's star-crossed "romance" is stomach-churning to say the least.[8]

The Enchanted Hunters Hotel has evil eyes peering from room paintings and when Quilty steps outside to the patio a seat cushion telegraphs a particularly large evil eye. Quilty shows he's "bent" in different ways when he flirts with the hotel manager Mr. Swine while simultaneously regaling him with his BDSM-flavored "Judo" experiences with his martial arts girlfriend, Vivian. "She's a yellow belt.... I'm a green belt. That's how nature made it." is odd for Quilty to mention as it indicates Vivian has the lower grade belt, yet she's the one that throws Quilty around in Judo. This blending of gender expectations provides another veiled hint of Vivian and Quilty being the same person, Nabokov.

Kubrick was, like many, seduced by Vladimir Nabokov's way with words and initially was happy when the author agreed to adapt his novel into a script for the movie. However, as time went on and Nabokov's treatment of the script grew ever more voluminous (400 pages) than his own book, Kubrick started having second thoughts. Nabokov himself recalled when he suspected Kubrick was changing his mind on how things were going: "I did not feel quite sure whether Kubrick was serenely accepting whatever I did or silently rejecting everything."[9] Gradually during the process Nabokov saw less and less of Kubrick until he later found out that Kubrick ended up not using much of his very lengthy treatment at all. *Lolita*'s producer James B. Harris said it had ended up "the size of a phonebook," rendering it impossible to implement. "It was voluminous and really overwritten and unwieldy," recalls Harris, "and very difficult to perceive as being the screenplay we could use."[10]

## Quilty and Humbert as Multi-Doppelgangers

In his various guises, Claire Quilty comes off as not just a double for Nabokov, but for two other characters as well. Proof of being Nabokov's twin are the suits and eyeglasses Peter Sellers' uses for Quilty's disguises that are similar to what the author has been known to wear. That Vivian Darkbloom (Nabokov's anagram he created for himself) and Quilty consistently mirror each other's movements while dancing, walking, or sitting is another clue to Quilty's doubly duplicitous nature as Nabokov. Again, her snake bracelet reinforces this connection. In the novel, Vivian Darkbloom is author of the book *The Woman Who Loved Lightning* and is seldom mentioned. In Kubrick's Lolita, Darkbloom is practically Quilty's shadow for a good portion of the film. Interestingly in *Lolita*, at the high school dance it is Quilty that is given credit for the now play "The Woman Who Loved Lightening" instead of Vivian, reinforcing Quilty and Vivian as both doppelgangers for Vladimir Nabokov. When talking to Charlotte at the Ramsdale Summer Dance, Quilty even quotes Nabokov the author later rephrased in an interview he gave for *Playboy*: "Lolita ... diminutive of Delores, the tears and the roses."[11]

As used in *2001* and *The Shining*, pairs of extras that walk by a main character can signify that character having a double or being a double for something or someone else. Mr. Heywood Floyd in *2001* had at least three doppelgangers, whereas some bellhops being the first to pass behind Nicholson's Jack (in exact opposite footsteps) inside the Overlook lobby reflects Jack Torrence's past servitude to the hotel. In *Lolita*, Stanley Kubrick stages doppelganger clues in the film for himself and Peter Sellers as being the merry puppeteers for Claire Quilty's character. At the Enchanted Hunters Hotel, when Quilty and Darkbloom are walking in the lobby towards the Manager's front desk, a conspiratorial duo of men point toward Darkbloom and Quilty as they pass by them from behind. This repeats again on the hotel's outside patio: the same duo, suspiciously similar to Kubrick and Sellers in terms of height and haircuts, now point to Humbert and Quilty as they walk on by. At the hotel and the Beardsley school play, Quilty also wears a camera, a piece of equipment more associated with Kubrick the former photographer than Quilty the playwright and sometimes pornographer. Kubrick even has his right-hand man, producer James B. Harris, stand in as Quilty's right hand man Bewster at the school play, so Sellers as Kubrick's Quilty is doing double duty as Kubrick masterminding Nabokov's characters. Backing this up even more is Sellers' imitating Kubrick's New York twang for Quilty's "actual" voice. All of the above exemplify the gleeful fun both the comedian and director appear to be having with Claire Quilty's character at Nabokov's expense.

Revisiting the nighttime scene on the hotel's outside patio where the two pairs of men pass by Humbert and Quilty also illustrate the two pedo-

## 19. What Underlies the Film Lolita     199

philes as doubles of each other. The leading, "thick like thieves" doppelganger pair have lighter suits, the two older men walking behind them wear darker suits. Both Humbert and Quilty themselves are in mismatched suits: Humbert wears a dark jacket with lighter slacks and a light-colored tie, and Quilty wears the exact opposite with a dark tie. This puts proof to the observation the two pedophiles are doppelgangers for each other as well as to Nabokov. Humbert writes with a quill fountain pen, both a verbal-visual reference to Quilty's name and a nod to Nabokov's own writing habits.[12] Charlotte stating to Humbert she does not "care if your maternal grandfather was a Turk" can refer to Nabokov's royal Tartar lineage[13] and Quilty quipping to Humbert that he looks like "a German refugee ... this is a Gentile's house, you better run along," brings up when Vladimir and his Jewish wife Vera had to flee Nazi Germany. While Quilty and Darkbloom are dancing at the high school, they are surrounded by two sets of older men; one duo in white tuxes and the other pair in black, whose presence suggest the importance of duality. One mature gent in a white & black tux (just like Humbert's) who's right behind Quilty dancing bears some resemblance to Nabokov, who not only has his black tie under his white collar just like Quilty's, but at one point claps his hands to keep time just as Humbert does later during Charlotte's flirtatious dance at home. The persistent layered referencing between Humbert, Quilty, and their creator Nabokov in Kubrick's *Lolita* happens too often to be ignored. Though calling Claire Quilty Humbert's shadow is nothing new, Kubrick's continual knowing jabs at Nabokov is telling of Kubrick's own opinions on the famous author's preoccupation with pedophilia.

    Case in point: at Camp Climax where Humbert disconcertingly meets Charlie Sedgewick, the one boy in an all-girls camp. Charlie's head is nearest a butterfly display case on the wall, about as unveiled a connection to Nabokov, a noted butterfly expert, as the author signing his own signature. A big "Camp Climax" banner points to this case as well, suggesting the butterflies symbolize the camp girls as trophies of Charlie Sedgewick, whose then-fitting anagram IS CHILDE WRECKAGE. The boy Charlie is a winking cipher for what would be for Nabokov a dream job. The table-tennis motif resurfaces at Camp Climax, where Humbert is seen playing around with a racquet near a stuffed otter. At the first hotel Humbert and Lolita stay at, they somehow get "Cpt. Love's" room who at the last moment canceled. This may shed light on why Quilty calls Humbert "Captain" when they first square-off at his mansion. It would be a great private joke to Quilty, seeing Humbert as "Captain Love," who struck zero when it came to Lolita (who only really loved Quilty), which would indicate Quilty was quite aware who Humbert was when he first entered his palatial lair.

    When Quilty shows up as Dr. Zempf in Humbert's Ohio home, he wears eyeglasses with double lenses and two gold pens in his left breast pocket. The scene's lighting shines on the golden pens brightly so they will be noticed. Dr. Zempf's coke-bottle glasses get verbal-visual reinforcement from Lolita's two empty coke bottles on the table (with double straws). Quilty's get-up is another clue that he is not just a doppelganger, but a multi-doppelganger. One of Dr. Zempf's shiny pens has a black case while the other's is white. When Dr. Zempf addresses Humbert, he pronounces the name as "Dr. Humbarts," which not only sounds like "mustard" to match Zempf's German name for mustard (*sempf*) but a verbal indication Humbert as well represents more than one person. After the Beardsley high school play, Miss Starch the piano teacher also calls "Mr. Humbers" in the plural which in addition, underlines "The Hunted Enchanters" play name change. Humbert earlier making Lolita a mayo-heavy sandwich conceptually connects to Quilty's "Dr. Mustard" as a repeating condiment theme.

The *Boelens* bottles also resurface throughout *Lolita*. We first see one on a chair's white shroud Quilty hides/sleeps under. Does this chair that reappears upstairs represent Howard Haze or Quilty's soon to be shot body? Boelens is found on Quilty's piano seat, rearranged on the ping pong table and later resurfaces next to Mr. Haze's elongated bust above his writing desk in Charlotte's living room. This black bust and the evil upstairs urn share similar silhouettes as both refer to Mr. Harold Haze. When Humbert is inside Pavor Manor at the end of the film, the chair's coverlet Quilty hides under now has a clear, white vessel resting on it instead of the usual dark bottle stand-ins for Quilty's/Haze's/Nabokov's presence.

When Humbert offers Lolita lunch, Lolita gets up, showing a thin, white cross on her back. When she moves, a most ghastly face with a black inverted pentagram on its forehead is revealed next to Harold Haze's strange black bust. The star is created by the ivy leaves on the bookshelf. It reaffirms evil both accompanies and binds Quilty and Lolita's father together. As Kubrick's Quilty is a doppelganger of both Nabokov and Dolores' dad it makes sense when Delores draws around the bust's eyes with a gold hand quill stationed at her father's writing desk, it is a tip Quilty stole Mr. Haze's ideas.

Quilty's cigarette ad in Lolita's room attests, "I can write without a pen but not without a Drome." Drome is a peculiar name for a cigarette brand, as most are sport surnames or animal names. Drome may also hint at dromedary, a verbal allusion to the popular cigarette brand Camel. We keep seeing Quilty smoke his Dromes (even offers one to Humbert at one point), so we are meant to pay attention to them for some reason. The ad also indicates the similarity between quill and Quilty's name as he "can write without a pen, but not without a Drome." Drome turns out to be an anagram of modre, which means "bite" in French and "murder" in German. Since Quilty's Dr. Zempf adopts a German accent while smoking his Dromes with Humbert, "murder" is the word to replace Drome in Quilty's cigarette advert. As the audience already knows Quilty dies, such veiled foreshadowing would be a wasted exercise, so another murder must be involved in Quilty's sordid past. Does the ad on Delores' wall suggest Quilty can't write without committing murder or stealing? In one instance, Delores even mocks Humbert about his locked-up journal, "What? Are you afraid someone's going to steal it and sell your ideas to Hollywood?" Whom might Quilty have murdered in the pursuit of his literary success? The evidence littered throughout Charlotte's house suggest the victim was none other than Mr. Harold Haze, an insurance salesman and aspiring writer who kept a writing desk in the Haze's living room as well as in the study Humbert now occupies. Despondent after Quilty's theft of his work, he ended up hospitalized and Quilty (the poison pen) poisoned him to ensure his silence.

Quilty does say "I'm dying for a drink" about three times at the beginning of the film, a repetitive dialogue device Kubrick has used many times as a signal to the audience. Humbert does the same, saying "Cross my heart and hope to die" three times promising Lolita he always will be there for her (the outcome of that threefold oath we already know). When Quilty drinks from a glass fouled by a cigarette, it links Quilty's Dromes to Quilty poisoning Mr. Haze's drink. Mr. Haze's stylized ebony bust also has a Boelens bottle sitting right next to it, another sly connection to Quilty and Nabokov as cold-blooded creatures. The awful satanic face appearing next to Mr. Haze's black bust above his black writing desk, whose murky lacquer sheen at times reflects demonic faces of its own, are more Luciferian imagery that infernally bind Mr. Harold Haze and Claire Quilty together.

In closing, I wonder if, in all the time that has passed since this movie was made in 1962, has anyone else noticed in the iconic poster of *Lolita* that her left heart lens is actually cracked? Such seems to be the fate of poor Delores, that in spite of Kubrick's solid attempts to flesh out her character and give her further agency, people tend to pay more attention and invest themselves in the film's mad monsters impersonating civilized adults. Even so, it is amusing to note as Kubrick places himself in his own film, the director makes it clear he is manipulating Nabokov the way Quilty manipulates Humbert. The main difference is when Kubrick does it, it is to hold up an unrelenting mirror to the author's pedophilic obsessions while giving Delores herself a more humanizing backstory and hopefully a new chance for a happier ending.

## 20

# Inserting Sources in *Spartacus*

It was after working with Kubrick for 1957's *Paths of Glory* that impressed and prompted Kirk Douglas to employ Kubrick again as director for his sword and sandal epic *Spartacus* (1960) as director Anthony Mann left the set when let go by Douglas, the film's starring lead and executive producer. As Kirk Douglas later made seemingly conciliatory arrangements with Mann to direct him in a future picture,[1] *Spartacus* co-star and uncredited co-writer Peter Ustinov thought Douglas wanted Kubrick all along, but could only ensure Universal fully getting behind his major picture with a seasoned director like Mann initially on board.[2] Though this incident provided Stanley Kubrick a once-in-a-lifetime opportunity to direct a big-budget, star-studded blockbuster, it also boded of difficult times to come with the resolute Kirk Douglas, who clearly saw the picture as his own project as it was produced through his own company Bryna, so the usual employer vs. employee relations clashed as it was hard for Douglas to accept that Stanley Kubrick was just as determined to do what he was hired by Douglas to do: direct.

Spartacus, a Thracian enslaved by the Romans and originally condemned to work and die in their hellish salt quarries, is fortuitously selected by Batiatus (Peter Ustinov) for his gladiator training facility that is effectively a prison. Towards the end of Spartacus' grueling gladiatorial conditioning, Batiatus' school is visited by Roman dignitary General Crassus' family, who wish to enjoy a battle to the death. While Spartacus is forced to fight the statuesque African warrior Draba (Woody Strode) he's grown to respect, Crassus (Laurence Olivier) presses Batiatus to oblige selling him the beautiful slave Varinia (Jean Simmons) who Spartacus has fallen in love with. Around Batiatus' opulent gallery box occupied by Crassus, Kubrick already has on display various Greco-Roman motifs now used as baroque shadow script, such as Roman X-style barricades, Roman eight-rayed window frames (perfect for the eight-point "morning star"), squared-S scroll clothing trim (also used in mosaic/statuary borders), and draping victory banners strangely colored in puce green. It is unlikely Kubrick developed his esoteric color code system this early in his career, but the weak green is aptly Kubrickian for signifying

In *Spartacus* (1960), Spartacus (Kirk Douglas) comforts escaped slave Varinia (Jean Simmons). Note her "Possessed Soul" sigils.

the corroding power of the Romans. Crassus, his wife Helena, her brother Marcus Glabrus, and his fiancé exhibit spoiled, decadent behavior during their expensive stay at Batiatus' school.

The slave girl Varinia who attracts the unwanted attention of Crassus, appropriately wears two linked dark green "possessed soul" sigils on her robe's shoulder straps, each framing a red diamond that doubles for (en-slaved) woman and the later hijacking "morning star" rhomb symbol which ensnares souls. Other female slaves are found wearing similar sigils throughout *Spartacus*.

Draba being killed for sparing Spartacus and Varinia's forced departure with Batiatus to be delivered to Crassus' estate adds to Spartacus' growing rage at endured indignities which both help fuel a gladiator revolt that succeeds in escaping, inspiring more slaves to rise up and raid their former masters wherever the gladiators went. During this confusion, Varinia escapes from Batiatus and joyfully rejoins Spartacus.

After finding his School of Gladiators in ruins, Batiatus seeks favor from his friend, the great Roman senator Gracchus (Charles Laughton), General Crassus' chief political adversary and obstacle from obtaining full power of Rome. Olivier's and Laughton's casting could not have been more perfect, as the two were known to hate each other in real life.[3]

The at times painful earnestness of the slave scenes in the wastelands can make one pine for Rome's spectacle and absorbing political intrigues, whose layered nuance reflect an engaging script by Dalton Trumbo based on the book *Spartacus* by Howard Fast, both writers who suffered under the McCarthy era Red Scare blacklist by refusing to give names. The screenplay was expanded upon by Kubrick, Calder Willingham, and Ustinov much to Trumbo's consternation. The sweeping panoramic views of Russell Metty's opening cinematography, capturing thousands of slaves toiling in the mines and Kubrick's masterful camerawork tracking the vastness of Spartacus' slave army on the move and the climactic battle scenes of imposing Roman military maneuvers executed by thousands of soldiers are among some of the most breathtaking wide-shot scenes put on film for combat.

Arriving to his grand estate (partial shots of Hearst Castle), General Crassus finds a gift of slaves waiting for him from a thankful governor. As Crassus assigns handsome young Antoninus (Tony Curtis) as his new personal servant, Gracchus turns out to be a more benevolent patrician towards his preferred harem of female slaves which Batiatus obsequiously teases him about. At one point Gracchus gently chides a slave named Julia to stop crying because "this is a happy house." As Julia's name is mentioned at least twice (a doubling), she may be a name cameo in honor of veteran set designer Julia Heron who worked on the film's interiors.

A lot can be missed in a Kubrick dolly shot. As Crassus strides past his rectangular pool to meet with Glabrus (an oily John Dall), shadowy fan shapes highlight a dark corner near a Priapus statue and Grecian-style dolphins bedeck the pool centerpiece. Surrounded by mainly nude male statuary, this pool has "rising-sun" borders at either end. The stylized snub-nosed dolphins and painted water horse above Crassus' atrium door are two disguises modern Luciferian agathodaemons (profaned cosmic serpents) inhabit. The snub-nosed dolphins reappear again gracing the corners of an elite Roman bath's central pool. Other beasts these deceptive agathodaemons later impersonate are monster serpents, dragons, fish, or two-legged lions, wolves, or griffons with curling, comet-like tails. Part of the Left Hand Path's appeal for the agathodaemon is that it was originally a beneficial Grecian serpent deity that doubled as a fair youth of garden plenty, a rather irresistible disguise for a palimpsest of Lucifer.

The fan-shape pattern pops up again as Crassus' trimmed shrubbery, in the orange-and-blue owl stained glass in *Barry Lyndon*'s shell grotto, the kitchen in *The Shining* and as unusual chain-link fencing in *Eyes Wide Shut*. When Crassus first sees Glabrus it is from behind a lit curtain, displaying a spiral-topped lamp stand's sharp silhouette. These spiral-topped hanging lamp stands make recurring appearances, such as in Crassus' and Antoninus' scene right after their famous "oysters and snails" sequence.

If now one was to take a stroll in any western city, look around: you may be surprised to note all the light fixtures, streetlights, wall lamps, iron fencing, and hanging shop plaques decorated with curly-ended S or C-for-comet scrolls. The lighting, lamps, fireplaces, chandeliers, and stairwells inside old buildings often have spiraling S and C scrolls too, a hallmark of baroque décor with sometimes more sinister meaning assigned to them. Taking such common locations into account, suggests the Luciferian upper classes strongly

Crassus (Laurence Olivier, left) and Marcus Glabrus (John Dall) frame Roman-coveted Near Eastern symbols now coveted as Luciferian baroque décor in *Spartacus*.

associate these scrolls with themes of light and ascent in addition to being satanic initials. Overlapping C's create S scrolls and linking C scrolls also conveniently make Luciferian rhombs.

While Crassus reprimands his second-in-command Marcus Glabrus for accepting Gracchus' strategically-expedient assignment of taking a good portion of Crassus' army away from Rome, effectively halting any possible military take-over of the city. This exchange takes place in Crassus' atrium, a dark blue room with painted yellow details which originated in the ancient Near East, such as Inanna's 8-petaled rosette, flipped scroll tendrils, flower-like "sun-ray chains," and hook-like, curling/branching boteh designs to be later seized as shadow occult sigils hidden in baroque décor. Kubrick ensures these bold yellow and red designs are either carefully framed by the two scheming Roman soldiers or in clear view next to them. Close-ups of Crassus magnify different details in the background. As they are kept in sight, it is plain viewers are meant to notice them. Crassus' gold palmette clasps become yet another appropriated 16th- and 17th-century western occult motif for victory and the eternal rising sun.

After Crassus propositions Antoninus at his bath, the scared young man runs away to join Spartacus' ex-slave army. Somewhat embarrassed by his light entertainment skills compared to the practical drudgery most slaves are subjected to, Antoninus is determined to make himself useful. His literacy wins him a position as Spartacus' reader, an ability Spartacus himself lacks.

Within this mighty amassing force of former slaves, Kubrick's cameramen make time for many little moments depicting the wide swath of humanity swelling its ranks, and women are not left out. Among the shots of celebrating little people, couples young and old making merry, the downtrodden from many lands listening to Spartacus speak, the ugly and the injured included among the hale and handsome, women are seen laughing among themselves, washing children, enjoying children at play, cooking, weaving, and making camp. During the beginning of the city slave riots, a freed woman is seen beating an old master for past wrongs until she is dragged away. Afterwards, when Spartacus arrives on horseback to greet newly escaped arrivals at his camp, he jovially remarks, "There are too many women." An elder lady, not knowing who he is, steps out to shame him, declaring, "Where would you be, you lout, if some woman had not gone through the pains of hell to get you into this accursed world? I can handle a knife in the dark as well as anyone, I can cast spells and brew poisons and I've made the death shrouds of seven Roman masters!" Spartacus joyfully lifts her up to welcome her and as he introduces himself she responds by embracing him. Before this humorous scene, Spartacus asks a new male slave of his skills, who replies, "I am a carpenter, a mason."

An underrated protagonist in this movie is Gracchus, the First Senator of the Senate who politically fights to protect Rome's limited democracy from military takeover and tyranny. While entertaining Batiatus, Gracchus' food-laden, goat-cornered table invokes either the Bacchus or Pan of nature's plenty and sensual pleasures. In the 15th and 16th centuries onward, the aristocratic European classes gradually co-opted the Bacchus/Pan goat/faun/satyr image as "masques" or "grotesque" effigies for disguising Lucifer's boss or Capricorn, the chief constellation for Left Hand Path followers. But long before Rome fell to its own vices and military overreach, Pan was revered as an essential male force in nature and had not yet been devolved into a mere symbol of hedonistic excess, similar to Bacchus/Dionysus. Due to the rise of Christianity and future 15th- and 16th-century Luciferian kidnapping, the image of Pan and other horned nature demigods were further demonized.

The traditionally baroque terms "masque" and "grotesque" are very telling of modern Luciferian artistic subterfuge. They enjoy Lucifer wearing the "masques" of other deities and classical heroes of humanity, be they bringers/messengers of light and knowledge, or those who dared to defy the gods on humanity's behalf, or impersonating the sun itself. Any "grotesque" carving or sculpture with S-shaped features or framed with S or C scrolls is no protective gargoyle, especially if it has a purposelessly wide gaping mouth (not a fountain spout or drainage fixture). The gaping mouth directly relates to the Luciferian use of a black/soul mirror (ovoid traditionally but not exclusively) for ascension; they equate stepping into the initially black abyss through the mirror to the wide open mouth of Lucifer/Satan, and is a perverse rip-off of the age-old Egyptian "Opening of the Mouth" religious ceremony originally created to help good souls find their way to the realm of the gods. Certain styles of baroque mirror and picture frames mimic stylizations of the ancient tools used in that ceremony, such as the adze and (for them) the temptingly symbolic peseshkaf "serpent's tongue" tool.

Recall the genius of *The Shining*'s Maze: the devil's gaping mouth holds a "✝" flanked by two S's actually reveals how Luciferians conceptualize their ascension process (through the mouth/mirror) and not just mocks the Christian cross. This is in part what light bringer lamps represent: Illumination through the Darkness. Remember when Jack Torrence squints at himself and then *opens his mouth wide* in the *mirror*. As he does it, a nasty devil head floats above Jack's on his headboard. Let us also not forget Claire Quilty's malevolently dark devil mirror. This pillaging of Egyptian religious articles and symbols goes deep within the unfortunate overlap of higher degree Freemasonry and Luciferianism, both of which Kubrick's select design teams have resolutely yet quietly compared through a battery of concealed approaches within *Paths of Glory, Dr. Strangelove, Clockwork Orange, Barry Lyndon, The Shining,* and *Eyes Wide Shut*. In *Spartacus*, Kubrick's subterfuge focuses more on bringing the Greco-Roman and Near Eastern aesthetic trappings that Luciferians appropriated to the fore.

*Spartacus* at times scores points for those more thick of limb (thanks to Ustinov's added lines). Gracchus makes the case for corpulence making "a man more reasonable, pleasant ... have you noticed the nastiest of tyrants are invariably thin!" Level-headed Gracchus understands the venial Batiatus and finds him amusing. In return, Batiatus genuinely likes Gracchus beyond their mutually beneficial business relations, often selling Gracchus slaves below his usual asking price. During their talk, both men compliment a pleased servant girl for gaining weight and while Batiatus playfully makes a grab for her, she good-naturedly scurries just out of reach. Though it is not spelled out, as the two portly men talk, two other women wait in the dark either as attendants or as evening company. A true diplomat, Gracchus himself treats those below his station with more cordial respect than Crassus, whether they be slaves or peasant farmers. A young Caesar, whom Gracchus has taken under his wing to counterpoint Crassus' Marcus Glabrus, sincerely respects the great statesman he looks to as a mentor.

Gracchus' estate is dominated by statues, mosaics, and frescoes of women. The long, painted hallway frescoes to his dining area also contain an unusual amount of women and appear to tell a story. It is no less than a copy of Pompeii's Villa of Mysteries murals, depicting a woman's Bacchic initiation. In the movie, Bacchus himself is reclining in the arms of Ariadne (the weaving goddess), whom he looks up to in an inebriated, loving fashion. The lady initiate in the original mural panels usually wears dark clothing. A blue-winged Victoria (the Roman Nike) is seen near a kneeling, orange-clad girl offering up a purple mantle while Nike readies a rod to strike the half-dressed initiate in black crying in the lap of another woman. Is the comforting lady the Goddess

Ceres (agricultural goddess of plenty) and the crying initiate invoking her daughter Proserpina (the Roman Persephone)? In the next panel the initiate's nude back is turned to us, showing no rod-marks as she dances. Between her and a lady in a dark stola is the Maenad's pinecone-topped thyrsus staff.

Other female figures have thyrsus staffs as well. Were at one time, fully-initiated Maenad priestesses cognizant of the pinecone's deeper pineal/Third Eye symbolism? The Villa of Mysteries panels give strong hints that this may be so. In one the original panels (not seen in the film) the initiate throws off her inky palla in fear of not only what Bacchus' tutor Selenus (an old satyr) holds in his hand; a gazing water goblet or mirror that another initiate looks into, but also a more frightening satyr mask being held over wise Selenus' head. Like the ancient Egyptians, the Bacchic/Dionysian mysteries appear to be aware of the revelatory powers of reflective surfaces when used properly. The mystery behind the movie murals true meaning and why Kubrick included them as Gracchus' stand-out friezes may be worth pursuing.

There are other Greco-Roman props and trappings Kubrick brings to attention more than once: the fasces, a bundle of rods in crisscrossed (X) wrappings, appears in the arms of standard bearers (lictores) near the Senate's entrance, the fasces Spartacus recognizes as "the power of the Senate" that he breaks in two for effect after successfully raiding Glabrus' army camp, and the gold fasces baton Crassus on the march waves in declaration of his new magisterial powers. The fasces is in continued use today as a western symbol of judicial authority over the public.

An unusual and decidedly non–Greco-Roman breastplate plaque centers Crassus' otherwise Roman-appropriate ceremonial uniform he wears just once during the pomp and circumstance of his troops leaving Rome to intercept Spartacus' ex-slave army. It is interesting that this one uniform Laurence

In *Spartacus*, General Crassus (Laurence Olivier) sees off his troops. On his breastplate peering out from behind a baldric strap is a gold devil/wolf head.

Olivier wore was on display in the touring Stanley Kubrick museum exhibit, for here the entire gold-on-white breastplate can be seen where in the film only part of it was shown. The top main section of this breastplate depicts a most demonic "wolf's" head that is *not* the standard historic depiction of a Roman-styled wolf at all. This head that is more devil than wolf is flanked by the now-recognizable boteh tendrils branching out into Luciferian spirals. On screen, Crassus' regalia reveals only the devil-wolf's horn-like ears and left eye glinting evilly in the sunlight among its gold spiraling vines. This may be among the strongest evidence of Kubrick partially using *Spartacus* as a vehicle to showcase where much of the occult elite's stolen symbolism originally comes from.

The movie's climax and tragic ending culminates in Crassus' forces winning the great battle against Spartacus' outnumbered warriors, re-capturing Antoninus, Varinia, her infant son, and unknowingly, Spartacus himself. When Crassus is reunited with his long sought-after slave, Varinia, a clever touch in Alex North's soundtrack reprises the same suite of music during Crassus' separate attempts to seduce Antoninus and Varinia. Varinia manages to keep him at bay by how she simply yet artfully holds up a mirror to Crassus with her words. Though he leaves her unharmed, the highly-polished floor betrays Crassus' wolfish intentions to the left of Varinia just before their scene ends.

The Roman army force-marches the surviving slaves to be crucified along the path to Rome. The Roman cross (crux), shaped like a T and called a tau ("t" in Latin) cross used in Catholicism, is hijacked as yet another Luciferian sigil Kubrick exposed in films like *The Shining, Full Metal Jacket,* and *Eyes Wide Shut,* usually hidden in architectural details or leaded glass.

In a final display of jealous cruelty, Crassus orders Spartacus and An-

A top-down view of Varinia (Jean Simmons) held captive in General Crassus' marbled villa.

toninus to fight to the death, the winner rewarded with crucifixion, an excruciatingly slow demise. This results in the debatably penultimate manly scene of two men demonstrating their love by trying to kill one another in order to spare the other from a far more gruesome death. In the end, an anguished Spartacus stabs Antoninus as quickly and humanely as possible. The two men declare their filial love to each other before Antoninus fades away.

Knowing his days are numbered with Crassus' triumphant return, Gracchus bribes Batiatus to steal Varinia away from Crassus as Gracchus makes arrangements for her and her son to be free citizens and significantly increases Batiatus' bribe money to ensure her safe delivery outside of Rome. "Now will you please leave before the soldiers come here," Gracchus waves them away. Batiatus entreats Gracchus to come with them, "Make sure I don't misuse the money," he jokes. Varinia kisses Gracchus gratefully goodbye and the two reluctantly leave Gracchus to his own devices. Unbeknownst to them, Gracchus had no real escape plans but is last seen unsheathing a long dagger as he retires to his bath one last and final time. Gracchus stoically realized that for him, running away from Crassus' determined soldiers would be a vain exercise. Especially if they were headed by ex-ally now turncoat Julius Caesar.

Due to frequent clashes and direction disputes with Kirk Douglas, Stanley Kubrick never felt *Spartacus*' final outcome was the film he wanted it to be. For example, he considered the ending of Varinia presenting the crucified Spartacus his free-born son was "a bit silly." Though the experience of making *Spartacus* strengthened Kubrick's resolve to work only for himself in the future, Stanley Kubrick did manage to leave his artistic and esoteric signature on the movie in spite of his conflicts with Douglas, scriptwriter Dalton Trumbo, and Cinematographer Russell Metty, whose particular job Kubrick simply took over. Concerned ringleader Douglas, along with the majority of *Spartacus*' cast and crew, were understandably completely in the dark about Kubrick's deeper subtle messaging throughout the movie.

If he managed to get them on his side, Kubrick's potential *Spartacus* cohorts in his more secretive cinematic endeavors could have been Art Director Eric Orbum, Production Designer Alexander Golitzen, and perhaps lead Costume Designer Valle. Though given that Kubrick was a late walk-in onto the set, it is more likely he kept the underlying esoteric reasons for his otherwise authentic-looking Roman set designs, props, and clothing details to himself. Unfortunately, whether Eric Orbum was in the know or not, the stress of producing the three-ring circus that was *Spartacus* may have contributed his fatal heart attack he suffered during the making of the demanding, large-scale film.

With its cinemascope vistas of Rome in all her ancient glory, scenes of impressive military might on the march, and the teeming downtrodden traveling en masse, *Spartacus* delivers in spectacle and exciting battle sequences, as well as engaging scenes showing the humanity of both the heroes and the villains. Olivier's Crassus is more complex than the typical sword and sandals shield-banging antagonist. Both men had to learn how to fight to survive and succeed in life, yet Crassus is simply flummoxed at the genuine love and loyalty Spartacus inspires in his followers versus Crassus' own purely politically strategic alliances and use of wealth to gain power and influence. When Crassus first walks into Batiatus' school he immediately falls for Varinia upon looking at her, yet it is Spartacus that earns her love through his willingness to be vulnerable and kind, without the need to be domineering.

# 21

# *Paths of Glory:*
# Where It Begins

Stanley Kubrick's 1957 film *Paths of Glory,* starring Kirk Douglas, is set in the year 1916 during World War I. Due to rash orders impelled by war office politics, three French soldiers are chosen to die for alleged cowardice on behalf of their troops who did not charge to take the German "Anthill"—a torn-up desolation scored with ditches, barbed wire, and trenches—when enemy fire was simply too great. The first part of the film introduces two top tier French generals, where Adolph Menjou's General George Broulard comes to convince George Macready's General Paul Mireau to order his sector of men to take The Anthill, a feat that had not been accomplished in two years since the war began. The film opens where General Broulard arrives at the now French army headquarters at Schleissheim Palace where he and General Mireau are stationed in conquered German territory held by the French.

General Mireau's own luxurious office is filled with the palace's 18th-century Baroque frippery. General Broulard makes note of all the finery, praising his comrade for his good "taste in carpets and paintings." Here Kubrick and screenwriters Calder Willingham and Jim Thompson insert dialogue nudging audiences to pay some attention to the actual interior sets and not just the actors themselves. General Mireau comments that he didn't do much to the room, since "most of this was here before I arrived." In fact, given the long history of the palace, much of the furniture and décor most likely have remained unchanged for centuries.

The first thing that stands out in Mireau's lavish accommodations is its elaborate marble or inlaid wood floor work. From end to end of the spacious office, the floor is wall-to-wall tiles with X's made of two points on each end, counting eight each, the Luciferian "morning star" number. If this was the only sinister suspect example in the room one could very reasonably ignore it, but X's also appear on the room's archway curtains, wall panel details, even a fireplace's iron grating within the same space. General Broulard himself sports an X-and-O made of linked "possessed soul" sigils when he enters the

## 21. Paths of Glory: Where It Begins

door and takes off his cap, so the audience can see the diabolical motif brocaded on the top of his military chapeau. The double doors Broulard walks through themselves have eighteen panels of glass each, a more than likely 6+6+6 reference that Kubrick continually repeats in the Overlook Hotel's architecture in *The Shining*.

As the two veteran actors Menjou and Macready stride around their opulent environs and hit their marks, they most likely have no idea they are doing this in part to show off the room's carefully positioned furnishings, which either carry pertinent messages of their own or direct the eye to other props that do. The potted palm that the generals circle during their conversation is a Near East symbol of rebirth and victory which makes it a popular illuciferian symbol.[1] Palmette designs originating from ancient Egypt and Sumeria, are a co-opted Masonic motif that moreover emulates the rising sun, another desired Luciferian meaning.[2] There are shots of this palm's vase that from certain angles look like grinning skulls or demons, depending on where the two generals are framed near it. The lights on its surface sometimes give the impression of malevolent pin-point eyes, impishly peering back at the audience. Even the base of its handles reveal an "S"-eared devil with a gaping mouth. Any so called "grotesque" or "masque" face with mouth open and "S" or "C"-shaped features are likely Luciferian motifs, especially if accompanied by any sort of curling baroque branches with spiraling tendrils. This same vase (or urn) is later moved onto a Masonic-style column left of the fireplace when Colonel Dax (Kirk Douglas) meets the two generals there.

In *Paths of Glory* (1957), Generals Mireau (George Macready, left) and Broulard (Adolphe Menjou) walk among sumptuous objects with centuries-old symbolic significance.

At one point during this meeting, General Mireau looks in the direction of a distant ornate table whose legs are sculpted into eerie, S-backed satyrs, a peculiar Luciferian furnishing that also quietly appears in *Lolita*, *Barry Lyndon*, and *Eyes Wide Shut*. Such specific period-appropriate decorative stylings would of course be created by craftsman and upholsterers knowledgeable of 16th- and 17th-century antiques. It would be interesting to know which of Kubrick's hires might have also been well versed in the symbolism inherent within such objects and were either brought on board with the full intention of exposing the illuciferian elite, or were production crew who simply assumed their period movie gig was just Hollywood business as usual. Such examples as the textile artists who designed the intricate, multi-faced, demon-filled wallpapers in *Barry Lyndon* and *Lolita*, more likely would *have* to know what they were making for it to be even half as effective as it was. It stands to reason that one of the lead cameramen for *Paths of Glory* could have been at least somewhat aware of why Kubrick singled out particular baroque building details at Schleissheim Palace and period furniture upholstery besides their aesthetic and historic appeal. When it comes to Luciferian baroque decoration, the Schleissheim Palace is indeed an embarrassment of riches, from its goat paneled plasterwork, black marble-inlay devil harpsichord room, multi-faced XOX wallpapers, and numerous golden boy Lucifers topping various embossed plaster scenes, furniture, and ceramic heaters. There's so much there Kubrick probably had quite a time deciding what to show and what not to show.

Another potent symbol is in a towering painting of a woman over Mireau's office fireplace holds a book in her lap that makes a strong diamond shape right over her pelvic area. So Kubrick must have been aware of the meaning of this ancient African feminine/ earth symbol at least as early as the mid 1950s. Such knowledge would indicate Kubrick was already well versed in metaphysical subjects at this time in his life. He would have had to be, to sprinkle even his earliest mainstream films with such shrewdly camouflaged esoteric clues.

Paintings too, appear to be of special importance in *Paths of Glory*, as we see large paintings prominently placed in scenes, such as a particularly large landscape or battle scene being moved by soldiers. If such turn out to be replicas of real artwork, knowing their subject matter and history might prove useful in providing other clues or messages, as has been the case with *Lolita*, *Barry Lyndon*, and *Eyes Wide Shut*. The palace ballroom where the trial takes place has an incredibly large painting mounted high above its central archways, which the cameraman makes sure to capture more than once.

No shot is extraneous. When General Mireau has words with Colonel Dax about being disloyal for allegedly insisting on a trial for his accused men, it is done on one of the palace's ornately-carved marble stairwells. But this is

## 21. Paths of Glory: *Where It Begins*

not done just for a pretty change of scenery. The stairwell's lozenge-shaped banisters are in fact coiling, S-styled cartouches, pilfered Egyptian hieroglyphics meant only to hold royal names. Given what we now know about the occult elite's baroque use of the letter "S," it is a fair question to ask if this S-cartouche is merely a motif just reserved for the German aristocracy, or does it also point to "royalty" far more diabolic? Though not shown in the film, Schleissheim Palace has window decks and wall panels topped with goat heads along with putti-as-Lucifer flanking or hoisting torches of illumination.

The military misconduct trial scene is held in the vast, bright ballroom within Schleissheim Palace. All of its elaborate baroque décor is plastered in white. In the center of all this whiteness is a large black marble circle on the floor, near where the soldiers on trial sit in chairs, attended by guards with lances. Understandably nervous about the situation at hand, the military defendants are completely unaware of the centuries old, weathered eight-pointed star they are positioned near. This black eight-point star links back to the eight-tined "X" floor tiles in General Mireau's sumptuous headquarters and their mutual reference to the "light bringer's" morning star appropriated from the far more ancient Sumerian goddess Inanna.

The black and white of the ballroom is another duality trope Kubrick is fond of indicating as a main overlapping theme in both freemasonry and Luciferianism he targets as well in *Clockwork Orange, Barry Lyndon,* and *Eyes Wide Shut.* The large black marble circle creates a sort of inverse spotlight on the accused corralled nearby its circumference. All the men attending this trial, from the acting judge to the military jury, General Mireau, prosecution (Major Saint-Auban), defense (Colonel Dax), prisoners, and surrounding soldiers, each one is strategically positioned and shot to draw attention to the ballroom's curious decorations. Lighting plays a large part in drawing attention to the features Kubrick wanted, for whatever reason, to point out. Among the things the camera focuses on are the ballroom's X-and-O wall paneling (near the army judge and jury), the "satyr" faces and winged serpents (devils and agathodemons) emerging from flipped S floral archways (located behind where Maj. Saint-Auban and Colonel Dax sit) sometimes webbed with "to work or to keep in darkness" nets. At times sunlight spears the black marble circle to expose its well-worn, eight-pointed star.

The prisoners' guards hold their staffs in ways that conveniently point to the distant archways behind them, revealing less ornate flipped S's and Lucifarian putti-framed entrances, matching the Lucifer-as-child table Dax occupies. Another use of actor positioning as signifier is when Ralph Meeker's accused Corporal Philippe Paris answers the overseeing judge's questions, his head strangely tipped so his army cap repeatedly motions towards the previously-mentioned Luciferian motifs above the rear archways behind him.

At one point Colonel Dax paces back and forth while passing standing French guards with rifles in the foreground. This shot required exacting camera work for Kirk Douglas' head to be perfectly aligned with passing XO wall paneling behind him, which are in turn reinforced by the guards' bayonets pointing exactly to the XO's as the camera dollies by. When Col. Dax finally stops to remark, "It makes me ashamed to be a member of the human race," his head is level with another XO panel. Further proof that this scene purposefully highlights these XO panels is a night party scene where the camera drifts through dancing couples, following a short man whose head height just clears right under all the XO wall paneling in the same ballroom. He has gone to inform General Broulard that Colonel Dax is waiting for him. It goes without saying these two scenes executed with such similar, flawlessly positioned camera work were carefully planned, beautifully done choreography.

As Maj. Saint-Auban prosecutes the soldiers on trial and Colonel Dax comes to each accused man's defense, the camera records General Mireau's reactions as he sits on a very elaborately embellished sofa. At one point the sofa is shot at a very low angle where ghoulish faces can be seen on the sofa's seat cushion upholstery and just above them, a forward-facing horned goat head with dim, malevolent eyes just left of Mireau (a scenario Kubrick virtually mirrors in *Barry Lyndon* with Lord Wendover). Above the goat face just left of Mireau is a squinting evil eye similar to the ones that appear in

General Mireau (George Macready) sits in the seat of his enemy's masters, an Evil Eye and front-faced goat-covered couch, in *Paths of Glory*.

## 21. Paths of Glory: *Where It Begins*  217

*Barry Lyndon* and General Ripper's office in *Dr. Strangelove*. The sofa's ornate backrest decorations hide flipped S's and other Luciferian motifs. Its pattern is important because this sofa is meaningfully featured again in a climactic scene in General Mireau's office when General Broulard and Colonel Dax make their final appearance there to challenge him.

When the soirée takes place in the palace ballroom later that night, it is lit in part by tall lamp stands in the form of candlelit funeral urns, another unusually popular Luciferian decorative motif. Some of the white plaster busts illuminated by the light could be Lucifer disguised as Greco-Roman deities. To ram this nefarious occult point home even further, the ballroom's curtains display patterns of S's, XOX's, and XXX's within their folds.

When Colonel Dax confronts General Broulard in the palace library during the fancy soirée the general hosts after the trial, many details can be gleaned from the room's furniture. Colonel Dax entreats for the lives of his men to be spared, and while both men argue their positions, one of the most prominent furnishings in the scene is the embroidered chair Broulard sits in (originally this chair the first thing one sees in the room). Kubrick designates this cushioned chair as the foreground object nearest to the camera, thereby heightening its importance.

Much of the time Broulard is out of this upholstered chair or leaning over it so its intricate pattern can be seen in detail. At first it looks like a mounted figure in a pastoral scene but if one steps back and soft-focuses, its design reveals eyes, some not so friendly.

The most shocking thing about the fabric General Broulard's chair however, is that it contains the hidden words "Six Six Six" all over, sewn in various ways. Even the mounted figure's horse becomes multiple letters for "SiX," especially its legs. Other shots of the chair reveal more letters. Colonel Dax's chair by contrast has a simpler eye-like pattern.

Once General Broulard drapes his arms over this chair as he reads something, the shadow his arms cast forms yet another unfriendly eye on the chair while simultaneously creating a focus on some of the chair's letters.

Behind the two men, Grecian temple-style paneling above a fireplace contains a low, understated black pyramid shape encasing an eye in its center, crowned with a sun-ray halo. There are times when General Broulard's head is positioned right below this eye pyramid so the audience's gaze can be directed towards it. Kubrick repeats this cinematic "association by proximity" conceit in *A Space Odyssey* where a pyramid-shaped light shines right over Dr. Heywood Floyd's head as he eats and in *Eyes Wide Shut* when Bill Harford rides a taxi and a building's pyramid top hovers near his head. Noting this repeated technique, Kubrick's filmic attempts to reveal to audiences the presence of the so-called Illuminati's influence in Western history here proves to go back decades, much earlier in his career than previously realized.

As Colonel Dax pressures General Broulard on the fact that General Mireau was going to fire on his troops for not charging (he was stopped by a sergeant who required the order in writing before proceeding), Dax and Broulard are walking near library bookshelf columns topped with gold flipped S's carefully lit to stand out. Depending on how the light hits them, the S's appear to frame abstract gold owls, invoking the Masonic mascot Minerva.

The tops of the bookshelves are studded with cherubs, also lighted to stand out from the background. The illuciferian set have a tendency to cast their Fallen Angel as either an Apollo-like youth, a sun-like lion, or even in the guise of a wannabe Zeus or Hercules-type, but more craftily appears as fair-haired cherubim, preferably in porcelain or gold and black material. Kubrick revisits these devilishly discreet manifestations in films like *Lolita*, *Barry Lyndon*, and *Eyes Wide Shut*.

The library's putti poseurs are seen with their left arms raised high in allegiance to the Left Hand Path. Some of them positioned right above the bookshelves' gold mirrored "S" satanic initials. Their raised arms are similar to the gold "cherub" in *Lolita* who gets mysteriously turned to its left when something evil is revealed in Charlotte Haze's living room bookshelf.

The second most prominently featured item in this palace library scene is its rug and floor, for Kubrick films much of the library from a high camera P.O.V. that captures the faint X pattern in the library rug and the same X

General Broulard (Adolphe Menjou, right) and Colonel Dax (Kirk Douglas) in the palace library in *Paths of Glory*. At top right, sun-rays radiate from an eye in a low pyramid, seen more clearly on screen.

## 21. Paths of Glory: *Where It Begins* 219

floor textiles found in General Mireau's quarters. This camera modus operandi is used again on rug scenes in films like *Barry Lyndon*, *The Shining*, and Ziegler's poolroom rug (spattered with red XOX's) in *Eyes Wide Shut*. Later, Kirk Douglas' Colonel Dax stops to pick up his coat from an old wooden chair painted in a black X-&-rhomb woven net (meaning "to be kept in the dark" or "to work in darkness") with a gold medallion at its center that from a short distance looks very much like a large eye as well.

Colonel Dax essentially corners General Broulard with his evidence showing that General Mireau was exceeding his authority; validating such evidence in witness sworn statements and Colonel Dax's own deposition. This drives an angry General Broulard to storm out of the library in a huff to rejoin his guests. Colonel Dax is left looking on in consternation, the scene slowly fades-to-black, highlighting one suspect "cherub" overseeing Dax's worried countenance. We can surmise that this Schleissheim library's putti poser is indeed no angel.

In General Mireau's luxurious office after the condemned soldiers' execution, the generals are enjoying a meal until Colonel Dax pays a final call. The generals praise Colonel Dax for his men dying so bravely and without shame, while Dax quietly bristles. General Broulard and Colonel Dax make it clear to General Mireau that he will be investigated for his order to shoot Colonel Dax's sensibly cautious troops for not charging on command, and the illuciferian sofa plus matching chairs are shown clearly in the background

Colonel Dax (Kirk Douglas) sits with General Broulard (Adolphe Menjou) and looks on as an inverted cross shadow points to the Evil Eye sofa's left-hand side. The painting the shadow falls over is no coincidence in *Paths of Glory*.

behind Dax and Broulard, with one chair in particular being moved when the camera cuts back to their shot.

Part of this intentional consistency error is to remind the viewer about these furnishings' strikingly unique upholstery and the secrets they contain; whose insidiousness is reinforced by the shadow of a giant inverted cross on the big mounted painting above them. This wide painting itself is of a gathering at night, lit by the torch of a fair-haired youth looking straight at the viewer. Some of the women at left in the painting appear sad or curtseying. The artwork's theme or allegory could be the subject of droit du seigneur, the Judgment of Paris, or the depiction of an upper-class ritual/party. Just by visuals alone, the painting's blonde boy holding a torch is an easy figurative stand-in for Lucifer, especially with the inverted cross shadow over him. Knowing what exactly this picture portrays and who it is painted by could reveal more interesting clues, as was the case for the 18th-century girl painting prominently featured in *Lolita*.

Sometimes this background wall's lighting changes so its upside-down cross shadow gets darker. Towards the bottom, the profaned cross shadow falls over an Evil Eye on the sofa under the painting. To make this symbolism even more apparent, the Evil Eye is at all times framed exactly between Colonel Dax and General Broulard so it is always seen. Meanwhile, in the scenes that cut back to Dax and Broulard, a chair is moved to draw more attention to the sofa's menacing Evil Eye cast within the back wall's ominously looming inverted cross shadow.

From all the cinematically covert tactics Stanley Kubrick subtly employs in undertaking the exposure of the Luciferian elite manipulating Western civilization, it is indeed impressive that such film craft was developed so early on within the young director's work. Kubrick's method of moving furniture or props around to attract an audience's eye in a cunning way has shown up in his other films such as *2001: A Space Odyssey*, *Clockwork Orange*, *The Shining*, *Full Metal Jacket*, and *Eyes Wide Shut*. These same films also contain scenes where either props or people are deliberately placed to engage focus on what Kubrick deemed crucial key movie elements or thematic visual concepts he encouraged his audiences to notice.

Considering all the above evidence, the question is not whether Stanley Kubrick ever tried to alert the public about the realities of corrupt occult power-brokers' chokehold on Europe and America, but when did he ever *not* know of this illuciferian presence? Before filming *Paths of Glory*, it is likely that he first became aware of such things when meeting his future third wife, painter and actress Christiane Harlan, at a high-affair costume ball in Munich:

Christiane Kubrick remembers: "He saw me on television in Munich. He called my agent and hired me. I met him at a studio, and then he went to an enormous masked ball where I was performing. He was the only one without a costume. He was quite baffled. He found a cousin of mine to help find me."[3]

It may well turn out that this was the pivotal event that started Kubrick's personal inquiry and subsequent cinematic recording of the nefarious grip such evil influence has had over Western civilization from this point on in his directing career with 1957's *Paths of Glory*. It was then sometime between *Spartacus* and starting *Lolita* that he came across Schnitzler's book *Traumnovelle* (thanks to Kirk Douglas' psychiatrist) and wanted to develop it into his next film that instead eventually became the last film he directed, *Eyes Wide Shut*.

His wife Christiane was well aware of the book's sinister, too-close-to-home subject matter and it should be understandable why she at first dissuaded him from turning the disturbing story into a movie. "Oh, please don't … not now," she told him, then, "We're so young. Let's not *go through this* right now."[4] (Italics mine.) The fact Christiane was actually relieved when Kubrick went from *2001* to developing the ultraviolent *Clockwork Orange* instead of *Traumnovelle* speaks volumes on the unsettling nature of the Austrian author's book, a rather Freudian (so arguably flawed to begin with) dissection of gender relations mired in an ominous occult undertow of intrigue.

From that day forward, all the rest of Kubrick's multifaceted films steadily contained clandestine diabolic alerts regardless of (or more to the point, because of) each movie's main subject matter targeting chosen aspects of human folly. Somewhere between meeting Christiane Harlan and producing *Paths of Glory*, Kubrick either had to somehow become a quick study in matters of the shadow occult to include such infernal elements so ingeniously into his 1957 war picture, or it was a topic he had already been mulling over for a while. Either way, *Paths of Glory* is Stanley Kubrick's first film showcasing his valiant, undercover attempts to forewarn audiences of the Western world's most unsavory inconvenient truth.

For this alone, if nothing else, we should thank Stanley Kubrick and the courageous crew people whose hand-picked talents helped craft his films' hidden symbols in embroidery, props, clothing, furnishings, lighting, and complex movie sets purposely designed to expose evil and most importantly, aid in humanity's spiritual evolution.

For those employed in these films who may have felt they were in some way used by Stanley Kubrick, perhaps now can feel reassured by the fact all their hard work indeed truly served a higher purpose.

As actor John Swindells (one of *2001*'s moonbus drivers) noticed when being introduced to the famous director for the first time, he observed Stanley Kubrick was "a very intense man, obviously with a hell of a lot on his mind."[5]

# 22

# Closing Remarks on Kubrick's Films Pre– and Post–*2001*

Probably the most stunning discovery in exploring Stanley Kubrick's body of work is how early on he started waging his quiet yet intense war baring the existence of the Deceivers, the higher echelon Luciferians that are more prevalent and influential in our modern-day society than previously realized by the public at large. In almost every Kubrick film, the director hid a selected variety of illuciferian symbols in the hopes that eventually they would be discovered and recognized for what they are. Kubrick consistently validated the value of women in his films by showing the ugliness in those that abuse them or take women for granted. Even films like *Clockwork Orange* actually reinforce women's importance in a layered, esoteric manner that does not bang people over the head with politically correct platitudes. Kubrick kept the surface story in his films often ambivalent or "take it as you see it," yet his underlying metaphysical symbolism most likely communicated what Kubrick himself thought about each of his films' subject matter, whether it be *Lolita, Clockwork Orange, Barry Lyndon, The Shining,* or *Full Metal Jacket.* It is fitting that Stanley Kubrick's last film, *Eyes Wide Shut,* can be viewed as a compendium of all the movies he ever made, as it covers a little bit of each topic that was a central theme in one of his previous films. Stanley Kubrick's movies usually had several themes running at once, but each picture had an overarching trope:

On a deeper level, *Lolita* treats its initial conceit of packaging pedophilia as an upbeat, consensual love story as the sad, monstrous farce it is. *Paths of Glory* and *Dr. Strangelove* took different approaches in attacking the highly illogical nature of military logic; the first being a straight drama and the other a savage satire. *Clockwork Orange* focuses on shadow government abuse of power in its ongoing pursuit of enforceable societal controls, whose processes in turn trickle down into the private sectors of the arts, the social classes, and the news media. *Barry Lyndon* traces an impoverished Irishman's furlough in the 1700s Seven Years War and the rise-and-fall of his fortune-hunting exploits. *Barry Lyndon*'s understory is the already-existing presence and impact of Luciferian influence in European history. What lurks underneath Stanley Kubrick's *The Shining* is the continuing coverage of this power's venomous hold within the history of now America's high society and allegorically how such can adversely affect the average American family. With brutal beauty and a deceptively secular approach, *Full Metal Jacket* revisits war as being a truly diabolical racket that keeps humanity from ascending. As a final bow, Kubrick's *Eyes Wide Shut* is a more modern focus on the sort of people *The Shining* presented as demonic ghosts of America's upper-class past. It is indeed grim to consider Stanley Kubrick may be proposing Luciferianism to be the *default religion* of the West's super-rich and powerful, from aristocracies on down. If this is true, then *Eyes Wide Shut*'s at times light-hearted, life-affirming tone downplays just how high the spiritual stakes are for the future of the human race.

Above all, in many of Kubrick's films symbolic keys to ascension are laid, with some movies hiding more clues of this age-old spiritual practice than others. Whether a person is secular or religious, and regardless of philosophical bent, the process of ascension Stanley Kubrick regularly alludes to in his feature films is open to all who seek to evolve spiritually and explore what lies beyond our physical realm.

So Seek. Try. Ascend.
And remember…

TRAVEL WISELY.

# Chapter Notes

## Part I

1. Walker, Alexander, *Stanley Kubrick, Director*, London, W.W. Norton & Co., p. 133.
2. Ciment, Michel, *Kubrick: The Definitive Edition*, New York, Faber & Faber, p. 128.
3. Howard, James, *The Stanley Kubrick Companion*, London, Batsford, p. 106.

## Chapter 1

1. Rice, Julian, *Kubrick's Hope: Discovering Optimism from 2001 to Eyes Wide Shut*, Lanham, Md., Scarecrow Press, 2008, p. 29.
2. Bogdanovich, Peter, "What They Say About Stanley Kubrick," *The New York Times Magazine*, July 4, 1999.
3. Author's phone conversation with actor Dan Richter, Jan. 3, 2018.

## Chapter 2

1. Walker, Alexander, *Stanley Kubrick, Director*, London, W.W. Norton & Co., 1999, p. 165.
2. Nelson, Thomas Allen, *Kubrick: Inside an Artist's Maze*, Bloomington, Indiana University Press, 2007, p. 107.
3. Castle, Alison, *The Stanley Kubrick Archives*, London, Taschen, 2016.
4. Kagan, Norman, *The Cinema of Stanley Kubrick*, New York, Continuum, 2003, p. 160.
5. In addition to *2001: A Space Odyssey*, many anagrams exist in Kubrick's other films such as *The Shining*, *Full Metal Jacket*, and *Eyes Wide Shut*.
6. Rasmussen, Randy Loren, *Stanley Kubrick: Seven Films Analyzed* Jefferson, N.C., McFarland, 2005, p. 73.
7. Nelson, Thomas Allen, *Kubrick: Inside a Film Artist's Maze*, Bloomington, Indiana University Press, 2007, p. 114.

## Chapter 3

1. Chion, Michel, *Kubrick's Cinema Odyssey*, London, BFI, p. 77.
2. Howard, James, *The Stanley Kubrick Companion*, London, Batsford, p. 108.
3. Frayling, Christopher, *The 2001 File*, London, Reel Art Press, 2016.
4. Ginna, Robert Emmet, "Stanley Kubrick Speaks for Himself," ew.com/article/1999/04/09/Stanley-kubrick-speaks-himself/.
5. Kerr, Michael, *Kubrick*, London, Picador, p. 92.
6. Anderson, G.A., "New Baltic Sea UFO Video—Hoax or Proof," hubpages.com/education/Baltic-Sea-UFO-Undentified-Submerged-Object-Update, July 16, 2012.
7. Bauman, Robert (alias), https://www.scribd.com/document/111799666/The-Ambassador, Oct 30, 2012.
8. Dr. Kalinin's blue sweater disappears in the scientists' scene, an inconsistency fixed by using an intercom announcement to explain.
9. This is, in fact, one of Kubrick's signature camera devices he has utilized since *Killer's Kiss* (for example, bus interior shots).
10. Castle, Alison, *The Stanley Kubrick Archives*, London, Taschen, pp. 419–424.
11. Loughlin, Gerald, *Alien Sex: The Body and Desire in Cinema and Theology*, Cornwall: Blackwell, 2004, pp. 64–102.

## Chapter 4

1. Walker, Alexander, *Stanley Kubrick, Director*, London, W.W. Norton & Co. 1999, p. 164.

2. Johari, Harish, *CHAKRAS Energy Centers of Transformation*, Rochester, Vt., Destiny Books, 2000.
3. Nelson, Thomas Allen, *Kubrick: Inside an Artist's Maze*, Bloomington, Indiana University Press, p. 117.
4. Good one, Stanley.
5. George Lucas mentions Kubrick's "very subtle" use of cinematic language in the documentary *Stanley Kubrick: A Life in Pictures*.
6. Kagan, Norman, *The Cinema of Stanley Kubrick*, New York, Continuum, 2003, pp. 156–157.
7. LoBrotto, Vincent, *Stanley Kubrick: A Biography*, New York, Da Capo Press, 1999, p. 286.
8. Corballis, Michael C., "Left Brain, Right Brain, Facts and Fantasies," *PLOS | Biology Journal*, Jan. 21, 2014.
9. cbsnews.com/news/mona-lisas-hidden-symbols-researcher-says-yes/, Jan. 12, 2011.
10. Bible, King James Version, Luke 17:21.
11. French, Karen L., *Gateway to the Heavens*, London, Watkins, 2014, pp. 62–66.
12. Frayling, Christopher, *The 2001 File: Harry Lange and the Design of the Landmark Science Fiction Film*, London, Reel Art Press, 2016.
13. Giardina, Carolyin, "2001: A Space Odyssey: Douglas Trumball on Kubrick's Search for 'Ultimate Perfection,'" hollywoodreporter.com, May 25, 2018.

## Chapter 5

1. Rice, Julian, *Stanley Kubrick's Hope*, Lanham, Md., Scarecrow Press, p. 36.
2. Kuberski, Philip, *Kubrick's Total Cinema*, New York, Bloomsbury, pp. 77–78.
3. Chion, Michel, *Kubrick's Cinema Odyssey*, London, BFI, p. 79.
4. Kuberski, Philip, *Kubrick's Total Cinema: Philosophical Themes and Formal Qualities*, New York, Bloomsbury, p. 130.
5. Chion, Michel, *Kubrick's Cinema Odyssey*, London, BFI, p. 79.
6. French, Karen L., *Gateway to the Heavens*, London, Watkins, pp. 63–66.
7. Nelson, Thomas Allen, *KUBRICK: Inside an Artist's Maze*, Bloomington, Indiana University Press, p. 111.
8. Edwards, Betty, *Drawing on the Right Side of the Brain*, London, HarperCollins, 2008.

9. Kagan, Norman, *Cinema of Stanley Kubrick*, New York, Continuum, p. 161.
10. French, Karen L., *Gateway to the Heavens*, London, Watkins, 2014, pp. 49–53.
11. Kagan, Norman, *The Cinema of Stanley Kubrick*, New York, Continuum, 2003, p. 161.

## Chapter 6

1. Ciment, Michel, *Kubrick: The Definitive Edition/Kubrick and the Fantastic*, p. 134.
2. Kagan, Norman, *The Cinema of Stanley Kubrick*, New York, Continuum, 2003, p.160.
3. Walker Alexander, *Stanley Kubrick, Director*, p.187.
4. Nelson, Thomas Allen, *Kubrick: Inside an Artist's Maze*, Bloomington, Indiana University Press, 2007, p. 128.
5. https://www.cnbc.com/2018/06/05/hanson-robotics-sophia-the-robot-pr-stunt-artificial-intelligence.html.
6. Frayling, Christopher, *The 2001 File: Harry Lange and the Design of the Landmark Science Fiction Film*, London, Reel Art Press, 2016.
7. Krohn, Bill, *Masters of Cinema: Stanley Kubrick*, London, Phaidon, 2010, p. 52.
8. Ljuijic, Tatjana, "Peldszus Regina," *Stanley Kubrick: New Perspectives*, London, Black Dog, 2015, pp. 215–217.
9. Kuberski, Philip, *Kubrick's Total Cinema: Philosophical Themes and Formal Qualities*, New York, Bloomsbury, 2014, p. 130.
10. Ljuijic, Tatjana, "Peldszus R.," *Stanley Kubrick: New Perspectives*, London: Black Dog, 2015, p. 201.
11. Duncan, Paul, *Stanley Kubrick: Visual Poet*, New York, Taschen, p. 113.

## Chapter 7

1. Anodea, Judith, *Eastern Body Western Mind: Psychology & the Chakra System as a Path to Self*, Berkeley, Celestial Arts, 2004.
2. Bosman, Leonard, *The Meaning and Philosophy of Numbers*, Berwick, Me., Ibis Press, 2005, pp. 96–99.
3. Bosman, Leonard, *The Meaning and Philosophy of Numbers*, Berwick, Me., 2005, p. 149.
4. Pennick, N., *Sacred Geometry, Symbolism and Purpose in Religious Structures*, Wellingborough, Turnstone, 1980.

## Chapter 8

1. Dashu, Max, *Witches and Pagans*, Richmond, Ca., Veleda Press, 2017, pp. 153–154.
2. Walker, Alexander, *Stanley Kubrick, Director*, London, W.W. Norton & Co., 1999, p. 190.
3. Schiavello, Michael, "The Connection Between Ancient Egyptian Mystery Schools & Freemasonry," https://www.gaia.com/article/, Feb. 13, 2017.
4. Friends of Christ King of France, "The LHR Bourbons French Masons," http://www.a-c-r-f.com/documents/LHR-Bourbons_francs-macons.pdf.
5. Tuckwood, Kenneth J., "Talks on Freemasonry," District Chairman of Masonic Education 2002–2003 UGLE.
6. Mackey, Albert Gallatin, *The Symbolism of Freemasonry*, Charleston, S.C., Forgotten Books, 1869/1882 (reprinted 2008).
7. Chion, Michel, *Kubrick's Cinema Odyssey*, London, BFI, 2001.

## Chapter 9

1. Squirt also wears inverted stars, whose original sacred meaning is "spirit into matter" but inverted pentagrams have been historically profaned to *imprison* spirit in the material realm in malevolent magic.
2. White, Rusty, "Ann Gillis: 2001 Interview," rustywhitesfilmworldobituaries.blogspot.com/2010/04/ann-gillis-2001-interview.html, Memphis Film Festival.
3. Nelson, Thomas Allen, *Kubrick: Inside a Film Artist's Maze*, Bloomington, Indiana University Press, 2007, p. 121.
4. Howard, James, *The Stanley Kubrick Companion*, London, Batsford, 1999, p. 100.
5. Pezzotta, Elisa, *Stanley Kubrick: Adapting the Sublime*, Jackson: University Press of Mississippi, 2016, p. 51.
6. Anderson, G.A., "New Baltic Sea UFO Video-Hoax or Proof," HubPages.com, July 16, 2012. Bauman, Robert (alias), www.scribd.com/document/111799666/The-Ambassador, 2012.
7. Lindsay, Jack, *The Origins of Astrology*, New York, Barnes & Noble, 1971, p. 237.
8. West, John Anthony, *The Traveler's Key to Ancient Egypt*, Wheaton, Il., Quest Books, 1995, pp. 73–74.
9. Schorn, Joel, *U.S. Catholic*, Vol. 78, No. 10, p. 46.
10. King James Bible, New Testament, Book of John: Revelations 17.
11. Herr, Michael, *KUBRICK*, London, Picador, 2001, pp. 9–10.

## Chapter 10

1. de Grummond, N.T., *Guide to Etruscan Mirrors*, Tallahassee, 1982, pp. 183–184.
2. Deutsch, Rabbi Eliezer Chaim, *Duda'ei ha-Sadeh*, Issue 78.
3. West, John Anthony, *The Traveler's Key to Ancient Egypt*, Wheaton, Il., Quest Books, 1995, p. 78.
4. Naydler, Jeremy, *Shamanic Wisdom in the Pyramid Texts: The Mystical Tradition of Ancient Egypt*. Rochester, Vt., Inner Traditions, 2005.
5. ritualabuse.wordpress.com/2013/12/19/kim-noble-activist-artist, Dec, 18. 2013.
6. www.geocities.ws/malcomtribute/acomagee.html

## Chapter 11

1. Asher Sinclair, Rabbi Yaakov, *Seasons of the Moon* (Iyar 5759), Jerusalem, Israel, Jewish Learning Exchange of OSI, May 15, 1999.
2. Frayling, Christopher, *The 2001 File: Harry Lange and the Design of the Landmark Science Fiction Film*, London, Reel Art Press, 2016.

## Chapter 12

1. Peldszus, Regina, *Stanley Kubrick: New Perspectives*, p. 217.

## Chapter 13

1. "Domestic abuse" is an unfortunate term that seems purposely designed to isolate and minimize the serious nature of such abuse.
2. Sakuramicheletakahashi.wordpress.com/2013/08/08/2013/satanic-celebrities-of-the-past, Aug. 8, 2013.
3. Fox, James, "Roman Polanski gives rare interview," https://www.vanityfair.com/style/2013/09/roman-polanski-interview, Sept, 25, 2013.
4. Weller, Sheila, *Girls Like Us*, New York, Atria Books, 2008, pp. 366–367.
5. Abbot, Kate, "How We Made Stan-

*ley Kubrick's The Shining,*" https://www.theguardian.com/film/2012/oct/29/how-we-made-the-shining, Oct. 29, 2012.

6. Wynalda, Steve, https://listverse.com/2015/08/03/10-crazy-things-stanley-kubrick-did-to-film-the-, 3, 2.

7. Bogdanovich, Peter, "What They Say About Stanley Kubrick," *The New York Times Magazine,* July 4, 1999.

8. MentalFloss.com/article/55893/25-things-you-might-not-know-about-shining.

9. In this book, "shadow script" is a catch-all phrase for any evil-intentioned magical motifs, insignia, and curse spell-work sigils.

10. Excavated by Dr. Henshilwood's team in Blombos Cave, South Africa, 1993.

11. https://En.wikipedia.org/wiki/Wolfsangel.

12. The Baphomet and Goat of Mendes was invented by self-styled French occultist Elphias Levi in 1856.

13. The Spiral can be found all over the world (Africa, Asia, the Americas, Europe, and the UK) as an ancient symbol for the womb or universal creative energies.

14. Examples of palmettes and their attached S scroll tendrils can be found as border trim on Athens' Erechtheum temple, Greece, 5th century BCE.

15. The Nazi Wehrmacht Infantry and Panzer troops that used wolfsangels were the 19th, 33rd, 206th & 256th Divisions.

16. Sutton, Anthony C., *Wall Street and the Rise of Hitler,* Forest Row, England, Clairview, 2010.

17. Wynalda, Steve, "Ten Crazy Things Stanley Kubrick Did to Film The Shining," Aug. 3, 2015. https://listverse.com/2015/08/03/10-crazy-things-stanley-kubrick-did-to-film-the-shining/.

## Chapter 14

1. Oscars Youtube Channel: "Ryan O'Neal on making 'Barry Lyndon' with Stanley Kubrick," www.youtube.com/watch?v=yVEqryTE2AY.

2. Michael Hordern also voiced the sun Lord Frith in the '78 animated film *Watership Down.* Now there's a fictional sun god worthy of respect.

3. Kerrane, Kevin, *The Art of Fact: A Historical Anthology of Literary Journalism,* New York, Simon & Schuster, 1998, pp. 321–322.

## Chapter 15

1. Boissoneault, Lorraine, "The True Story of Brainwashing and How It Shaped America," SmithsonianMag.com/history, May 22, 2017.

2. Though never convicted of any crime, many parents would think twice about leaving their girls alone in the same room with the likes of Vladimir Nabokov (when alive) and Woody Allen, who married his adopted daughter.

3. Ronson, John, "After Stanley Kubrick," *The Guardian,* Aug. 18, 2010.

4. Freemasoninformation.com/masonic-education/books/the-beginning-of-masonry//the-masoni-symbolism-of-color/.

5. HMP Wandsworth was built in 1851 (originally Surrey House of Correction) and is currently still the largest men's prison in the UK.

6. One of Lucifer's prime sigils contains two large X's, the base of one breaking into two smaller x's. It also has the hijacked Canaanite "mouth" glyph which doubles as satanic initials.

7. Freitag, Dr. Steven M., "The Use of Light and Sound Technology with Hypnosis," Feb. 26, 2005.

8. Clegg, Robert I., *Mackey's Revised Encyclopedia of Freemasonry,* Chicago, The Masonic History Company, 1929, pp. 140–46.

9. Chaitkin, Anton, "British Psychiatry, from Eugenics to Assassination," *EIR,* Vol. 20, No. 40, Oct. 7, 1994.

10. *Eyes Wide Shut's* repeated Italian references suggest decadent 17th- and 18th-century Venice as the root history of *Traumnovelle's* mystery.

11. Alleged mind control survivors' artwork such as Kim Noble/Ria Pratt and Lynn Schirmer feature checkerboard patterns and dissociative states.

12. Marthe, Emalie, "The Monarch Mind Control Mystique," vice.com/en_us/article/9bne7e/the-monarch-mind-control-mystique, Aug. 2013. Besides the prevalence of neon wigs in *Clockwork Orange,* such wigs and "sex kitten" imagery reappear again in Kubrick's *Eyes Wide Shut.*

13. International Society for the Study of Trauma and Dissociation, "What is dissociation?," www.isst-d.or/?contentID=76, 2002–2003.

14. FAQ: "Symptoms and signs of

dissociative disorders," www.nami.org/learn-more/mental-health-conditions/dissociative-disorders.

## Chapter 16

1. Abrams, Nathan, *Stanley Kubrick: New York Jewish Intellectual*, New Brunswick, Rutgers University Press, 2018.
2. Castle, Robert, "Don't Follow Leaders: Animal Mother in *Full Metal Jacket*," www.brightlightsfilm.com, July 31, 2004.

## Chapter 17

1. Ebert, Roger, "Cruise Opens up About Working with Kubrick," *Chicago Sun Times*, July 14, 1999.
2. En.wikipedia.org/wiki/Babalon.
3. Rice, Julian, *Stanley Kubrick's Hope Discovering Optimism from 2001 to Eyes Wide Shut*, Lanham, Md., Scarecrow Press, 2008, p. 29.
4. Boissoneault, Lorraine, "The True Story of Brainwashing and How It Shaped America," Smithsonian.com, May 22, 2017.
5. Such as is exemplified in Biljana Djurdjevic's paintings *Dummies* ('06), *Bad Behavior* ('05), and *Systematic Examination* ('05), *Living In Oblivion* Series.
6. Boar head on stick in front of Belvedere Palace fountain, Travelladda.com/all-list-city-places/Austria/Vienna/Vienna/experience-all#image-10375.
7. Koons, *Ushering in Banality*, 1988. Amsterdam, Stedelijkt Museum, 2012 Exhibit.

## Chapter 18

1. http://www.wackyuses.com/weirdfacts/wrigleys.html.
2. http://www.wackyuses.com/weirdfacts/wrigleys.html.
3. Lydon, Peter, director, *The Peter Sellers Story*, BBC Arena documentary, 1995.

## Chapter 19

1. Keams, Juli, http://idyllopuspress.com/idyllopus/film/lo_selfportrait.htm.
2. Ksiezopolska, Irena, https://lfq.salisbury.edu/_issues/46_2/kubricks_lolita_quilty_as_author.html.

3. Nastasi, Alison, "20 Things You Didn't Know About Stanley Kubrick's Lolita," flavorwire.com/521766/, June 6, 2015.
4. http://artobserved.com/2013/07/ao-onsite-devils-heaven-the-2013-watermill-center-summer-benefit/.
5. https://me.me/i/lady-gaga-and-marina-at-the-20th-annual-watermill-center-11768369.
6. "The Five-O Interview," Hollywood Five-O, Inc., Fall 2002
7. "FBI Arrests Man for Sex Kidnap," *The Oregonian*, 1950.
8. https://www.theparisreview.org/blog/2016/04/19/who-wrote-lolita-first-an-interview-with-michael-maar/
9. www.vice.com/en_us/article/nnqjm/ragged-odds-and-ends-0000340-v21n6, 2014.
10. Pinkerton, Nick, "Interview: James B. Harris (Part One)," *Film Comment*, 2001.
11. Toffler, Alvin, *Playboy*, Jan. 1964 (actual interview done in 1963).
12. Oakes, Phillip, "Vladimir Nabokov interview," *The Sunday Times*, London, June 22, 1969.
13. Wikipedia.org/wiki/Vladimir_Nabokov#Life_and_career.

## Chapter 20

1. Feinberg, Scott, "Kirk Douglas: 'I am always optimistic,'" *Hollywood Reporter*, June 2008.
2. https://variety.com/2001/digital/features/spartacus-2-1200467733/.
3. https://variety.com/2001/digital/features/spartacus-2-1200467733/.

## Chapter 21

1. En.wikipedia.org/wiki/Palm branch.
2. Meyer, Franz Sales, *A Handbook of Ornament*, New York, The Architectural Book Pub. Co., 1907, pp. 31 and 92.
3. Bogdanovich, Peter, "What They Say About Stanley Kubrick," *The New York Times Magazine*, July 4, 1999.
4. Ebert, Roger, "Cruise Opens up about Working with Kubrick," *Chicago Sun Times*, July 15, 1999.
5. Cairns, Robert, "British Actor Recalls Life in the Glorious Profession," *South China Morning Post*, Jan. 6, 2005.

# Bibliography

## Print Sources

Abrams, Nathan, *Stanley Kubrick: New York Jewish Intellectual*, New Brunswick, Rutgers University Press, 2018.

Anodea, Judith, *Eastern Body Western Mind: Psychology & the Chakra System as a Path to Self*, Berkeley, Celestial Arts, 2004.

Asher Sinclair, Rabbi Yaakov, *Seasons of the Moon*, Jerusalem (Iyar 5759), Israel, Jewish Learning Exchange of OSI, May 15, 1999.

Bogdanovich, Peter, "What They Say About Stanley Kubrick," *The New York Times Magazine*, July 4, 1999.

Bosman, Leonard, *The Meaning and Philosophy of Numbers*, Berwick, Mn., 2005, p. 149.

Cairns, Robert, "British Actor Recalls Life in the Glorious Profession," *South China Morning Post*, Jan. 6, 2005.

Castle, Alison, *The Stanley Kubrick Archives*, London, Taschen, 2016.

Chaim Deutsch, Rabbi Eliezer, *Duda'ei ha-Sadeh*, 1978.

Chaitkin, Anton, "British Psychiatry, from Eugenics to Assassination," *EIR Journal*, Vol. 20, No. 40, Oct. 7, 1994.

Chion, Michel, *Kubrick's Cinema Odyssey*, London, BFI, 2001.

Ciment, Michel, *Kubrick: The Definitive Edition*, New York, Faber & Faber, 2003.

Clegg, Robert I., *Mackey's Revised Encyclopedia of Freemasonry*, Chicago, The Masonic History Company, 1929.

Corballis, Michael C., "Left Brain, Right Brain, Facts and Fantasies," *PLOS | Biology Journal*, Jan. 21, 2014.

de Grummond, N. T., *Guide to Etruscan Mirrors*, Tallahassee, 1982, pp. 183–184.

Deutsch, Rabbi Eliezer Chaim, *Duda'ei-ha-Sadeh*, Issue 78.

Duncan, Paul, *Stanley Kubrick: Visual Poet*, New York, Taschen, 2008.

Ebert, Roger, "Cruise Opens up About Working with Kubrick," *Chicago Sun Times*, July 14, 1999.

Edwards, Betty, *Drawing on the Right Side of the Brain*, London, HarperCollins, 2008.

"FBI Arrests Man for Sex Kidnap," *The Oregonian*, 1950.

Feinberg, Scott, "Kirk Douglas: 'I am always optimistic,'" *Hollywood Reporter*, June 2008.

"The Five-O Interview," *Hollywood Five-O, Inc.*, Fall 2002.

Frayling, Christopher, *The 2001 File: Harry Lange and the Design of the Landmark Science Fiction Film*, London, Reel Art Press, 2016.

French, Karen L., *Gateway to the Heavens*, London, Watkins, 2014.

García Mainar, Luis M., *Narrative and Stylistic Patterns in the Films of Stanley Kubrick*, Rochester, NY, Camden House, 2011.

Herr, Michael, *KUBRICK*, London, Picador, 2001.

Hopper, V. F., *Medieval Number Symbolism*, New York, Cooper Square, 1969.

Howard, James, *The Stanley Kubrick Companion*, London, Batsford, 1999.

Johari, Harish, *CHAKRAS Energy Centers of Transformation*, Rochester, Vt., Destiny Books, 2000.

Kagan, Norman, *The Cinema of Stanley Kubrick*, New York, Continuum, 2003.

Kerrane, Kevin, *The Art of Fact: A Historical Anthology of Literary Journalism*, New York, Simon & Schuster, 1998, pp. 321–322.

King James Bible, New Testament, Book of John: Revelations 17.

Koons, *Wintry Pig*, 1988. Amsterdam, Stedelijkt Museum, 2012.

Krohn, Bill, *Masters of Cinema: Stanley Kubrick*, London, Phaidon, 2010.
Kuberski, Philip, *Kubrick's Total Cinema: Philosophical Themes and Formal Qualities*, New York: Bloomsbury, 2014.
Lindsay, Jack, *The Origins of Astrology*, New York, Barnes & Noble, 1971.
Ljuijic, Tatjana, "Peldszus Regina," *Stanley Kubrick: New Perspectives*, London, Black Dog, 2015.
LoBrutto, Vincent, *Stanley Kubrick: A Biography*, New York, Da Capo Press, 1999.
Loughlin, Gerald, *Alien Sex: The Body and Desire in Cinema and Theology*, Cornwall, Blackwell, 2004.
Mackey, Albert Gallatin, *The Symbolism of Freemasonry*, Charleston, S.C., Forgotten Books, 1869/1882 (reprinted 2008).
Meyer, Franz Sales, *A Handbook of Ornament*, New York, The Architectural Book Pub. Co., 1907.
Naydler, Jeremy. *Shamanic Wisdom in the Pyramid Texts: The Mystical Tradition of Ancient Egypt*. Rochester, Vt., Inner Traditions, 2005.
Nelson, Thomas Allen, *Kubrick: Inside a Film Artist's Maze*, Bloomington, Indiana University Press, 2007.
Oakes, Phillip, "Vladimir Nabokov interview," *The Sunday Times*, London, June 22, 1969.
Pennick, N., *Sacred Geometry, Symbolism and Purpose in Religious Structures*, Wellingborough, Turnstone, 1980.
Pezzotta, Elisa, *Stanley Kubrick: Adapting the Sublime*, Jackson, University Press of Mississippi, 2016.
Pinkerton, Nick, "Interview: James B. Harris (Part One)," *Film Comment*, 2001.
Rasmussen, Randy Loren, *Stanley Kubrick: Seven Films Analyzed*, Jefferson, N.C., McFarland, 2005.
Rice, Julian, *Stanley Kubrick's Hope Discovering Optimism from 2001 to Eyes Wide Shut*, Lanham, Md., Scarecrow Press, 2008.
Ronson, John, "After Stanley Kubrick," *The Guardian*, Aug. 18, 2010.
Schorn, Joel, *U.S. Catholic*, Vol. 78, No. 10.
Sutton, Anthony C., *Wall Street and the Rise of Hitler*, Forest Row, England, Clairview, 2010.
Toffler, Alvin, *Playboy*, Jan. 1964 (actual Nabokov interview done in 1963).
Tuckwood, Kenneth J. "Talks on Freemasonry," District Chairman of Masonic Education, 2002–2003.
Walker, Alexander, *Stanley Kubrick, Director*, London, W.W. Norton & Co., 1999.
Weller, Sheila, *Girls Like Us*, New York, Atria Books, 2008.
West, John Anthony, *The Traveler's Key to Ancient Egypt*, Wheaton, Il., Quest Books, 1995.

## Online Sources and Other Media

Abbot, Kate, https://www.theguardian.com/film/2012/oct/29/how-we made-the-shining, Oct. 29, 2012.
Anderson, G.A., "New Baltic Sea UFO Video-Hoax or Proof," hubpages.com/education/Baltic-Sea-UFO-Unidentifid-Submerged-Object-Update, July 16, 2012.
http://artobserved.com/2013/07/ao-on-site-devils-heaven-the-2013-water-mill-center-summer-benefit/.
Bauman, Robert (alias), https://www.scribd.com/document/111799666/The-Ambassador, Oct 30, 2012.
Boissoneault, Lorraine, "The True Story of Brainwashing & How It Shaped America," SmithsonianMag.com/history/, May 22, 2017.
Castle, Robert, "Don't Follow Leaders: Animal Mother in *Full Metal Jacket*," www.brightlightsfilm.com, July 31, 2004.
cbsnews.com/news/mona-lisas-hidden-symbols-researcher-says-yes/, Jan. 12, 2011.
https://www.cnbc.com/2018/06/05/hanson-robotics-sophia-the-robot-pr-stunt-artificial-intelligence.html.
En.wikipedia.org/wiki/Palm_branch.
FAQ: "Symptoms and signs of dissociative disorders," www.nami.org/learn-more/mental-health-conditions/dissociative-disorders.
Fox, James, "Roman Polanski gives rare interview," https://www.vanityfair.com/style/2013/09/roman-polanski-interview, Sept, 25, 2013.
freemasoninformation.com/masonic-education/books/the-beginning-of-masonry//the-masoni-symbolism-of-color/.
Freitag, Dr. Steven M., "The Use of Light and Sound Technology with Hypnosis," Feb. 26, 2005.
Friends of Christ King of France, *The LHR Bourbons French Masons*, http://www.a-c-r-f.com/documents/LHR-Bourbons_francs-macons.pdf. Freemasoninforma

tion.com/masonic-education/books/the-beginning-of-masonry//the-masoni-symbolism-of-color/.

geocities.ws/malcomtribute/aco/magee.html

Giardina, Carolyn, "2001: A Space Odyssey: Douglas Trumball on Kubrick's Search for 'Ultimate Perfection,'" hollywoodreporter.com, May 25, 2018.

Ginna, Robert Emmet, "Stanley Kubrick Speaks for Himself," ew.com/article/1999/04/09/Stanley-kubrick-speaks-himself/.

Keams, Juli, http://idyllopuspress.com/idyllopus/film/lo_selfportrait.htm.

Ksiezopolska, Irena, https://lfq.salisbury.edu/_issues/46_2/kubricks_lolita_quilty_as_author.html.

International Society for the Study of Trauma and Dissociation, "What is dissociation?," www.isst-d.or/?contentID=76, 2002–2003.

Lydon, Peter, director, *The Peter Sellers Story*, BBC Arena documentary, 1995.

Marthe, Emalie, "The Monarch Mind Control Mystique," vice.com/en_us/article/9bne7e/the-monarch-mind-control-mystique, Aug. 2013.

Nastasi, Alison, "20 Things You Didn't Know About Stanley Kubrick's Lolita," flavorwire.com/521766/, June 6, 2015.

Oscars Youtube Channel, "Ryan O' Neal on making 'Barry Lyndon' with Stanley Kubrick," www.youtube.com/watch?v=yVEqryTE2AY.

ritualabuse.wordpress.com/2013/12/19/kim-noble-activist-artist, Dec. 18, 2013.

Schiavello, Michael, "The Connection Between Ancient Egyptian Mystery Schools & Freemasonry," https://www.gaia.com/article/, Feb. 13, 2017.

https://www.theparisreview.org/blog/2016/04/19/who-wrote-lolita-first-an-interview-with-michael-maar/

https://variety.com/2001/digital/features/spartacus-2-1200467533/.

www.vice.com/en_us/article/nnqjm/ragged-odds-and-ends-0000340-v21n6, 2014.

White, Rusty, "Ann Gillis: 2001 Interview," Memphis Film Festival, rustywhitesfilmworldobituaries.blogspot.com/2010/04/ann-gillis-2001-interview.html.

www.LynnSchirmer.com/.

Wynalda, Steve, "Ten Crazy Things Stanley Kubrick Did to Film The Shining," https://listverse.com/2015/08/03/10-crazy-things-stanley-kubrick-did-to-film-the-shinin, Aug. 3, 2015.

# Index

abuse as consistent Kubrickian theme: child 96, 129, 137, 142, 144, 170, 194–5; cycle of 137; domestic/family 81, 170, 195; mind control, gaslighting, conditioning 73, 90, 124, 127–9, 130–1, 138–140, 169–170, 196, 202, 228, 223; rape 74, 85, 127, 171, 192
*A.I.* (film)  45, 162, 174
artificial intelligence (A.I.)  7, 30, 38, 43–45, 232
Alex "DeLarge"  72–74, 123–144, 170, 192
anagrams (Kubrick wordplay)  14–5, 68, 82, 107–8, 130–1, 136, 158–9, 167–8, 186–7, 191, 194, 198–9, 200, 225
Ankh  18, 29, 34–38, 44, 48–50, 54–55, 61, 67, 72, 94, 100, 135, 148, 165–166, 172–173; as grid-field 30, 34, 44; as life-vessel 31, 37–38, 48, 61, 67; as thought-space 30, 32, 37, 67
ankhs  19, 31, 32, 34, 37, 40, 44–6, 50–52, 60, 61, 79, 85, 111, 134, 165, 171, 178, 180, 183, 185, 189
architecture  90, 96, 100, 116, 126, 148
*Aries* (*2001* moon shuttle)  11, 20–3, 25–7, 29, 32, 34, 37–3, 42, 46–7, 50, 53–4, 58
ascension  32–3, 38, 48, 56–9, 61–3, 70, 105, 144, 152, 157, 169, 191, 206–7, 223
associative proximity as filmic device  80, 154–5, 173, 181–2, 187–8, 190–1, 208–9, 213, 215, 217–8
astronauts: on Clavius moon 7, 11, 3, 13–5, 17, 19, 20–4, 28–9, 34, 36, 39, 41–2, 46–7, 52, 54, 68, 184; on *The Discovery* 7–8, 13–4, 16–21, 25–6, 28–9, 30–2, 34–40, 42–9, 51–5, 57–8, 67, 76, 179
Athena  66–7

Balibari, Chevalier de (*Barry Lyndon*)  114–116
*Barry Lyndon*  1, 3–4, 81, 83, 103, 111–122, 128, 156, 186, 188, 191, 204, 207, 214–5, 217–9, 222–3, 233; *Eyes Wide Shut* 81, 103, 112, 116–8, 122, 188, 204, 214, 218; *Full Metal Jacket* 185–6, 223; (as it relates to) *The Shining* 81, 83, 112, 188, 191, 204, 207, 219, 223
Berenson, Maria (Lady Honoria Lyndon)  115–118
blue: as dark consciousness 129, 141, 171; as the heavenly realms 59, 157, 163, 166; as higher awareness/consciousness 59, 151, 170–1; as the masonic/traditional masculine color 41, 59, 151–2, 157, 163; as used in Kubrick films 27–8, 39–41, 46, 59–60, 62, 129, 141, 144, 151–2, 171
Bowman, Dr. Dave  3, 7–8, 16, 19, 20–1, 23–4, 26–30, 32, 34, 37–45, 49–64, 67–9, 71, 76, 95, 161
Braun, Wernher von  47, 184
Brow symbolism  26, 28, 31, 66, 128, 166, 173, 200
Burgess, Anthony  124, 132, 192
Brodsky, Dr. (*A Clockwork Orange*)  79, 138
Bull, Peter (Amb. de Sadeski)  177

C as consciousness container  28–9, 37–8, 48, 178
Campbell, Joseph  9, 166
Castle, Alison (author)  vi, 225, 231
Chion, Michel (author)  17, 36, 63, 231
Ciment, Michel (author)  44, 231
Clarke, Arthur C.  9, 13, 23–24, 179
Clavius moon base  7, 11, 3, 13–5, 17, 19, 20–4, 28–9, 34, 36, 39, 41–2, 46–8, 52, 54, 58, 65, 68, 184
*A Clockwork Orange*  1, 3, 4, 38, 40, 56, 61, 72–4, 79, 81, 84, 90, 96, 98, 105, 113–4, 117, 122–44, 147, 148, 151, 153–8, 161, 165, 167, 169–71, 173–6, 180. 189, 192, 194, 207, 215, 220–22, 228; futurism as subtext 4, 124, 126, 130–1; government societal controls 90, 128–130, 136, 140, 142–3, 189, 222; sleeves, importance of 74, 129, 138, 156
color code  20, 35–41, 58, 63, 65, 68, 84, 92, 105, 108, 130, 132, 141, 151, 153–4, 157, 164, 169–70, 202
consciousness, glyphs of  26–34, 166
continuity/intentional errors as Kubrickian device  20, 22, 113, 118, 150, 152, 158, 163, 220
Corri, Adrienne (as Mrs. Alexander, CO)  74, 132, 144
Crothers, Scatman (Dick Halloran, *Shining*)  82, 85, 102
Cruise, Tom  167, 169, 229, 231

235

# 236 Index

darkness as a Kubrickian theme 93, 100, 117, 155, 163–4, 171, 184, 207, 215, 219
*Dawn of Man* (*2001*) 7, 9–11
dialogue, as used in Kubrick films: repeating phrases 19, 69, 201; revealing layered context 19–21 66, 78–79, 94, 150, 192, 212
Discovery 1B (*2001* craft to Jupiter) 7–8, 13–4, 16–21, 25–6, 28–9, 30–2, 34–40, 42–9, 51–5, 57–8, 67, 76, 179
*Dr. Strangelove* 4, 19–20, 79, 90, 148, 175, 176–188, 191, 207, 217, 222
D'Onofrio, Vincent (actor, *Full Metal Jacket*) 146
doppelgangers 14–16, 21–23, 28, 67–8, 125, 164, 192, 198, 199–200
Douglas, Kirk: *Paths of Glory* 212, 214, 216, 218–19, 221; *Spartacus* 3, 184, 202–3, 210, 231
diamonds: Earth symbol 41, 53, 59, 63, 69, 77, 95, 97–8, 116, 133, 135, 152, 155, 157–8, 165, 168, 187, 214; feminine symbol 69, 76–7, 95, 98, 135, 157, 165, 187, 214; nested rhombs/double diamonds 79, 82, 86, 88, 100, 111, 135, 144
Droogs 74, 124, 126–7, 129, 137, 138, 140, 170
duality: as doubling, mirroring 12–3, 96, 158, 204, 216–7; as fabric of reality 11–16, 18, 21, 24–5, 29, 35–6, 40, 42, 43, 45–7, 49, 52, 55, 61–3, 66, 69, 79, 107, 125, 127–8, 136, 217; as a masonic concept 127–8, 151, 517; as masonic dualistic chessboard/checkerboard 55, 61–3, 73 107, 125, 127–8, 133, 138, 170, 188, 199, 215; as polarity of good & evil 44, 07, 125, 141, 147, 156; as representing the body 43–50, 49, 73
Dullea, Kier (Dr. Dave Bowman) 18, 31
Durkin, Larry (*Shining*) 107
Duvall, Shelly 74, 82, 85

Egyptian/African influence in Kubrick films 29, 35, 49–50, 54, 57, 61, 67–8, 71–5, 97, 99–100, 104, 114, 117–9, 122, 126, 135, 157, 202, 206–8, 213–4, 215, 232–3, 228
Ermey, R. Lee (Sgt. Hartman) 146, 150, 153, 159
EVA (extra vehicular activity) 8, 19, 20, 24–26, 28–30, 32–4, 36, 38–40, 43, 48–50, 54, 56–60, 62–3, 67, 76, 187
evil as a Kubrickian theme 15, 44–5, 79–80, 82, 86–7, 90–1, 93–5, 118–121, 128–30 133–7, 139–141, 153–8, 166, 170–8, 180–5, 187–8, 189–197, 213–21
evolution 5, 9–10, 17, 24, 29, 32, 39, 41–2, 45, 57, 61, 63, 69, 75, 78, 95, 221, 223
*Eyes Wide Shut* 3, 4, 9, 17, 19, 40, 56, 57, 61, 70, 74, 80–1, 91, 93, 96, 98, 101, 103, 113–4, 116–8, 119, 122, 124–5, 139–40, 144, 147, 161–174, 175, 179–80, 183–4, 188–9, 191–4, 204, 207, 209, 214–5, 217–23
eye/eyes, the importance of: Hawk Eye/War Hawk themes 122, 181–3, 185, 135; of Horus/Ra 71–5, 97, 122–3, 131, 189; as proof of the spiritual dimension in Kubrick films 187,

191; the Third Eye as a Kubrickian theme 26, 28–33, 40, 47, 49, 51, 53–5, 58, 63, 65–6, 72–4, 76–8, 81, 94, 118, 137, 147, 149, 157, 158, 166, 179, 191, 208

fabric of reality 21, 24, 41, 55, 66, 68–9, 77
the feminine principal (as sacred) 67–9, 70, 76–7, 93, 98, 141 157, 163, 164–5, 166, 187
films: Kubrick films' connections to Kubrick's other films 122, 140, 142, 154, 155, 173, 175, 184–8, 207, 220. 222–3
Floyd, Dr. Heywood (*2001*) 7, 10, 13–15, 19, 20–23, 28, 31, 33, 36, 40, 53, 57, 63, 65–6, 68, 173, 198, 217
Frayling, Sir Christopher (author) 34, 225, 226, 227, 231
Frazier, James 166
freemasonry 15, 57, 59, 61–2, 73–4, 84, 90, 92–3, 97, 100, 105, 112, 115, 117–118, 120–2, 126–134, 141–2, 152, 163–4, 172–3, 180, 185, 188–9, 207, 213–5, 218. 232–3
*Full Metal Jacket* 3–4, 10, 38, 40, 56, 70, 74, 79, 90–1, 145–60, 176, 178–9, 185–7, 191, 209, 220, 222–3, 232
futurism as subtext see *Clockwork Orange*

geometry, sacred 41, 60, 226
gold as ascended embodied life 38, 55, 59, 68, 105, 132, 141, 166
Gold Room 90, 94–5, 101–2, 109; *see also* Overlook Hotel
graphic symbols of consciousness 26–34, 37, 41, 49, 59, 65, 92, 152, 166, 171
green: as creativity 39–40, 42, 45, 59, 64, 83, 93, 105, 108, 141; as growth/evolution 39–40, 45, 59, 67, 93, 141; as perversion/corruption 40, 93, 105, 108, 134, 141, 144, 149, 153, 155, 171; as use of intuition 29, 39–40, 45, 64, 105, 141
grid: as fabric of reality 11–13, 18–9, 21–2, 24–5, 30, 37–8, 41–2, 46–7, 52, 55, 62 66, 69, 165; as masonic checkerboard pattern 46, 61, 73, 127, 138, 155, 188, 228

HAL 9000 7, 14, 16–8, 20–1, 24, 27–8, 30, 34, 38–45, 47, 49, 52–3, 66–7, 157, 166
Hallorann, Dick (Overlook Hotel caretaker) 80, 82, 85, 97, 102, 104, 106–7, 109
Harewood, Dorian (*Eightball*) 148, 150, 152, 154
Harlan, Christiane 220–1; *see also* Kubrick, Christiane
Hartman, Sgt. 131, 132, 136, 138, 145
Hayden, Sterling 177–8, 182–3
Heron, Julia (set designer) 204
Hordern, Michael 112, 228
Humbert, Humbert (*Lolita*) 171, 178, 189–201

I as 'I Am' in *2001* 27, 28, 35, 45, 47, 57, 157, 160, 166

# Index

I-Space Field 12, 19, 29, 36–7, 47, 50; as thought-space field 29, 30, 32, 35, 38, 67
iL as iLeft or iLand 21, 56–8
Illuciferian definition 90–91
Illuciferian/s 95, 97–8, 103–4, 109, 112–5, 117, 119, 121–23, 126, 128–132, 142–3, 148–9, 152, 155–6, 168, 171–3, 189–191, 213–4, 218–220, 222
insanity/madness as a Kubrickian theme 4, 44, 87, 90–1, 101–2, 148, 155, 176, 185
intuition, Kubrick's value of 29, 39–40, 42, 45, 56, 59, 62, 64, 105, 141, 164
Isis 60, 61, 66–70, 116

"Joe" the tenant in *Clockwork Orange* (Clive Francis) 134, 144
Jones, Chuck (cartoon director) 108
Jones, James Earl (the Bombardier, *Dr. Strangelove*) 181, 187
Julian (writer's aide, *Clockwork Orange*) 129, 130, 134
Jupiter (*Discovery* Mission, *2001*) 7, 8, 14, 21, 33–4, 48, 58
Jupiter space 14, 58

Karlin, Miriam (as Cat Lady, *Clockwork Orange*) 126–8, 134–7, 144
Keams, Juli 190, 229, 233
Kean, Marie (*Barry Lyndon*'s mother) 117
Khachaturian, Aram (composer) 17
Kidman, Nicole, (see Alice Harford, *Eyes Wide Shut*)
*Killer's Kiss* 3, 12, 184, 225
*The Killing* 3
King, Stephen 81, 108, 109
Kubrick, Christiane 157, 158, 169, 177, 178
Kubrick, Katherina 65, 162
Kubrick, Vivian (Squirt, *2001*) 30, 65, 122
Kruger, Hardy (Cap. Potzdorf, *Barry Lyndon*) 113–4

Lange, Harry 17, 34, 48, 76, 226, 227, 231
Leonardo da Vinci 32–33, 42
Ligeti, Grygory (composer) 8, 17, 54
light see Special FX
lighting in Kubrick films 12, 14, 18, 24, 27, 29, 31, 33–4, 44, 49, 55, 61, 63, 79, 84, 97, 99, 128, 132, 147, 158, 162, 167–8, 179–181, 184, 187–8, 191, 200, 204, 215, 220–1
Lockwood, Gary (Dr. Frank Poole, *2001*) 12, 16, 18–20, 23, 26–30, 34, 38–41, 44–46, 48–9, 51–3, 65, 68
*Lolita* 3, 4, 79, 114, 125, 166, 171, 175–8, 188–201, 214, 218, 220–2, 233; character (Delores Haze) 189, 190, 192, 193–4, 196–7, 199–201; film 3, 4, 79, 114, 125, 166, 171, 177, 188–9, 195–6, 198–9, 201 214, 218, 220–2, 229, 233; novel/author 175, 192–3, 195, 198
Luciferian: animals, appropriated imagery 163, 204, 215, 218; baroque motifs 60, 98, 116, 119, 126, 162, 174, 202, 204–6, 212–15; diamond (use of) 87, 95, 97–8, 101, 103–4, 116, 126, 135, 149, 158, 168, 187, 193; hidden shadow script techniques 74, 83, 84, 86–7, 90–1, 93, 95, 97, 100, 117, 124, 126–7, 182; masonic overlap 119, 121, 122, 123–4, 128–34, 138, 142–3, 164, 173, 180, 188, 207, 213, 215, 218; spiral (use of) 98–9, 114, 116, 119, 162, 171, 204, 209, 213; star/sun (use of) 93, 95, 97–8, 104, 114, 115, 117, 126; stolen cultural symbols 61, 95, 99–100, 104, 116–8, 131, 135, 162–4, 165, 205, 207, 209, 213, 215
Ludovico treatment (*Clockwork Orange*) 79, 127, 129–30, 132–3, 138, 142
Lusthog squad (*Full Metal Jacket*) 74, 159, 186
Lyndon, Lady Honoria (*Barry Lyndon*) 124, 125
Lyon, Sue (*Lolita*) 125, 190, 192

Magee, Patrick (actor): de Balibari in *Barry Lyndon* 114–6; as Mr. Frank Alexander (writer) in *Clockwork Orange* 74, 124, 126–7, 129–30, 132–4, 136, 140–1, 144; as the Chevalier
magenta: the higher seat of consciousness color (*2001*) 41, 58–60, 144, 147; as used in *Clockwork Orange* (murky magenta as abused sexual love) 93, 133–4; as used in *Eyes Wide Shut* 93; as used in *Full Metal Jacket* 153
Major "King" Kong (*Dr. Strangelove*) 177, 187–8
Mason, James (H. Humbert) 125, 192
Masons 15, 57, 59–62, 73–4, 84, 90, 92–3, 97, 100, 105, 112, 115, 117–8, 120–22, 126–34, 138, 141–3, 151–2, 157, 163–4, 167, 172–3, 180, 185, 188–9, 192, 206–7, 213–15, 218, 227; see also Freemasonry
Masters, Tony 34
Maze, Overlook 83, 86–7, 91, 93, 95, 99, 101, 106, 109, 207; see also Overlook
McDowell, Malcom (Alex DeLarge, *Clockwork Orange*) 74, 124
message motif 10, 33–4, 48
mirrors: frequent appearance of 72–3, 74, 116, 133, 142, 169, 170, 179, 191, 194, 231; importance of 25, 31, 39, 56–7, 62–3, 67, 71–4, 83–4, 93, 99, 101, 115, 140, 157, 169–70, 191, 206–8
misogyny/machismo addressed in Kubrick films: in *Barry Lyndon* 112, 117, 120–1; in *Clockwork Orange* 124, 126–8, 134–8, 139, 142–4, 170; in *Dr. Strangelove* 176–8, 186–7; in *Eyes Wide Shut* 164–5, 170, 172, 173; in *Full Metal Jacket* 150, 152, 156, 158–9; in *Lolita* 189, 195, 222; in *The Shining* 82, 98, 142, 170; in *Spartacus* 203, 206, 209; in *2001: A Space Odyssey* 65–6; see also women
Modine, Matthew ('Joker,' *Full Metal Jacket*) 131–140, 142–145
monolith 1, 7–10, 14, 18–25, 27, 30–1, 38, 40, 42, 44, 46–8, 53–5, 57–8, 62–3, 77–8, 84, 93, 101, 140–1, 151, 165–6, 168, 184
Moonwatcher (Dan Richter) 10, 225

# 238 Index

Nabokov, Vladimir 124, 189, 191–2, 194–5, 197–201, 228–9, 232
Nicholson, Jack 10, 74, 80, 82–6, 91, 93, 95–6, 99–103, 106, 108–9, 142, 177–8, 182–3, 187–8, 198, 207, 232
Nora Brady (cousin/love interest in *Barry Lyndon*) 111–2
numbers, esoteric importance of in Kubrick films 51, 53–5, 69, 231
nurture/nurturance as Kubrickian theme 37, 98, 127, 134, 143

O'Neal, Ryan 111, 122, 228
orange: as life functions (*2001*) 38, 46, 52, 58, 60, 207; as used in *Barry Lyndon* 112, 113, 128, 204; as used in *Clockwork Orange* 84, 128, 129, 130, 131, 134, 141, 142, 143; as used in *Full Metal Jacket* 153, 158–9; as used in *The Shining* 84, 92–3, 94, 96, 100, 104–5;
Ordway, Herbert 18, 48
Orion III (*2001* spaceplane) 11, 13, 18, 26, 31–2, 46–7, 57
Overlook Hotel (*Shining*): carpets 92, 94, 101, 105, 109; Colorado Room 82, 91, 96–7, 107; corridors 83–4, 92, 94, 101–2, 104, 109; furniture 84, 90, 93, 100–1; Gold Room 90, 94–5, 101–2, 109; maze 86–7, 91, 93, 95, 99, 106, 109; Room 237, 84, 92–3, 99, 105

Pan 116, 206
Pan American emblems in *2001* 10, 26, 28, 47, 70
*Paths of Glory* 3–4, 61, 90, 114, 116, 118, 120, 168, 175, 180–1, 184–6, 188, 191, 194, 202, 207, 212–22
pink: murky pink as insecure or compromised consciousness 92, 94, 129, 130, 138, 141, 153; as nurturing love 129, 143–4; as seated consciousness 37, 40–1, 58–9, 64, 65, 148
Polanski, Roman 84–5, 124, 192, 227, 232
Pollack, Sydney *see* Ziegler, Victor
Poole, Dr. Frank *see* Lockwood, Gary
portal motif 26, 31–2, 47, 65, 76
Prowse, David (Julian, *Clockwork Orange*) 129
purple: as ascended consciousness 41, 53, 59–60, 63, 66–9, 76, 105, 207; as Earth sanctified 41, 60, 69, 147–8, 152; as the sacred feminine 69, 76, 165–6, 179; as sacred sexual love (red+blue=purple) 132, 134, 143, 144, 169, 179
Pyle, Private Leonard (*Full Metal Jacket*) 74, 79, 146–7, 153, 156, 158–9

Quigley, Godfrey (prison chaplain, *Clockwork Orange*) 1, 129
Quilty, Claire (Peter Sellers, *Lolita*) 79, 125, 178, 189–201, 229, 233

red: as a danger signifier 83–4, 92, 105–6, 147, 153; as a masonic color for earth/woman 59, 69, 95, 151, 157, 163–4, 165, 203; as a Satanic/Luciferian signifier 83, 95, 97–8, 100–1, 103–4, 105, 107–9, 126, 130, 132, 146–7, 168–9, 172, 219; as the seat of consciousness 35, 36, 37, 40, 49, 59, 152; as sexual love 134, 143, 144, 170
Reed, Tracy (as Miss Scott, *Dr. Strangelove*) 179, 186
Rice, Julian (author) 9, 35, 225, 226, 229, 232
Richter, Dan (Moonwatcher) 8
Rossiter, Leonard: as Captain John Quin (*Barry Lyndon*) 111; as Dr. Dimitri Smyslov (*2001*) 15, 20, 65–6
The Room Beyond (at end of *2001*'s Star Gate), 4, 50, 53, 54, 56, 161, 163–166, 172, 174
Room 237 84, 92–3, 99, 105; *see also* Overlook Hotel

Scott, George C. 177, 186
Sellers, Peter 99, 149, 151, 152, 200, 202
Servile Slave War (*Spartacus*) *see* War
Seven Years War *see* War
sexual orientations, portrayal of 129, 144, 164
shadow script: definition 228; examples of 12, 22, 74, 84, 106, 107, 119, 149, 170, 180, 182; real life examples of 61, 99–100, 191, 214–5, 128, 228, 229
*The Shining* 3–4, 17, 20, 38, 40, 38, 56, 61, 74–91,–92, 93, 95–101, 103–9 112–114, 117–8, 122–124, 129, 134, 139–144, 147–149, 151, 153–155, 157–8, 165, 169, 170, 180, 183, 188, 191, 198, 204, 207, 209, 213, 219–20, 222–3, 225, 228
*Spartacus* 3–4, 175, 184–5, 188. 202–11, 221
special effects: light FX as signifiers 22, 26, 37, 61, 146–7; light's spiritual dimension in Kubrick films 27, 29, 31, 33–4, 49, 55, 56–64, 99, 133, 140–1, 147, 162, 167–8, 181, 187–8, 191, 220–1; Star Gate 8, 18, 21, 24, 26, 29, 34, 56–60; to indicate danger 21, 43–4, 67, 101, 102, 140–1, 147–8, 168
Square the Circle 55, 56, 60, 162
Squirt *see* Kubrick, Vivian
Star Child 4, 25, 54–56, 161, 167, 187
Star Gate 4, 18, 22, 25, 28, 31, 37, 41, 53–55, 80, 159, 161–166, 172–174, 187, 193
Strauss, Richard 17
Szavost, Sandor (*Eyes Wide Shut*) 164, 173

T as Third Eye 26, 31, 58, 63, 77, 81, 87, 157; *see also* eye/eyes
Tanit 59, 61, 66, 68, 70
tapirs (*2001*) 7, 9–10
Third Eye 26, 28–9, 31–2, 40, 49, 51, 53–5 58, 63, 65–6, 72–3, 76–8, 81, 94, 147, 149, 157–8, 166, 179, 191, 208
T/I/bone as tool 10, 26, 50, 78
thought-space field 30–32, 34, 50, 52, 171; as I-Space 11, 19, 30, 43, 46, 50, 51
Torrance, Danny (*Shining*) 74, 80–3, 85–7, 92, 95–6, 98, 102, 105–6, 109, 139, 142–3, 151

Torrance, Jack (*Shining*) 74, 82–6. 90–3, 95–6, 99–103, 106, 108–110, 142, 198, 207
Torrance, Wendy (*Shining*) 74, 80, 82–4, 86–7, 91, 93, 96, 98–9, 101–2, 105–6, 108–9, 142
Trumball, Douglas 18, 34, 226
Turkel, Joe (bartender, *Shining*) 85
tycho magnetic anomaly (TMA-1 site, *2001*) 14–5, 21–5, 28–30, 32, 36, 38–9, 42, 46, 53–55, 68, 184
*2001: A Space Odyssey* 1, 3–10, 12–15, 17, 19–21, 23–4, 26–9, 31–2, 34–7, 40–2, 45, 50–1, 53, 56, 58, 60, 65–71, 77–80, 83–4, 92–3, 95, 105, 108–9, 111, 122, 125, 131–2, 140–1, 143, 145–9, 151, 153–8, 161, 165–7, 169, 171–3, 175, 179, 184, 187, 191, 198, 220–1, 225–7, 231–3

U/C: as container 28, 31, 37–8, 48, 178; as "I" or ego projection 28
Ustinov, Peter 202–3, 207

V-for-vessel 28, 31, 42, 61, 63, 67, 69, 76–7, 159, 127, 172, 179, 190, 193, 200–1; vessel-as-body/vehicle 31, 61, 63 69, 76, 159, 172, 177–8–79, 190, 200; vessel as recurring Kubrickian theme 69, 92, 98, 127, 177–9, 190, 200–1
Vav 69, 76–7, 166
vehicles, spacecraft: *Aries 1B* (moon shuttle) 11, 20–3, 25–7, 29, 32, 34, 37–3, 42, 46–7, 50, 53–4, 58; The *Discovery* 7–8, 13–4, 16–21, 25–6, 28–9, 30–2, 34–40, 42–9, 51–5, 57–8, 67, 76, 179; *EVA* (extra vehicular activity) pods 8, 19, 20, 24–26, 28–30, 32–4, 36, 38–40, 43, 48–50, 54, 56–60, 62–3, 67, 76, 187; Moon-bus 14–5, 20, 22, 26, 29, 31, 37–9, 41–2, 48, 52–4, 68, 151, 221; *Orion III* spaceplan 11, 13, 18, 26, 31–2, 46–7, 57; *Space Station V* (Earth avatar) 10–12, 14, 17, 40, 47–8
Vietnam 4, 145, 148–9, 152–5, 157–9, 185
Vincent D'Onofrio (Pvt. Pyle) 132
Vitali, Leon 128; as Lord Barringdon 118–9, 120–1; as Red Cloak 166, 173

Walker, Alexander (author) 6, 12, 26, 44, 60
war: Kubrick's covert cinematic campaigns 169, 175, 188, 220–1; Servile War (ancient Rome) 175, 202; Seven Years War (Europe & its colonies) 111, 113, 185, 222; Vietnam 4, 145, 153, 185; World War I 4, 175, 184, 212; World War II 34, 82, 177
wedge motif 32
Weegee (photographer) 184
Wendover, Lord Adolphus (*Barry Lyndon*) 117–9, 217
white: as the essential self/life 28, 35–7, 72, 154, 178; as innocence 143–4, 154, 177–8, 200; as light/part of or beyond duality 12, 15, 18, 35, 37, 40, 42, 49, 52, 63, 68, 73, 125, 144, 188, 199, 215; as nurturance (milk) 98, 126–7, 134; as thought 29, 30, 35, 37, 40, 47
Winters, Shelley (*Lolita*) 193
women in Kubrick films: *Barry Lyndon* 112, 117, 120–1; *Clockwork Orange* 124, 126–8, 130, 132–3, 136–8, 142–4, 173; *Dr. Strangelove* 180, 196; *Eyes Wide Shut* 164–5, 168, 171, 172, 173; *Full Metal Jacket* 147, 150, 152, 156, 158–9; *Lolita* 98, 190–1, 193, 195; *Paths of Glory* 220; *The Shining* 74, 81, 83, 85, 142, 170; *Spartacus* 205–6, 207; *2001: A Space Odyssey* 9, 40, 52, 65–8, 69–70, 72, 166; *see also* misogyny
Wynn, Keenan (Col. Bat Guano) 186

X: as shorthand for inverted hexagram 92, 98; as used in various shadow script 84; as XOX, or XO/OX 94–5, 97, 99–101, 104, 109, 112–5, 120, 125, 130, 132, 134, 136, 171, 173, 182, 187, 191; as XX 95, 134, 149, 168, 188, 192, 196, 214, 216; as XXX 94–5, 104, 113, 128, 130–1, 133, 149, 150, 154–6

Y as life vessel 31, 69
Y as Vav 76–77
Y as Yoni 69, 76–7, 135, 165, 172
yellow: as death 38, 101, 105, 141, 171; as embodied life 37–9, 54, 171; sanctified yellow=gold 38, 105

Ziegler, Mrs. & Mr. Victor (*Eyes Wide Shut*) 162–4, 172–3